Writing Academic Papers in English
Graduate and Postgraduate Level

Kenneth Eckert

Copyright © 2024 Kenneth (Ken) Eckert
Version 6: June 2024
Previous name: *Writing Academic Papers in English: For Korean Writers*

Moldy Rutabaga Books
http://keneckert.com/mrbooks
All rights reserved.
Print ISBN: 978-1-7750234-6-3 International Edition
Or 978-1-7750234-2-5
E-book ISBN: 978-1-7750234-3-2

CONTENTS

1 STARTING OUT		1
1.1	Why Do We Write?	4
1.2	Why Bother if AI Can Write?	6
1.3	Making an Argument	9
1.4	Three Parts of Writing	14
1.5	Three Steps of Writing	17
1.6	Part Science and Part Art	21
2 PLANNING		23
2.1	Fear and Your Body	25
2.2	Choosing a Topic	26
2.3	Refining a Topic into a Position	30
2.4	Discussion Frames	36
2.5	Note Taking	42
2.6	Outlining	45
3 THESIS ARGUMENTS		49
3.1	Stress-Testing Your Argument	50
3.2	Thesis Statements	54
3.3	Being Clear	57
3.4	Chunking and Phrasing	60
3.5	Thesis Statement Placement	66
3.6	Titles	74
4 STRUCTURE		77
4.1	Paragraphs	77
4.2	The Five-Paragraph Model	80
4.3	Proportionality	88

4.4	Transitions and Signposting	91
4.5	Conclusions	92
4.6	Beyond Five Paragraphs	98
5 EVIDENCE & RHETORIC		**105**
5.1	Aristotelian Rhetoric	106
5.2	Appeal to Logic (Logos)	107
5.3	Faulty Logic	109
5.4	Appeal to Emotion (Pathos)	116
5.5	Appeal to Authority (Ethos)	120
5.6	Two Types of Ethos	121
6 EXTERNAL SOURCES		**125**
6.1	Something's Missing	128
6.2	Judging Sources	131
6.3	Protecting Yourself	138
6.4	Scholarly Search Engines	146
6.5	Search Terms	150
6.6	Fine Tuning: Avoiding Bias	151
7 MLA & APA FORMAT		**157**
7.1	Title Pages	160
7.2	End-Text References	165
7.3	In-Text Citation	173
7.4	Citing Literature	182
7.5	Chicago, IEEE, and Footnotes	185
7.6	Figures and Tables	189
8 QUOTING		**195**
8.1	Seven Ways to Quote	195
8.2	Quoting Fictional Characters	204
8.3	Quotation Grammar	207
8.4	Quotation Sandwiches	219

8.5	Advanced Quotation 'Waves'	222
8.6	Plagiarism	227
9 EDITING		237
9.1	Rest Before Editing	237
9.2	Two Levels of Editing	241
9.3	Cutting the Dead Wood	243
9.4	Raising Academic Tone	255
9.5	Sexist Writing	257
9.6	Peer Editing	258
10 SEMINAR PAPER & DISS SECTIONS		261
10.1	Section Headings	264
10.2	Abstracts	267
10.3	Tables of Contents	272
10.4	Literature Reviews	273
10.5	Methodology & Results/Discussion	277
10.6	End Materials	281
11 THE THESIS/DISS PROJECT		283
11.1	Advisors and Committees	285
11.2	The Diss Proposal	288
11.3	Emotional Skills: Common Dangers	292
11.4	The Diss Defense	297
11.5	Optimizing Your Defense	299
11.6	Grading Metrics	305
12 BEYOND THE DISS		307
12.1	Revising Your Diss	308
12.2	Academic Journal Articles	312
12.3	No: Rejections and Revisions	317
12.4	Conference Papers	325
12.5	Preparing a Conference Paper	327

12.6	Edited Collections and Monographs	329
13 OTHER PROFESSIONAL WRITING		335
13.1	Digital and Self-Published Books	335
13.2	Technical Writing	340
13.3	Business Writing	341
13.4	Cover Letters and Resumes/CVs	343
13.5	Online Writing	350
13.6	Wikipedia Writing	353
14 GRAMMAR CLINIC		355
14.1	The History of English	355
14.2	Language Interference	357
14.3	Articles A & The	359
14.4	Numbers, Prepositions, and Passives	361
14.5	Word Class and Miscellaneous Errors	364
14.6	Grammar and Native Speakers	364
FINAL COMMENTS		369

ACKNOWLEDGMENTS

When I began teaching composition in Korea in 2003, I worked with industry textbooks, but found that they were inadequate for graduate and advanced writing. I began to generate class materials, eventually forming the genesis of this book, which has been in regular revision since 2011. I am grateful for all those educators who freely traded around their handouts and materials, as well as to students who continue to ask questions and motivate me to repair and expand upon this work. *Soli Deo gloria.*

My specific thanks to undergraduate and graduate students who have given me permission to use anonymous excerpts of their course papers as writing samples. Additional thanks to colleagues who in earlier drafts made editing suggestions and corrected my Korean. I am responsible for remaining content or usage errors.

The opinions expressed here are my own and do not necessarily represent Hanyang University.

KENNETH ECKERT

1 STARTING OUT

If people cannot write well, they cannot think well, and if they cannot think well, others will do their thinking for them. – George Orwell

There are many manuals to help students write, but few deal with academic writing at the graduate or high-undergraduate level, and still fewer which address the particular needs of nonnative users of English. This book explains how to better plan, research, write, and edit an argument seminar paper, thesis/dissertation, or postgraduate scholarly publication in MLA, APA, or IEEE format. While it is tailored to English language learners and especially Koreans, the information here is meant to be helpful for any writer. This updated version also discusses some of the ethical challenges and opportunities of AI-written text.

I don't want to begin by discouraging people, as this isn't the goal of this book, but what are the most common problems I see with student papers?

Six Common Reasons Academic Papers are Failures

1. The paper is filled with grammar mistakes. If your essay has brilliant things to say but no one can understand your sentences, it is a failure.
2. The paper has no clear thesis argument and merely wanders between ideas talking *about* things. If you present information or describe a subject without taking a discernible position,

there's little reason to continue reading it.
3. The paper's subject is too broad. The argument attempts to cover too many topics within the space of the paper, and ends up with only a thin and weakly-connected list of topics.
4. The paper's evidence is weak. The paper does not quote or cite its claims, instead presenting vague statements or generalizations.
5. The paper imitates the phrasings and structure of a speech or presentation. The essay has a casual, slangy tone, or is filled with "I think" and "I feel" statements, and is too focused on the writer and not the subject.
6. The paper does not follow expected or assigned citation standards. Non-standard title pages and sloppy reference lists signal unprofessional writing to the reader.

Who are You?

I hope this book will be helpful for you, but it might be helpful to indicate some of its target readers. I will feel guilty if you have already bought this book and it is not applicable—although I should warn I have already spent my thirty-eight cent royalty on fast living. I originally wrote this book as a seminar course text for senior and graduate students at Hanyang University ERICA, Korea, and so most of its readers have been non-native speakers of English (L2). Every expat English instructor claims to have an instruction book in them, and as Christopher Hitchens wagged, that's usually where it should stay—but among the endless sea of mediocre writing textbooks I observed at teaching conferences such as KOTESOL, the majority were tailored to low-level situations such as writing paragraphs about one's favorite food, or a vacation. The remainder jumped to theoretical monographs on linguistics or language acquisition, which are fine but do not teach you how to write a paper.

During two decades of teaching I have found few writing books which address the middle needs of graduate students and seniors, and basically none for specifically English language learners. To my alarm, neither my Korean nor my international

1 STARTING OUT

graduate students seemed to receive any guidance on how to write seminar papers, their thesis/dissertation projects, or postgraduate projects. Even as an English major, I received no explicit course instruction on this. I have learned more, alas, about writing by *teaching* it. The materials I evolved to address this need formed the genesis of this book. Over time I have added discussions on scholarly and professional writing-related tasks such as conference papers, journal articles, and monographs, as well as curriculum vita and online writing.

Native (L1) and non-native (L2) speakers bring to argument-based writing different strengths and weaknesses. Native-English speakers tend to have more experience in such projects from freshman composition courses and other classroom scenarios. The difficulty for such students is that they may be overconfident or dismissive of the need to improve their writing skills, believing that knowing how to speak English means one can write at an academic level. This is no more true than the supposition that knowing English qualifies one to be a public speaker in it.

Korean graduate students and other non-native speakers typically bring to their programs prior experience writing essays in English on personal topics or opinions on preferences or current events. It is less difficult to convince non-native English learners to take writing seriously, although for some students language fluency is the goal, and writing fluency is a nice-to-have but not a primary aim.

Moreover, learners of English, and even native speakers, often imitate the forms and phrasings of a spoken presentation in their essays, with their typical questions and pauses and colloquialisms, because this is what they have learned. But every language has a gap in style or grammar between its spoken and written forms. French in fact has verb tenses used only in writing (*temps littéraires*). English has no exclusively literary tenses but the stylistic difference between its spoken and written forms can be large, and in serious writing a textual and not verbal skillset must be acquired.

Writing instruction books inevitably compare themselves to

the grandfather of writing manuals, Strunk and White's *The Elements of Style* (1918). I have always felt uneasy with the drill sergeant school of writing instruction which seeks to make academic writing a joyless exercise in self-abnegation. But I have also never liked the 1970's touchy-feely school which sees writing as a personal journey, if not therapy. If you are a graduate or senior student, you are likely writing in order to get a project done to finish a degree. If you are nearing or beginning an academic career, you wish to get published. The purpose of writing is not to have fun. But neither is it wrong if sometimes its byproduct *is* enjoyment.

Further, for those in a hard science or STEM (science, technology, engineering, and medicine) field, your priority is the subject content and even less knowledge of writing as a theoretical discipline. I write with humility on this field because it is not mine; but I hope to convince such writers that not only will this book help with the performative task of writing a thesis/dissertation, but that engaging with the concepts and methodologies of composition studies will be interesting and good intellectual exercise. I regret not taking mathematics seriously in high school, and I now see that even if I don't use trigonometry often, the subject was attempting to teach me a mental rigor and discipline. I believe this is conversely true for those outside the humanities. The science-humanities rivalry in academia is a recent one, and in the ancients and medieval eras, all knowledge was 'science' and precious. The word in its Latin roots had this broader meaning, still preserved in words such as 'conscience' or 'omniscient.'

1.1 Why Do We Write?

Perhaps I betray my bias in a book about it, but writing is one of the most important inventions in human history. Agriculture, democracy, printing, germ theory, cars, and the internet are all crucial innovations, but the preservation and transmission of knowledge about them rely on writing. The European Middle Ages were nowhere near as 'dark' as the cliché implies, but it is

1 STARTING OUT

not coincidental that when literacy and the interchange of books declined, the growth of civilization slowed.

I will expand on this while discussing rhetoric and Aristotle, but formal argumentation is one of the oldest scholarly traditions in Greco-Roman civilization, going back some 24 centuries, and continuing in the scholastic debates held in medieval European universities. Three topics covered in this book—grammar, logic, and rhetoric—are the components of the *trivium*, the basic program of a medieval European university education. These are the oldest academic subjects in the west, taught since the sixth century in various institutions.

Rhetoric in the ancient and medieval world was of course usually spoken and not written. The undergraduate essay has been a classroom staple only since the nineteenth century. Yet its roots also have a far older pedigree. The writing of academic treatises dates to antiquity, and we might call the first scholarly scientific 'paper' in English that of Chaucer's on the astrolabe, a navigational device, in 1391. The first published academic journals go back to 1665, and by the early modern era dissertations had shifted from oral to written form, although the emphasis on original research really begins in the early 19th-century Berlin model. Written discourse since then has remained a fundamental component of scholarly activity.

It may be only too obvious that you must write such papers. What I am attempting to convey here is why, and I see at least three good reasons. The first is already alluded to, that your dissertation is a preparation for academic life. I realize not every reader will be a scholar, but second, writing skills will help your career and possibly personal life. If you can write effective and clear work memos or papers for conferences and meetings, you will be a more valuable employee and more likely to accrue leadership roles and promotions. When people write badly and are misunderstood, careers are jeopardized, online relationships end, wrong orders get placed, bridges fall down, lawsuits happen, and businesses lose money. A recent study claims that U.S. businesses spend $3-4 billion a year re-training employees to write competently.

Third, what you are learning *while* you are writing is extremely valuable. English majors are constantly asked, as I was, how writing a paper on a poem is useful for anyone. The answer is that you do not exercise in a gym to prepare to lift dumbbells on the street—you are training your muscles for future needs. You are doing the same in the classroom. Education is partly about content, and partly about process, the skills one learns while working on specific tasks, just as I regret seeing in high school the reasoning abilities that mathematics develops. Similarly here, being a good writer will not only help you master a content subject, but also inculcates independent work habits and a breadth of cognitive and linguistic skills.

In brief, even for those not in the humanities, written communication is a vital skill which develops our highest reasoning faculties. I realize he is a controversial figure, but Canada's Jordan Peterson is astute in saying that "the best way to teach people critical thinking is to teach them to write." The challenges and temptations of using AI software like ChatGPT to make essays are serious. But again, this yields product but not skills. Doing the writing yourself is the best way to learn advanced critical thinking and communication abilities.

1.2 Why Bother if AI Can Write?

But why learn to write papers at all if AI bots and chat generators can do it? This wouldn't have been asked as recently as a few years ago, until late 2022, when the closest thing to an asteroid hitting the dinosaurs hit the field of writing and composition studies: Chat GPT. Its use reached 100 million users within *weeks*, and journalism overnight thundered that "The College Essay is Dead," as *The Atlantic*'s Steven Marche did. Very soon, I had students cheating by submitting blog posts, assignments, and papers entirely written with AI prompts. My colleagues, well used to a sort of gallows humor regarding the field of English studies and literature, soon began (half-) joking with each other: What are we going to do for a living now?

Academia and scholarship is still catching up with AI

generators, but to me there are three broad paradigms I'm already seeing in writing instruction:

Fight it and treat it as a cancer. Some instructors I've seen see AI generators purely as a glorified plagiarizer, slicing and vomiting up the work of others into simulated knowledge, and refuse to allow students to use it. Some use the newly-developing AI detectors to identify and punish/fail such papers.

Incorporate it as a tool. Some professors I know reluctantly, or enthusiastically, see AI as a useful tool for automating lower-level drudge work in writing, while arguing that the finished product still requires a traditional human skillset.

Give up. Some academic chat on social media calls paper writing an obsolete skill, that for better or worse will soon be as rarefied as long division. Such people advocate abandoning teaching writing altogether and focusing on other learning activities.

But this book is about your writing, not my teaching of it, even if the two actions intersect. Yet for students, the questions are similar—is it worth learning this skill, or is it a dinosaur talent just as calculators and keyboards have inevitably made hand-written arithmetic and penmanship out-of-date?

If I try to tell you that words are beautiful and powerful, even in an essay, and that there is pride in crafting and having ownership of them, you may be chiefly concerned with the product as a means to an end. If I try to tell you that the rigor and mental precision of writing is as valuable as the textual object, just like learning a foreign language gives you an acuity and vocabulary that using a translation app can't, you may say that these are nice high-flown ideas, but impractical when real-world tasks are at hand—and that you must compete with other people who don't have these ethics. But I do make two cases for learning to write. If I fail, this book fails in its justification. But I think my reasons are good ones.

Extrapolation Error. Extrapolation error—more on that in the chapter on evidence—is a logical error where short-term changes are assumed to always apply. For example, cafés were rare in Korea in the 1990s. Let us say there were 100 coffee shops in 2000, 1,000 in 2010, and according to current estimates, there are now about 100,000 in the country. If we graph this growth, we find there are one million in 2030, and ten million in 2040, which is ridiculous—by the century's end, there would be nowhere to live except in a café. Common sense tells us that the trend will eventually stabilize.

It may be that AI generation engines will hugely increase their complexity and power, as is predicted. This doesn't mean that AI writing will necessarily evolve to match or surpass human output in terms of subjective human-judged quality. It may be that AI text will plane out and improve only very incrementally, just as calculators have basically changed little since the 1980s. There are present experiments with AI-written academic work, and even fiction. But such software does not understand the context or meaning of what it produces, and the fiction lacks any human feeling for realistic character depth or motivation. I have colleagues who assert that this will change. But it may not, and there may be hard limits that are reached.

Who Will Direct or Judge the AIs? I know this isn't a philosophy book, but I distinguish between an educated pessimist and a lazy one. The thoughtful pessimist argues that we are headed towards broad unemployment and social problems because of AI. Such a vision might be right, though I think it's alarmist. The lazy pessimist just says, why bother, there won't be any jobs—in order to avoid work. It is like the stylish cynics I mention later in the book who think literary analysis is pointless because "a story can mean anything." The position is only taken to evade effort.

There are likely to be wide-ranging job losses because of AI, and we may be headed towards a future of guaranteed minimum incomes where employment is prestigious, not onerous—and that may be the best case scenario, as opposed to poverty and unrest. But if so, our future socioeconomic cleavages will probably be between people content to let AI give them an easy but basic life, and the people who want to lead—who can determine what the AI should do, who can evaluate its work, and who can communicate and liaison with people.

I know which group I would rather be in. And while most societies don't pay much more than lip service to the liberal arts and humanities, being able to think clearly in text and to arrange, support, and advocate ideas will very likely remain crucial career and personal skills.

In short, in this book I will take approach #2, which is to see AI content generators as a tool that can automate and bolster the writing exercise, but which shouldn't replace one's own work and responsibility for the final product. I don't use these generators myself, as I am vain and see my writing as to an extent expressing and representing myself, and because I am particular and don't want to surrender any part of my writing to a machine—but perhaps in a generation this will be as quaint as using a typewriter instead of a computer keyboard. Nevertheless, I will occasionally refer to AI tools in this book for those who see value in adopting them for basic work tasks, such as brainstorming ideas, recommending outline structures, formatting reference entries, or making grammatical or stylistic suggestions. My caveat is that you should still know how to do these things well enough so that you can intelligently tell the tools what to do, and can evaluate what the tools are outputting.

1.3 Making an Argument

This book is about argument research writing in particular, as opposed to the many other forms of writing people do. Much writing is expository, which means that it chiefly describes or conveys information. Journalism, an instruction manual, an encyclopedia entry, a social media post, or an ingredient list on a can of soup may seek to explain or guide without asserting any particular viewpoint. Another category is creative writing, such as a novel, a poem, or a movie script. You might also have experience of non-academic persuasive writing, where you attempt to convince someone—to get married, to travel in Spain, or to drink a brand of beverage. Some writing situations might be more than one type, of course, such as a blog or Facebook post where someone relates their day, tells a joke, or gives advice.

In basic description, an argument research paper—the subject of this book—may take the specific form of an essay, journal article, or book, but it has three qualities: one, it has an academic tone and register in its writing and subject; two, it normally involves incorporating information outside the writer's own ideas, such as books, websites, survey or experiment results, or other serious sources; and three, it does not merely describe the subject: it states an argument or analysis regarding it.

All of these points will be expanded on, but the third needs re-emphasis. Again, there are other valid and valuable types of writing. I study and write literature and am not dismissing it. But most academic writing, and the focus of this book, is argument-based research writing, which states and supports a serious position with reasons and evidence.

I also stress the aspect of argumentative writing because some students import a false ethic of fairness to such papers— they see a moral responsibility to present both sides, or they feel it would be wrong to dictate to the reader what to think. Such is the nature of expository writing, such as journalism or informative writing, such as a Wikipedia or newspaper article: to be objective and avoid injecting one's own opinions. But academic argument writing does not endeavor to be fair and balanced; it commits to a position and provides evidence that the position is correct, similar to an editorial or opinion article or post. A courtroom prosecutor or defendant cannot argue both sides of the case out of a belief in impartiality, asserting that the defendant might equally be guilty or innocent. He or she must pursue a side, and a verdict must be given.

*What **is** an Academic Argument?*

What *is* an argument? This also may appear too basic or easy a question, but it isn't. One of the drawbacks of the English

1 STARTING OUT

language is that it has a massive vocabulary but sometimes its words are not precisely differentiated, with a common one having dissimilar connotations. The word 'argument' is such an example. In common parlance it involves anger, such as a hostile interchange on Facebook with people exchanging emotional or insulting statements regarding a heated political issue, or a situation where two drivers involved in an automobile accident are disputing who was at fault.

But an academic argument is not necessarily or normally belligerent. It is a formal position to be proven or investigated: Hamlet is (not) insane; this country should (not) sign a free trade agreement with Brazil because x; posts on social media can help promote budget cosmetics; the solvent caused the level of rusting to decline here, but not there. I won't be naïve here—there *are* petty academic fights, and political or ideological battles in scholarship. But the purpose of writing in academia is ideally and typically the generation of useful new ideas or viewpoints, not personal victories.

I have previously noted that academic papers are not speeches, but they are partly like debates. There are indeed similarities and overlap between the rhetorical techniques applied in both activities. In both academic argument writing and debating, one attempts to build and prove a position with reasons, evidence, or examples. In both one tries to appeal to the interests and abilities of the audience in order to convince.

Where the two enterprises usually differ is how one views the opponent. A debate as a formal activity may seek to win by convincing a jury or audience that one team has performed better. In its most degraded practice, such as in noisy American talk-shows, the aim may be to monopolize the discussion, to goad opponents into losing their temper and discrediting themselves (in Latin a 'stultiloquentia'), or to bully them into silence.

Offending or humiliating your opponent into quitting the exchange may be seen as victory in such situations, but it is not the proper province of scholarly writing. Its ideal aim is not to defeat anyone, but to win over the reader to your position, in what composition or rhetorical theorists also call Rogerian argumentation; or we might also call our optimal goal a positive-sum outcome (everyone benefits) instead of the zero-sum aim of debate or angry arguing (I *or* you win).

One of my favorite analogies for academic argumentation is that of a courtroom where a group of judges confers on a case, attempting to convince the others. My most enjoyable arguments have been with close friends over coffee and donuts, certainly not occasions for anger or hurt feelings. An argument paper assumes that its readers have some base information about the subject or a thoughtful curiosity about it, and are expecting you to provide some helpful interpretation about it. Your relationship to them is optimally a concerned or at least benign stance.

But My Culture Doesn't Do That

Non-western writers may nevertheless feel intimidated by the goal of advocating argumentative stances, particularly Korean or Confucian-culture students who live in societies that traditionally prioritize consensus. Richard Nisbett's *The Geography of Thought* (2003) is a helpful analysis of this which analyzes how the culture of ancient Greece gave western thought its analytical and argumentative stamp, and how Asia developed an emphasis on relationships and harmony.

This raises a sensitive question: isn't asking Asian writers to pursue western-style argumentation cultural imperialism? Maybe. I will only counter that, when in Rome, one does as the Romans. If one were composing a Japanese haiku, it would be prudent to consider the norms and audience of the genre. Similarly, if you are writing about western culturally-influenced subjects in the English language, using western notions of rhetoric is going to be inevitable. Moreover, your readers may be native English speakers, and audience is always a vital consideration in crafting a paper. For those who disagree, it might be better to seek a book written in a different language addressing other cultural contexts. I can only write about the one I know.

Moreover, Asian rhetoric wasn't created by Martians; it has similarities and overlaps with any other tradition, the English one included. Pointless writing that fills space while saying nothing is as worthless in Asia as it would be elsewhere. Your argument may certainly seek to demonstrate a relationship of harmony or synthesis of various viewpoints. I will discuss this again later when we come to contrastive rhetoric, but so long as you have a position, *how* you develop it can be done with as much culturally-influenced directness or tact as you like.

But I'm a Student Writing for Experts

You may also object that you are a student working in an acquired language and are unqualified to assert different or original viewpoints on subjects you are still mastering. What if my professor or the experts disagree? But the experts had to learn their craft at one time as well. At an undergraduate or graduate seminar-paper level, your professor knows your writing is a learning exercise, and hopefully sees no threat in an opposing viewpoint; many of my colleagues enjoy such challenges. As well, at a thesis or dissertation level, you may be *right*, and you may have astutely observed a corner of information that you are uniquely expert on. You also have individual interests and experiences that will provide you a different personal understanding of a subject. You have as much right as anyone to defend this interpretation.

Thus you need to have some confidence to write an academic argument paper, because you must believe that your assertions are worth defending. Once again, this is not necessarily done with egotism or aggression. But without a position the essay has no reason to be read by anyone apart from the suffering professor. Just as a politician who sits on a fence can be infuriating, if you won't commit to a stance in your paper out of timidity or safety you will test the patience of your readers, who are also committing their time to reading it. I have had engineers tell me that there's little latitude for argumentative positions in their papers—they deal in facts. But facts are interpretable. A claim that results are valid or correct is itself an argumentative position, as is a statement on their meaning or relevance.

Tip

"Do you love me?" "Well, there are reasons to say yes or no, and everyone has to decide." Your partner will be annoyed by this evasive response. Equally, in an argument paper you need to commit to a position.

1.4 Three Parts of Writing

Our brains seem comfortable thinking in threes, and movies and novels often form trilogies: *The Matrix*; *Lord of the Rings*; *The Divine Comedy*. Human minds tend to prefer 'chunking' ideas into small, digestible pieces, a topic I will return to later. Not all academic arguments have three sub-reasons, but for ease of discussion in this book I will divide many concepts into threes, and this first triplet concerns the building blocks of academic writing: grammar, structure, and content. I compare this to a camera tripod, which will fall over if one leg is missing—and similarly, all these three parts of writing are necessary to a successful paper.

Grammar involves writing meaningful sentences with correct punctuation according to accepted rules of usage. Grammar rules are not natural laws; they are arbitrary conventions agreed on by the language's speakers. But without some commonly-recognized system giving meaning to word combinations, communication cannot occur.

Learning a foreign language's grammar can be tedious, just as the basics of playing a guitar or piano are not always fun, but as proficiency is gained some of these skills become automatic, allowing one to concentrate on other matters. You normally do not think about correct speaking or writing in your own native tongue—the sentences flow out, and your intuition warns you when something is ungrammatical or unnatural, even if you cannot understand why. The 'little bird' in your head tells you that something is wrong. Similarly, no native speaker of English ever fully masters grammar, but many of its processes become unconscious.

Grammar is the most basic issue in writing, and for some people it is their main concern when writing in any language, native or foreign. This can be a problem in itself for academic writing, as grammar is only one leg of the tripod, and I often find students unaccustomed to or resistant to considering the further two components.

Structure is arranging sentences and paragraphs into a meaningful and connected sequence. Do the sentences in a text fit into a coherent whole with a natural flow? A smartphone text message may be only a few lines: "Hi David, come to the pizza house tonight at 7, bye for now, Hyejin." Yet this message contains a comprehensible structure and order: greeting, message, and closing. If these parts were randomized ("Bye for now, Hyejin, come to the pizza house tonight at 7, hi David") even this brief text would be more difficult to understand.

In academic writing there are more formalized sections of introductions, bodies, and conclusions which indicate the parts of the paper and give readers a recognizable structure which allows them to focus on your paper's ideas. And at the higher level of longer papers there is more structural complexity, with abstracts, literature reviews, methodologies, results and discussions, and appendix sections.

Structure also involves how topics and concepts flow in an understandable sequence from beginning to end. If a paragraph's first sentence is about *Hard Times*, the second sentence is about asphalt, the third sentence is about orangutans, and the fourth sentence is about Max Planck, the sentences will seem disconnected and confusing to the reader, even if they are grammatically flawless. Your readers are trusting you with their time, and by the fifth sentence of this chaos they may refuse to continue investing it.

I am not sure that reading journal articles is ever great fun, but I have read enjoyable ones, where the pages flew by and I was at the end without noticing. Often this was certainly not because the material was easy, but because the ideas felt organically connected and flowed into each other. Conversely, a paper where I mutter, "Where did *this* come from?" can be tiring as I struggle to follow an unclear line of reasoning.

Content is the third aspect of academic writing, which refers to the information and meaning the writing carries. If the paper is about airports, does it actually discuss airports and state and prove its argument regarding them, in such a way that the reader can understand your ideas or be persuaded by them? Again, it is possible to write grammatically correct sentences which form a coherent unit that moves fluently from one idea to the next, but if the paper is about airports and only deliberates on basketball, or it fails to prove its arguments, or it confuses or frustrates the reader, or it contradicts its own arguments, or it merely discusses a silly or emotional personal preference regarding airports, the paper may be a failure in doing what it was intended to. I once wrote an undergraduate paper on the nature of evil in *Paradise Lost*, and lost sight of the text, instead drifting off to a philosophical discussion of evil. The paper may have been interesting in its own right, but did not address the topic, which was to interpret the poem. It was content, but the wrong content.

Audience

A vital component of content is considering who the text is written for—and that is why I am unhappy with the '70s writing-as-therapy hippies, as they sometimes over-focus on the writer's personal fulfilment (I exaggerate for some humor). A text that doesn't target the reader's interests or needs is a failure, regardless of how you benefitted from writing it.

If your instructor only wants you to practice your writing skills and the content isn't really important, there is less problem if your essay is framed to satisfy your own interests and knowledge level. But normally academic papers are written for others, and so a content-related issue is that of writing purposes and audience. Why is the paper written, and for who? If you're a freshman, the answer may be no more than that you are writing it because Prof. x is requiring it; but hopefully you have already intuited that the paper was assigned for you to model a real-life writing situation where Prof. x is no longer there, and your audience is broader.

It is thus misguided to write your paper as though its audience were literally and solely your professor or committee. I've had students begin their essay with "Hello, Professor Eckert! How are you? The weather has been getting cold lately..." A good course paper will imagine an unseen group of addressed readers, as the real thing won't be imagining one—scholarly writing *will* be for a collegial group of known or unknown readers. As a rule of thumb, when I was a university student I conceptualized my readers as my classmates—peers and colleagues with similar levels of knowledge who might have an interest in perusing my paper.

Thus it's not wrong to take pleasure in your own work, but good writing in general firstly satisfies the needs of your readers in being informative, efficient, convincing, and lucid. Unless you are writing a personal diary, it is not sufficient that you understand your own text. Your reader must also understand it, or else the entire endeavor is a failure. Becoming annoyed with others for failing to grasp your meanings is rather missing the point, like trying to persuade someone that they don't have a stomach ache, or that they love you. The responsibility is on you to be clear and the reader has a lesser responsibility to work to see your ideas. In short, the reader's time should be seen as more valuable than your own.

1.5 Three Steps of Writing

The three writing parts of grammar, structure, and content deal with how we see the components of an academic paper. We might think of these parts as spatial units, although I realize the analogy is imperfect. The next set of three I will discuss, of planning, writing, and editing, is basically chronological—that is, it happens in time. Unlike the former triplet, the three steps of writing are in progressive sequence, just as steps on a stairs or a ladder are. Similarly, if one needs to step back for some reason, that is fine—but eventually one eventually needs to cross all three steps to get to the top, and none can be jumped over without problems.

Planning is reasonably self-explanatory. For every major project we make it comprehensible and achievable by laying out its parts or steps. I will repeatedly use the analogy of architecture for planning, but in constructing a building we consult a plan, a blueprint, to guide the tasks. Similarly, paper planning involves considering your paper's subject, size, and audience, and making decisions on how the paper will be arranged to meet these goals in the time that you have. This process might be done mentally, roughly sketched out, or carefully detailed on paper or a screen.

The bad news about planning is that you need to do it, and as writing projects get longer, the necessity of planning becomes more urgent. The good news is that it makes little difference how you plan and the actual format or arrangement is your business. Your outline need not be a formal bullet-point schedule; it can be any sort of textual or visual plan which helps you organize your ideas—it could even be a sound or video recording on your smartphone. An outline can be serious, tightly organized, or a mess of scribbles, arrows, and notes. No one is ever going to see it. It can perform its job for you, and then you can throw it away if you wish.

It *is* possible to over-plan, as I perhaps did during my master's. In a sense I was avoiding writing the thesis by composing a rather excessive 32-page handwritten outline. What if I had begun to write after all this expenditure of time and labor, and realized I had made a serious mistake, and needed to make considerable changes—or worse, was too proud or impatient to do so? You can always return to your outline and alter or re-write it. If you want to drive to California and discover that you are headed toward New York, it would be ridiculous to continue out of obstinacy, intending to drive around the earth somehow and reach California from Eurasia. If your outline proves inadequate and you see that your ideas or information are faulty, it is obviously better to stop and revise or begin again.

For this reason, do not be locked into the mindset that planning, writing, and editing forms an ironclad sequence of steps. As I noted with the stairs analogy, sometimes you might need to step back and forward between different activities. During writing, you might need to briefly return to your planning stage, or you might be in editing mode when you realize you need some rewriting.

Writing. The writing and typing of your paper might not be beginning-to-end either. Writers are seldom equally good at writing every part of a paper, and as an undergraduate I was weaker at introductions. My solution was to hurriedly write any sort of rubbish as an introduction to warm myself up and build my confidence—by seeing something on the page—and then delete and re-write it later on. I now find as I age that conclusions are for some reason harder to write. The reader will never know or care in what order you wrote the paper, and in comparison to the old nuisances of typing on paper, with word processors it is easy to move text around easily between sections.

Don't fret if you find that your ideas inevitably evolve after you begin writing; part of writing is discovering and refining as you progress. Most people "write to think," developing their materials as they are handwriting or typing, and it is a mistake to believe that writing is merely transcribing what we have previously decided to communicate. It is my own experience (and yours may vary) that what I intend to write beforehand is inexact and incomplete, and improvement happens while I am doing it.

The writing stage is hugely important in the humanities, where central ideas and arguments are still being worked out and tested. In STEM and technical fields, the writing stage often tends to be briefer. If the results are concluded, the paper may feel like a write-up or afterthought, where one fills in the section boxes. Nevertheless, I don't encourage this mindset, for as textual projects get longer and more complex, the writing issues will multiply.

Editing. Close, careful editing makes text leaner and more effective, and catches mistakes. A much better practice than one-step writing is to create a draft, rest, and return later to hunt down grammatical or typographical errors, or to change, move, or remove pieces of text that do not fit, duplicate something already written, or which waste space. This is a skill which requires discipline, because we tend to fall in love with our writing. We do not want to change it and we think it is beautiful the way it is on the bright, clean paper with the shiny paper clip. But this sort of reflex is going to make you a better writer, and is an integral third stage in the writing process.

It is sobering, or perhaps encouraging, to view online images of early novel drafts written by famous writers. F. Scott Fitzgerald, one of the greatest American authors of the twentieth century, published *The Great Gatsby* only after lengthy revisions done with his editor, Maxwell Perkins. In turn, Fitzgerald helped younger Ernest Hemingway as the latter matured as an author. These were two experienced writers—at the time Hemingway already had worked as a journalist—but even they benefited from editing help. In fact, sometimes very competent writers have more need of editors, as they can develop egos which prevent them from seeing their own work dispassionately. As much as I like Harry Potter, Rowling's later books get over-long.

Equally so, you and I need editing help, or at least we need to edit ourselves. But my experience is that you need to give yourself time between the stages of planning and writing your paper, and revising it. Your brain needs to rest between those stages so that you can view it freshly as a reader. I have repeatedly revised this book over a decade, and it is (hopefully) improved every time when I revisit it and see opportunities for improvements and repairs that I didn't see before. I also know, sadly, that whatever I do, there will still be remaining errors in this book I may recognize in the future.

At the undergraduate level, you will typically write your paper and then the instructor will grade it and add some comments. At the graduate level you will often submit numerous updated versions until your advisor feels the thesis is ready to defend. The revising you do between these drafts is a form of editing—and if you are an undergraduate and only receive your essay back once with a final grade, the comments on the paper are still personalized advice which will help you improve future writing. It is natural to be disappointed or angry if the comments are critical—you might complain over beer about your unfair professor just as I once did. But once you calm down, such comments can be helpful to you in assessing what you are doing right and wrong.

1.6 Part Science and Part Art

As you are going to see, academic writing is part science and part art—that is, there are rules and conventions, but also some scope for personal style. AI can imitate, but it's not *you*. Some writers are tightly organized and others are more freewheeling and spontaneous. When I have students over multiple semesters, I begin to recognize their favorite argument approaches, discursive styles, and other patterns. No one can really teach you how to dance or how to write the perfect paper. I can only show you what I do as a model for you to try or evaluate.

Nevertheless, academic papers are fairly regimented in format and layout, particularly in the social science and hard science disciplines. Just as I always worry that the STEM people will scoff that my methodology is too sentimental or impractical for their serious paper on robot code, others may object to what seems like arbitrary rules and grumble, "*Who says* that papers have to be arranged or written in such a way?" I once had a hostile student in Las Vegas accuse me of being complicit in some outlandish elitist power conspiracy to dictate writing standards, in order to guard Eurocentric class privilege.

These are difficult ideas to address. Composition theory is a young field and hasn't resolved many such questions, although it does consider some writing ethics as reflecting a western-influenced methodology. But whether some standards are only capricious or arbitrary guidelines, there are fairly universal and inevitable patterns in written argumentation that reflect human cognition. People everywhere tend to understand an essay better when the writer first presents the subject, then discusses it, and then has some form of closure, and they are going to understand papers more easily which have a recognizable organizational pattern. Whether such rules are good or right by whatever postmodern standard we apply does not overrule the reality that human brains work as they do.

Many of the rules I lay out will indeed seem random. Perhaps it is obvious that we can't prove an argument that wasn't yet stated, but why do page numbers need to be on the top right? These are admittedly conventions of style or institutional standards, and you will not go to jail for violating them. But neither will you go to prison for wearing socks on your ears and your tie on your toes at a job interview—you are just unlikely to get the job for flouting accepted modes of conduct. In the same way, there are expected practices in writing so that you conform to a community, and your paper may be otherwise rejected or viewed as unserious by others. These professional normative prescriptions allow your writing to be admitted into a dialogue.

Yet the tired cliché for creative arts that one needs to know the rules in order to break them is somewhat also true for academic writing. Typical practices and conventions for elements such as topic sentences and paragraphs are somewhat open to personal style once you become more expert in understanding their logic and functions. It is then time to begin discussion of these topics, beginning with more extensive detail on the first step of writing, of planning.

2 PLANNING

By failing to prepare, you are preparing to fail. — Benjamin Franklin

You can't write about the entire world in 750 words, though students certainly try. Much of planning is *narrowing*—specifying with increasing detail what you are going to write about by removing, as a sculptor does with stone or wood, all of the topics and ideas you are *not* going to write about. Typically, a paper which had a weak and vague plan is easy to recognize: it wanders, repeats content, or tries to discuss too much, resulting in an essay which discusses nothing, because there is no space to develop anything usefully.

Broadly, planning is the process of deciding your topics, arguments, and scope, and then amassing and organizing the information you will use in your paper. The sequence I use is to choose a topic, research and organize my sources, and then make a working argument and outline for the paper. Along the way, I am narrowing my topic down to a manageable size for the project I am working on. We're human—sometimes the finished arrangement springs out at you immediately, and sometimes steps are confused or repeated. How you produce your paper's plan need not be exactly the same every time; it is only important that you *have* a plan. Doing so will help to organize your actions and develop a comfortable and predictable workflow for them.

So far so good. I have never had someone actually challenge

the need to plan, or assert that leaping into a paper with spontaneous abandon is superior. But it is typical for novice writers to pay lip service to it, similar to how we feel exercise and good diet are fine pursuits for *other* people. Such writers may phone in their outlines by scribbling a brief, superficial list.

But I can think of several reasons why planning should be a serious step in writing. The first is, as I have mentioned, the skillset and rigor learned *during* the process of writing is also valuable. Hurriedly stamping out a one-sentence outline may be adequate for a very brief essay, but such a habit becomes increasingly insufficient for longer works, and not planning a dissertation or book would make for an incredibly frustrating experience. Learning to formulate a detailed plan will serve you well at the seminar paper or dissertation stage, just as building a pup tent or greenhouse may involve minimal planning, but an office tower cannot be finished with plans kept in your head.

Second, the time expended on planning will probably be compensated for by time saved during writing. Sometimes when I give timed essay exams, I see two types of students. One thinks, "I have an hour—I need to hurry and start writing." The other takes five or ten minutes to plan. These latter students look as though they are doing nothing, but they are deliberating or making scribbled notes before they write their essays. Even though they have sacrificed some exam time to plan, their essays may be equally as long, for they are easier to write; and they usually rate better grades because they are more focused.

This works against our human tendency to do the easy thing, not the efficient or the best long-term thing. Philosopher Johann Goethe once wrote that what makes people unhappiest is trading what we really want for something we want right now. This applies entirely to writing, where people avoid spending thirty minutes planning their paper, when having one might save days of confusion later. To use architectural terms again, it is like being too impatient to consult a blueprint for a house and rushing out to nail boards together as you find them. What time is saved will be lost when everything falls down, and the need to repair everything or begin again will outweigh any initial time savings.

A further issue is that the paper itself will again likely read as disorganized or substandard to others without a determined order of topics. You may start writing about x, move on to y, and then come back to x again, forgetting that you have already written about it. At the end of the paper you may have a meandering mess which, additionally, forget to address z entirely. This may be thus both structural and content problems. I re-emphasize that your professor and the class is a practice scenario, and in the professional world your paper operates in a competitive economy, where readers may refuse to continue a confusing essay if others are available.

2.1 Fear and Your Body

I will add a last argument for planning and then cease my sermonizing, but I do so to help you. Lacking a plan makes writing much more stressful and intimidating. Without one, you may end up staring at a blank computer screen, frozen and unable to begin, and it is demoralizing to see the cursor blinking and not know where to start. The temptation is to spend "only a few" minutes on Facebook and return, which may end up wasting your entire evening.

If you have a good outline or other preparation, the paper is already in motion, and you will be better situated to proceed. Even if you do feel blocked on a bad day, you have something tangible to refer to which will help you resume your work. I noted that I overdid my master's thesis outline by having 32 handwritten pages, but the positive side of this was that the actual writing was minimally stressful, for I had basically pre-determined all of the content. Each day of writing involved far fewer decisions, as I merely needed to follow my plans.

Many social media memes romanticize the writing activity as a sort of beautiful suffering, where you must agonize over a typewriter late at night with a cigarette and bourbon. I believe this to be nonsense, and being unhappy or anxious has never helped me create better scholarship, or even better fiction. I can only speak for myself, but I recommend you endeavor to make your workflow less stressful and unpleasant where possible, in order to both allow you to concentrate on your task, and to weaken the avoidance association you create between *writing* and *pain*.

One recommendation is that you write often, about anything, so that you will increasingly associate writing with enjoyment. Perhaps one reason I never found academic writing intimidating is that from childhood I wrote stories, poems, and letters. On a regular basis I still write e-mails, blog posts, and social media comments. Optimally, you might pursue a writing activity that you do not need to force yourself to do, even if unrelated to your academic subject. This will of course improve your writing quality generally, but will also build your confidence level when confronting course papers and dissertations.

As well, there are owner's manuals for every electronic device and appliance, but not for us. Another means of reducing the fear impulse is to take the time to examine and improve how our own minds and bodies approach writing tasks in order to make them more comfortable to us. Ernest Hemingway advised writing drunk and editing sober for best results. For a scholarly paper I would not advise this, and my own writing after beery nights in college resulted in bad poetry. My experience is that I accomplish more when my mind is clear and I'm physically most alert, and for me that is late morning. Through experimentation you can observe what your body best prefers—whether you write best at a particular time of day or night; if you need dead silence, or you need the white noise of a café, or music; if caffeine makes you alert or jittery; if you need to be warm, or cool, or outside, or with other people. Learning to accommodate your own mental and physical inclinations may again lessen the expectation that an impending writing task will be unpleasant.

2.2 Choosing a Topic

Before we begin to write a paper, we need to decide what it will be about. In some programs, your professor or partners may assign you your topic. There is a downside in not being able to choose, but there is an upside: you don't have to choose, and your

2 PLANNING

work of deciding is avoided. As the expression and Maya Angelou book goes, there's a reason why the caged bird sings. If so, you can begin working on your project, even if you are not entirely on board with the topic. In STEM fields, topic choice may be easier, as a gap in research on a subject may be more clearly identifiable. But this is not always the case, and my experience is that it happens less often in other disciplines.

If a topic is not given or indicated, how do writers come up with ideas for papers? The easiest way is when ideas are presented to you on a silver platter, explicitly or in context, when you hear or think of something that piques your curiosity and you jot it down. A professor may say something stimulating which gives you a ready idea—one of my published papers did originate in a professor pondering in class, "I wonder why no one has written on this yet?" The lab or group you are in might be working on something from which you find an interesting aspect, or a supervisor may give you advice or recommend a topic. The audience you are writing for—your peers, the professor, or the public—might also affect or direct your choices.

Or, none of this may happen. You may have to cold-bloodedly concentrate on developing a suitable and workable paper idea, and endure false starts and dead ends. Literary theorist Kenneth Burke wrote that "Thinking which does not include thinking about thinking is merely problem solving, an activity carried out very well by fish." You may need to not only think about your paper topic, but consider or experiment with how you might better structure or enable your thinking process.

What I Do

My own go-to approach to planning a paper is to decide on a broad topic such as a work of literature or an idea, and then research the subject to build a basic foundation of knowledge. Then I try to come up with a tentative position on the subject: I think x may be about y. This may jump out at me while I am reading, or it take some time to germinate, and I may need to do things such as wash dishes or walk to let my mind wander and make connections.

But that is what I do, and not what you must. Every writer has a favorite technique to generate ideas, and others rely on chance flashes of insight. Every grad student has a story about a classmate who sat on a couch for months and then suddenly leaped up and wrote a thesis in a weekend. At times, you might need to sit or lie down and force yourself to concentrate, or you might let your mind float. While I discourage students from writing papers the night before, I admit that for some the adrenaline of pressure helps them. It does not help me, and if your printer cartridge runs dry an hour before class your delaying might also result in a late paper.

Some theorists advocate brainstorming, involving writing down every thought as it randomly floats into your head, to help fertilize your mind with ideas. Such ideas were in vogue in the 1970's, and composition scholars such as Peter Elbow recommended forcing yourself to write continuously about the subject without stopping, filling up some pages to warm up your thinking, and then going back and repeatedly editing down the text as you attempt to solidify what is worth using. Another idea is *webbing*, which my previous graduate professor Stephen Brown at UNLV writes about. In this you write your topic in a circle or square, and then randomly think of connecting ideas related to it, writing them on the page with arrows or more circles.

I also know writing theorists who insist, "research first, then argument." Their reason is that some writers fix on a position and then discount or ignore information which counters it. While that is possible, I find this rule too simple, for if you have not even the genesis of an opinion or interest area, it may be impossible to narrow the research you need to do. As an extreme example, there are some 5,000 new articles and books on Shakespeare a year. No scholar could read even this new production, let alone the backlog from previous centuries. It would be better to pre-specify at least some topical corner regarding Shakespeare in order to reduce the reading, although there may of course be subfields so tiny or undocumented that it is possible to simply read everything.

2 PLANNING

My advice remains that you should develop a working position or concept regarding your topic and then affirm or modify your thinking as necessary as you go, and do your best to avoid becoming biased against contradicting information. This gives your research some necessary structure but does not restrict or blind you from changing your plans if you later decide the argument is impractical, unoriginal, or contradicted by the evidence. You may need to start over. This is not a failure and it sometimes happens; discovering what won't work is still progress. I don't mean to discourage anyone, but if you believe research writing should never have false starts, you are perhaps expecting too much. It is disappointing, but it's life, and optimally the work done can be salvaged and redirected elsewhere.

Can You Use AI?

Probably. I promised I would try to incorporate AI tools into this book, and possibly you could use AI generator prompts to produce potential paper ideas. As you can guess, simply parroting the output via copy and paste will probably yield robotic-sounding banalities, but it might be helpful to randomly springboard or brainstorm based off what the generator suggests.

What About Group-Written Papers?

I don't think anything I've written here would be substantively different for a group paper project. You still need a central position grounding your essay. I would guess, though, that group-written papers introduce their own pluses and minuses. On the benefit side, you will have partners who can contribute ideas, support, and feedback. The cost side is that you will need to agree on your paper's focus and arguments, and that may require interpersonal abilities and flexibility as much as composition skills. I would recommend your group clearly establish early on how you will proceed and divide tasks to avoid conflicts; in a solo project you can have your own workflow and style, but in a group your habits may need to mesh together.

2.3 Refining a Topic into a Position

 **Tip**

Choosing a broad topic to appease the professor and minimize your commitment requires less initial work: "My paper is about China." Great. But in the long run, a focused, narrow topic is usually easier to research and write about.

To repeat, refining your topic is largely narrowing it, removing what your paper is *not* about, and increasing specificity as you move from a general subject to a focused position, again considering the parameters set on your project such as audience and length. The cliché 'general audience' is often used—but there really is no such thing as a general audience. In a professional situation such as a journal article or conference you may have a more precise idea of your audience's level of knowledge and expectations, and you might personally know some of the people involved. You may know something about your department's or discipline's culture, and how much conservative or risk-taking it may be in subjects or arguments. But at a course level, as mentioned, I would imagine I am writing my paper for other students, which will help me to gauge what my potential readers already know and how to address them.

The other variable in refining is paper length or word count. A common difficulty my students have with topics is choosing one appropriate to the size of the essay. This skill requires some experience, and I won't claim it is mastered immediately, but it is important. A fifty-page research paper about thumbtacks will be difficult to write without boring the reader, but a three-page paper might be right. Yet being too narrow is in practice rare; most students and graduate candidates overshoot with their topics, resulting in shallow, hurried discussions. I cringe whenever students write about globalization, probably the largest socioeconomic change in the world in the last century. To attempt to treat globalization in three pages is ridiculous—nothing profound is likely to come from that short space. What you are likely to produce is a skim or list of ideas without giving any compelling discussion or proof of anything.

I understand the temptation. I overestimated my topic size numerous times as a student. A broad topic is easier to think of, and sounds more impressive than a paper about the globalization of left-handed gardening scissors. It feels more useful and important to solve the very big problems. But the paper about scissors will likely be easier to write, as there are fewer sources to read and a smaller set of concepts to organize and arrange.

One wild card in this is originality: whether you are expected to produce *new* arguments. In a course paper you probably aren't, and it likely matters little if fifty other students have written on the same thing. In a thesis or diss topic more novelty is expected, and it becomes necessary to strike a balance between the popular and easy subjects—with mountains or prior research to wade through—and esoteric ones with little written on them. It is possible to choose so obscure or recent a subject that there is too little research to base anything but a speculative essay on. But this doesn't happen often in my experience. As little as a generation ago the challenge in research was finding enough information. Now the usual obstacle is the torrent of online sources to sift through. The more common problem is that after doing initial research you may find yourself feeling that you have bitten off more than you can chew.

As well, you may not believe it is interesting for others to read a paper about something highly specialized, but in my experience that is the case. Some of my favorite authors, Malcolm Gladwell and Leavitt & Dubner (*Freakonomics*), write essays on such focused things as ketchup or cheating teachers in Chicago; the articles are much more memorable reading than a general essay on fast food or education. I've read countless semi-identical papers about plastic surgery, but if someone writes about "freckle surgery for elderly store greeters," I'm curious. I'm going to take an interest in that paper, as it is something new. I realize your paper is not journalism and that its potential readers will be academics, but follow the analogy. I know you may be worried that your family or friends will roll their eyes in disgust on your paper topic on a seemingly miniscule concern, but they are probably not its target audience.

If I have convinced you of the benefit of close narrowing, how to get to this point is the concern. Constricting a particular topic may come organically to you without overthinking it, and my proposed techniques here may seem too contrived, which is a fair objection. If so, you don't need them. But I indicate them as starting points, after which you can hone or prettify the results.

Narrowing Strategy 1: Choosing a Sub-Argument

This may make more sense when I discuss thesis statements, but ordinarily at the planning stage you might divide your paper's argument into sub-arguments or sub-topics which you will address throughout the essay. Numerous times throughout my graduate programs I submitted proposals where my professor warned me that I was taking on too large a topic, and recommended that of my three sub-arguments I choose one and make this the basis of my paper.

Narrowing Strategy 2: Using Limiters

This strategy might be easier to demonstrate than to define, but for a vague or oversized topic it may be possible to restrict the discussion to a particular category of that topic. For example, taking the subject of globalization, there are common filters which might reduce the scope of this subject, just as filter terms and check-boxes on internet sites or search engines do.

Limit by globalization's effects on
- Concept: politics, marriage, travel, pollution
- Demographics: the elderly, females, fathers, redheads, students

- Geography: a single country, a city, a type of landscape, rural, urban
- Industry: agriculture, entertainment, banking, tourism
- Time: a specific time period or year
- Case study: a particular example which effectively illustrates it (IBM's 2005 sale to Lenovo; Covid-19)

Optimally, if the filtered topic remains too large, multiple filters could be applied (globalization's effects on married redheads in Bern who work in banks?), or within an individual category, two elements could be compared (globalization pre-1914 and 1918-1939; Spanish Influenza vs. Covid-19).

If the last term is not clear, a case study focuses on one single example of something and attempts to understand it or draw conclusions from it. A business paper might examine a company's actions or responses (a new product approach, bankruptcy, technological changes) and attempt to derive explanations or lessons for the future. In international relations, one could study a political or cultural phenomenon. For example, in a single-case-based study you might ask, "Why did the French give up and leave Vietnam?" In a comparative-case–based study you might ask, "Why does Germany have better relations with post-war allies in the twenty-first century than Japan does?" Again, the focus is on scrutinizing that particular situation as a means to gain broader insights.

The examples here regard international relations or the social sciences. A STEM student may object that such papers are typically concerned with whether the experiment or process works or not, and there is little need to filter. If so, fine. But how did you choose the experiment?—and in what key *way* does the experiment work or not, and who or what might be affected by its success or failure? For example, in a paper describing a process to apply an electric charge to metal-reinforced concrete to retard oxidation, if process x causes result y, does y apply everywhere, or only in certain situations? Is x the best way to obtain this result, and on what grounds (cost, safety, ethics, speed, green-ness, reliability)? The topic could also be filtered by application (what type of structures: buildings, bridges, subways?) or geography (hot climates, cold climates, humid ground, unstable ground)?

I suspect that within certain disciplines, there are standard questions or contending schools of thought which provide ready limiters for intended topics. There indeed are in my own field of literature, which are usually called lenses or 'readings,' not in the common sense of the word, but the more restricted meaning of a type or school of interpretation. Some common ones are:

- Plot: What does the plot mean? What events in the narrative have significance to the text or its messages?
- Characters: Is there a special meaning to a character, or in a relationship between two or more characters? Does a character change or react to an event in an interesting way?
- Symbolism: Is there a political, ethical, historical, feminist, religious, allegorical, or other level of interpretation in the text which you see?
- Scene analysis: Does one scene or passage help to explain or change the meaning of the entire text?
- Poetics: Is there an unusual way of phrasing words or arranging words in the text, or making them rhyme or create an image pattern? Why?
- Biographical/historical: Can the text be explained by examining the author's life, or by the historical or cultural circumstances it was written in?
- How can the text be interpreted by feminist, queer/LGBT+, eco-green, Marxist, modernist, postmodernist, psychological, or other theoretical approaches?

All of these ideas might help you to find an interpretation of the text which goes beyond a wide but shallow summary. For example, instead of analyzing theme x in *Do Androids Dream of Electric Sheep?*, you might analyze one character in the novel, arguing how that character exemplifies or advances that theme. Or, if this is too broad, you might multiple-filter and select one

2 PLANNING

scene or significant section of the novel where one that character does so. (Again, admittedly, you could perhaps ask an AI generator prompt to help you with this.) For example:

Harry Potter & the Philosopher's Stone demonstrates the value of courage.

This is okay, but vague and unoriginal. Try filtering by character.

Hermione in *Harry Potter & the Philosopher's Stone* demonstrates the value of courage.

This is better. Try continuing to filter by scene.

Hermione, in the first train scene in *Harry Potter & the Philosopher's Stone*, demonstrates the novel's value of courage.

This is stronger, and I am curious. What is it about that particular scene which you think has importance? This was a student's paper which earned her an A+. Or:

An important theme in *Dubliners* is selfish people taking advantage of the innocent.

This is also imprecise. What people? Why? Try filtering by story.

An important theme in "The Boarding House" in *Dubliners* is selfish people taking advantage of the innocent.

This is more specific. It can still be improved. Try filtering by characters, or concept.

An important theme in "The Boarding House" in *Dubliners* is Polly selfishly taking advantage of Mr. Doran, as it mirrors what happened to Polly's mother.

This is interesting and I want to see how the writer connects these two threads.

Tip

Don't forget the minor fictional characters. Some of my best papers were written about Gertrude and not Hamlet, or Neville instead of Harry Potter. It's also easier to research and focus on them, because you only have to re-read and think about a smaller area of text where they appear.

2.4 Discussion Frames

As with topic limiters, discussion frames or styles may be more easily demonstrated than explained. Chiefly, what I mean is the logical shape of the argument at an abstract level. Perhaps the most common discussion frame is comparison, to say x is like or not like y. A related frame is evaluation, to say x is better than y. There are many more, but I will restrict myself here to ones which may be of relevance to academic writing situations—with the normal proviso that if these frames give you a fertile new viewpoint or inspiration, well and good, and if you find them too artificial, they are merely suggestions.

Here are some common frames which might help you to spatially or logically arrange your argument, to either create a claim or suggest a way to fill a research gap:

Comparison

As stated, here you compare things and argue that they are similar or different and something may be learned from the comparison—or that one is better or worse somehow: "a large university is better than a small one because a, b, and c." This format is also called 'compare and contrast' in undergraduate papers. The essay may make a value judgment or simply explain how two things are similar (compare) or different (contrast): Hester in *The Scarlet Letter* is x as opposed to her daughter Pearl who is y. Under my 'limiters' rubric I listed case studies, and multiple case studies could also be compared against each other: How did the legal case Smith vs. Foster (1976) compare to Merced vs. Yang (1989)?

Such papers require a basis of comparison—in what way are x and y comparable? The concepts compared should not be too similar—if you compare two pencils there is little to say—or too different: if you compare Lady Gaga and a train because both are made of atoms, or Beowulf and Atticus Finch because both are fictional characters, the comparison will not evince very much. The best comparison papers suggest a connection that is interesting or informative, such as a comparison of Sherlock Holmes and Hercules Poirot on the basis that both are detectives.

My least favorite comparison papers are where the writer 'argues' that "both large and small universities have benefits and drawbacks, and everyone has to decide for themselves." Everything has benefits and drawbacks, and everyone already needed to decide for themselves on them, and this statement says nothing new of interest.

Analysis

In this frame you prove a position by breaking down things or concepts into parts, in order to explain how they interact or to derive a conclusion: "Examination of blood glucose levels in these patients suggests that they might benefit from low-carbohydrate diets." These papers are often good for breaking down an engineering or design problem, such as identifying why an engine component failed, or a business paper might analyze a specific business or event and make an argument about its qualities or results: "We can see that Acme Products' marketing advertisement uses the visual strategies of a, b, and c." A social science paper might look at a political event or natural disaster and unpack its components. This frame approach can also be done with literature: "Through examining the evidence, the likeliest ending for *The French Lieutenant's Woman* becomes clearer."

Process Analysis

In this variation analysis is considered chronologically, and the position might be an explanation of how a sequence or group of multiple events or steps combine to create a result, or the relationship between them: "The programmed instructions x and y will result in the robot arm doing z." This sort of paper is more common in hard science or social science topics, but could be done in literature also: "a, b, and c form a series of events which subsequently cause Eveline to panic in *Dubliners*."

A variation on this is a *Cause and Effect* approach, how x causes y: "Because of these events, Durian Air went bankrupt." Often the task is to show that two things are not coincidental, but that one leads to another: Napoleon did x in 1812, y happened. Because Macbeth did not listen to what the witches said, z occurred. Either the cause or the effect could possibly be emphasized in the paper, although again the point is to demonstrate the sequential relationship between the two factors.

Prediction

In this paper one takes a position predicting future events: "Next year the Euro will decrease in value because of a, b, and c." For many topics this discussion frame is limited, and the paper might not be worth reading next year after the prediction is no longer relevant; but for quickly-changing subjects such as current events or politics such papers can be interesting.

Problem-Solution

Here a writer describes a solvable problem and proposes a solution: "The best way to diminish inner city traffic congestion is by a, b, and c." These papers often involve political or technical issues. Many of my past STEM (science, technology, engineering, medicine) papers were technically problem-solution in design, as they identified some material or medical difficulty and then proposed a process to solve it: autonomous cars are not safe, so here is an experiment for an improved guidance system; gas sequestration is dangerous, so here is a safer process for storage; medical charts aren't always available, so here is a secure system to improve access. Theoretically, one could again emphasize either the problem *or* the solution, and the problem could be taken for granted and only briefly covered (one doesn't need a long defense why fatal autonomous car accidents are bad). But a paper stating only solutions without even *mentioning* the problem would likely confuse the reader.

Students often like this frame, but as with compare and contrast papers, problem-solution essays can be poorly managed. The most common problem I see in non-STEM papers is obvious or unrealistic solutions: "the best way to solve traffic jams is to develop flying cars" is not a useful argument, as this is not a realistic short-term outcome. Nor is "campus alcoholism can be solved by more responsible drinking habits" or "prostitution will be diminished by teaching men to have healthier attitudes to sex." Great. These answers say little that is interesting or new unless they discuss how to make these outcomes happen. As well, you may need to anticipate and answer the question, if your solution is so wonderful, why hasn't someone tried it?

A case study approach (more on this soon) might also work well in problem-solution essays. For example, if your paper is about school bullying you might examine how a some school district in Texas or Scotland dealt with bullying, and then examine how it might be applied to your situation. Business paper writers also often like such papers as they have practical relevance. A paper on how to make hiring or supply management more efficient, again showing corporate examples of such policies being attempted, might have valuable real-world implications. The writer of a thesis on how to make corporation x function better might be especially attractive as an employee to that corporation after graduation.

Interpretation

What does something *mean*? This sort of frame involves explaining the meaning or significance of a text, act, or some communication. I don't want to give you the idea that this is the only or chief mode for literature students, but such a style often fits papers on literary criticism, where a problem of understanding a written text is involved. Why does Steinbeck have a chapter about a turtle in *The Grapes of Wrath*? What is the character function of Paul's father in "Paul's Case"? Is *Utopia* meant to be political philosophy or satire? Why did Lorraine Hansberry use a certain type of scene construction? Or, in a social science paper, one might try to understand what one of North Korea's policy announcements means, or what a politician's visual gestures mean. Such papers take a position by attempting to answer such questions, and in a way this form is again similar to analysis.

Challenging Conventional Wisdom

This is perhaps my favorite structure. It involves disputing an orthodox assumption about something. "Most scholars believe that x is true, but this paper shows that y is a better explanation"; or, "The critical consensus is that the author meant a in her book, but a closer reading shows that she meant b." Or, perhaps it is less aggressive for a less confident newcomer to a field to write something like this: "No one seems to have noticed that a is related to b."

Recently, I read an essay where the author argued that people *should* show favoritism in hiring friends; although I disagreed, the logical process which the writer used was interesting. This is a more advanced type of paper to write, because you first need to learn the orthodox view before you counter it, and have evidence to show this is the majority viewpoint. You need to fairly represent what the conventional wisdom is before you confront it, so that you avoid a "scarecrow" argument: "Most people believe Mayella Ewell is evil, but the text shows..." This isn't an honest statement—you need to prove that most readers believe Mayella Ewell [*To Kill a Mockingbird*] is a villain before you build a case against that belief.

Case Study

This somewhat overlaps with other categories, because a case study paper could be a comparison, analysis, or problem/solution paper, and so on. The difference is that as indicated in the discussion on filtering, in a case study you focus specifically on an example of something and attempt to understand it or draw conclusions from it. The reasoning may be more *inductive*, meaning that you are trying to generate larger principles or explanations from examining a specific incidence of something. A business paper might examine a company's decision or some event (a labor strike, bankruptcy, technological change) and attempt to derive explanations or lessons from it for future application.

Another way of categorizing case studies is by those mentioned earlier—you might write a single case study, which looks closely at one (or a small set) of incidents and makes judgments, as opposed to a multiple case study, which looks at a larger set and attempts to derive comparisons or patterns. But admittedly, the latter approach is starting to sound more like a flat-out comparison paper than the specificity that a case study usually has.

Single case study: What can we learn from the failure of X Cosmetics? What can we learn from this fuel cell process?

Multiple case study: What common pattern can we see in these airlines that failed? Among these hydrogen fuel cell processes, why did some work better than others?

When I taught low-level academic writing, I often designed the course so that students practice these different discussion frames in order of difficulty throughout the semester, following Bloom's taxonomy of reasoning skills. Benjamin Bloom orders cognition into a hierarchy of complexity, moving from knowledge, comprehension, application, analysis, and evaluation, to synthesis—creating new knowledge. Comparison papers may come earlier to you because they are generally conceptually easier, and frames involving analysis or original synthesis of ideas may take a groundwork of practice to move up to.

But one is not better than another, and in time you will find your own favorite patterns or forms. There are also argumentative positions which do not fall neatly into one frame, or which overlap others. These frames are here to help, not to restrict. It's my experience that argument formulation usually suggests itself based on the topic, and it's seldom that I've had to myself consider which frame to use. But again, I include them for those who want to try them or who wish to learn about some of the concepts underlying argumentation.

2.5 Note Taking

As you read about your subject, I recommend taking notes to remember ideas and quotations you might use in your paper. There is no single best way to do this. I prefer writing on paper, but many type their notes, and when I wrote my dissertation I had two monitors, and used one for planning and notes and the other for writing. I can only relate various strategies which I have developed over the years and which work for me. This might be done before, during, or after an outline plan is made.

Why bother with even more planning? Why not just read some texts or websites and then write the paper? The reason is likely predictable: if writing about a small text or experiment with few sources, the relevant ideas and where they are may be remembered, but this becomes impossible in the longer works you are learning to write, when the training wheels will be gone. Nearly every student has paused while writing a paper and thought, "yesterday I read the perfect quote on this which will fit right here"—and then wasted time searching through a pile of photocopies or browser tabs to find that quotation, perhaps even ultimately forgetting what was being looked for or how it fit into the paper. I did this as well. Having notes already prepared on what was written, and where, would reduce this process to seconds, allowing you to incorporate the source while the idea remains clear in your mind.

Planning Workflow

I don't want you to think there is only one optimal sequence of actions in planning, because everyone is different, and because I don't employ the same practices in every writing project. I will only tell you what I typically do, which is to:

1. Decide on a rough tentative topic or position
2. Tailor research and reading to this, making notes
3. Prepare a more specific argument and outline

But again I stress that my process might vary, and there may be backtracking on steps. As well, I don't always consciously think about these steps or separate them, and they might all gradually unfold together. Again, there is no correct way to plan, so long as it helps organize your content and prepare you to more effectively write, and with less anxiety about the project.

To trace this workflow in more detail, in my second step of reading and note-taking I usually begin by searching out books, journal articles, and internet resources on my particular area of interest. While selecting materials, I may do a quick scan or triage—meaning that I divide the sources into ones which are not relevant, those which have some minor data or evidence I can use, and the ones which may be important or critical for my paper. I don't want to waste time on sources which aren't helpful, even if they might be interesting for other reasons. I can always note the title for another time, or take a smartphone photo of the cover if it's in print.

I then proceed to a fuller reading of the sources. As I read, I have a sheet of paper ready, or the computer screen where I note down ideas, quotations, or facts which may be useful later, along with the title of the source and page numbers or other details. This doesn't need to be perfect, so long as it helps you find the lines of text. Here is an actual example I once made, where "contemporary novelists" is a short form of the article title:

> <u>contemporary novelists</u>
> Ishiguro cites Proust, Chekhov, Bronte as influences 123
> Ishiguro also left Nagasaki 123
> — a meditation on sublimated pain - lost her homeland, husband, daughter 123
> — all Ish's characters are looking back to explain themselves 125
> a vivid narrator memory compromised by contradictions 127
> Etsuko grieves and copes by fixating on the past 130
> more sources 140
>
> <u>narrative skepticism</u>
> — the modernist concern of knowing 167
> pale light suggests a self-deception realized 177
> suffer from obsessive, compulsive repression 189

All this allows me to quickly find what I want later when I am writing the paper and wish to implement some quotation or piece of information. If I have a longer and more complex project I may have several sheets of paper with these notes, and I might even use numbers or colored highlighters to indicate which part of the paper the entry is related to. I use paper sheets, but some people use index cards or sticky notes, and of course a smartphone or computer file would function as well.

I find lately that I am using a word processor more for note taking, because I can type faster than I handwrite. Here is a newer fragment of notes I took on a paper on Agatha Christie's *Murder on the Orient Express*.

Forever England - Alison Light
*Christie became synonymous with lavish reconstructions of 'period' as she became hyper-English 62
"the high priestess of nostalgia" 62
But doesn't Christie undermine this Victorian niceness with her

murders? 61-62
Unlike Holmes's world, we take for granted that genteel families are rotten? 67
Tropes and linguistic cues are mixed and slightly parodied 68
Christie's archness and "refusal of seriousness" like Waugh 68
Poirot is not a gentleman? He is plain and bourgeois? *Not sure.* 78

I am hoping you will notice two things. One is that you are probably finding these notes gibberish, as they are brief and contextualized. While that's to be expected if you have not read the novel or the work of criticism, the notes are compressed information even for me. I write short notes so that I am not overwhelmed by pages and pages of words when writing, and the cost of doing so is that the notes are not very clear months later. But by then the paper is done—and if I need to revise, I will do the best I can.

Second, I hope you will see that I sometimes briefly have a small conversation with the notes, indicating where I think the argument is important (there is an asterisk *), or where I'm doubtful or I disagree with the claim (there is a question mark, or I've written "Not sure." That doesn't mean I have disrespect for the book or author, but that I want to note points of disagreement that may be important later—and on which I might change my mind.

2.6 Outlining

It might be helpful to discuss outlining as a typographical matter, although there may be little to say. An outline is simply a graphical or textual map of the paper. If your outline is four scribbled words you will get what you pay for. But otherwise, there is really no wrong way to compose one, and an outline can be in any format that you find useful or easy to write. If it is full of scribbled arrows, smudges, and erasures, so what? If it helps you to write the paper, it is correct. Your outline's appearance and design make no difference to the reader, who will never see it. My outlines are conventional with numbers and key-words, but a more scientific or mathematical thinker might prefer a flowchart or a more symbolic arrangement on the paper. A visual person might have connected circles with different-colored words or lines. Again, an AI chat generator *might* be helpful at helping you visualize these ideas spatially or textually.

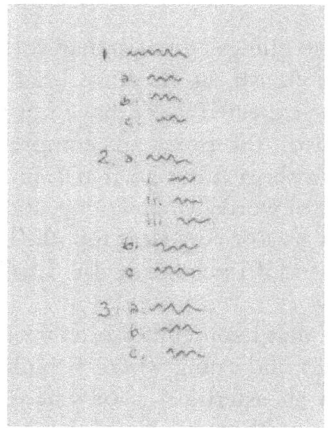 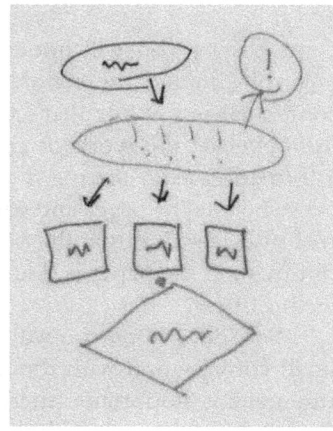

Number / point-form style   Spatial / color style

If I may fudge a little, however, in not prescribing what an outline should be, but describing what an effective one often is—from my experience having students write outlines, they usually have too little information in them. If they write a point form outline, they tend to have only first-level headings:

1) Thesis: No character in *Brave New World* is heroic
2) Lenina
3) Bernard
4) The Savage
5) Conclusion

For a quick scribble before writing an in-class exam, this is perhaps adequate. For a planned paper, it's bad—it gives minimal help to guide the writer in building the paper or remembering its

2 PLANNING

ideas. It would provide more guidance with second or third-level headings (or a corresponding hierarchy or complexity if visual shapes or something else is used). Point 3 might read as:

3) Bernard
    a. Bernard is flawed and self-pitying
    b. Bernard does not really love Lenina
    c. Bernard betrays his friends to try to save himself

A longer paper might break down this structure further, and list page numbers from the book for later reference:

c. Bernard betrays his friends to try to save himself
   i. He gives no help when the others are attacked (188)
   ii. He blames the others to the World Controller (205)
   iii. He breaks down and cries in childish whining (207)

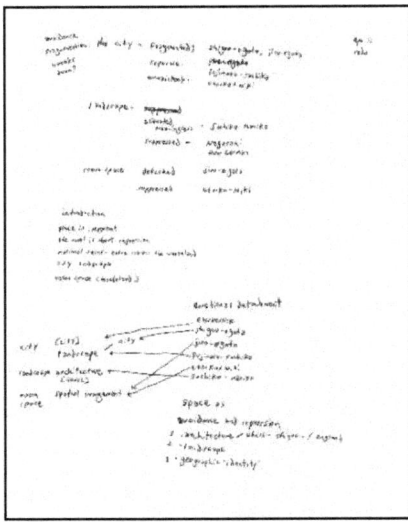

One of my own outlines, a combination number/spatial style

To summarize, planning saves more time later than it initially costs. The romantic stereotype of Mozart is that he wrote in a passionate frenzy toward a finished masterpiece, and that of Beethoven is that he plodded meticulously with endless corrections. These are musical clichés and not totally historically true; but so far as they go, most people probably fancy that they are like Mozart, whereas they are probably more like Beethoven. Nevertheless, people have seen images of Beethoven's score manuscripts, which are full of scrawled notes and alterations and erasures, and nobody seems to think worse of him for it. What matters is the music, just as what matters is your final paper.

3 THESIS ARGUMENTS

I'm not a Bob Dylan fan, but Dylan once told John Lennon, "Your music is nice, but it doesn't *say* anything." This apparently stung Lennon into taking the Beatles into new directions. I still occasionally encounter a paper which is well-written, which 'discusses' an issue and cites quotations and examples, but nowhere states a viewpoint on the issue. It doesn't say anything.

Similarly, in literature courses I receive papers which are little more than plot summaries, without analysis or interpretation. It is like a friend who describes a movie watched the day before but never offers any opinion of whether he or she liked it, or why. Why tell me then, if these facts are on Wikipedia? Just as a court trial without a verdict is useless, so is an argument paper without an argument. It is also distressing to grade, for the paper may reflect hard work, but it is not what was assigned.

As I mentioned, in graduate seminars I encounter STEM students who say that this is very nice for the humanities, but how can a scientific paper have a subjective interpretation? The experiment worked, or it didn't. Fair enough—but perhaps such a text should just be called a report—and if that's what the instructor wants, fine. But to me there is still scope for an argumentative position, such as on the experiment's relevance or application. Even a claim regarding validity or replicability might make the paper more compelling. I am not in such fields, but it feels to me that asserting what the results mean, or how we might understand or apply them, is a pretty crucial professional activity. Who better than the person who conducted the experiment?

3.1 Stress-Testing Your Argument

Assuming you do have an argument to make, a good writer might test it by subjecting it to an imagined opponent's potential objections. Perhaps these next testing questions belong with the earlier discussion on discursive frames in Chapter 2, but they relate to the problem of phrasing a position into real words.

Test 1. Obvious or Factual Claims Usually Don't Make Good Thesis Arguments

Thesis statements which report an obvious or objective fact are not wrong, but they're seldom very interesting. I once read an editorial titled "The best way to prevent a coronavirus recession is to beat the coronavirus." Groundbreaking. But this can also happen with academic essays:

In *The Remains of The Day*, Stevens gradually feels guilty for serving a lord who was revealed to be a Nazi sympathizer.

This paper will show that the height of the tsunami wave generated by the experiment tank was two meters.

Again, these aren't bad, but the first is just a plot summary. Every reader knows that Stevens feels guilty for the reason given, for this is what the novel is about. There is little more to say or prove—what can possibly follow after this beside more plot summary? The second one isn't a commonly known fact, and will only be shown by your results, but again, so what? The thesis gives the reader no real viewpoint or opinion. The height of the wave was two meters, but there is no indication why this is important or controversial. These two might work better as this:

In *The Remains of The Day*, Stevens gradually feels guilty for serving a lord who was revealed to be a Nazi sympathizer, but he convinces himself that Miss Kenton has wasted her life, not him, to avoid accepting it.

This paper will show that the height of the tsunami wave generated by the experiment tank was two meters, but that Kumar's process is only effective with seawater, not fresh.

I made this up—there's no Kumar's process—but both examples now have an interesting interpretation that the reader might be curious to see proven. Again, STEM writers may cavil that the procedure worked, and that's a fact—what do you want me to say? But if it were merely a fact, you wouldn't have needed to demonstrate it. There must have been some knowledge gap in what you did—why, how, or for what reason or application you did the procedure that wasn't known before—that might be remarkable to state.

Corollary: A Non-Falsifiable Argument May Also Be a Poor One

An argument consisting only of facts is problematic, for there's little left to do—but an argument which can't theoretically be *dis*proven should also raise doubts. I will cover logic more later, but for now, as counterintuitive as it sounds, sound academic arguments should be refutable: that is, it should be possible to disagree.

The *Ramayana* is an interesting poem because it was written by time-traveling space aliens.

The remote-assisted brake controlling system failed because there is a conspiracy by the world bankers to prevent autonomous cars.

These are again silly examples to demonstrate the point. Both claims are so outlandish that there is no solid ground to oppose them on. A position where you can't anticipate any way that someone could disagree may be just a potent argument—but it may also indicate something is very wrong. C. S. Lewis once wrote that a belief in invisible cats can't be disproven—your inability to see them proves there are invisible cats. This is why conspiracy theories can be so seductive, as they are often designed in such a way that nothing can refute them. If you believe the government is hiding space aliens from the public, a lack of evidence for space aliens proves how successful the government is at hiding them.

Test 2: Is the Argument Serious and Provable?

A good academic argument is useful to other scholars. If my position is that my belly-button itches because it's a) full of lint, and b) I don't bathe enough, I might be able to summon compelling evidence and reasons for it, but it's of course a ridiculous topic.

An academic argument normally is supportable with serious evidence, and not merely the writer's personal emotions or preferences. Arguing that one author deserved the Nobel literature prize more than another because you like that author's works better is not a suitable argument—nor is saying one musician's music is superior to another's based on your private tastes.

There are two caveats; one is that if you were writing a personal essay for a music website or other where you feel your likes and dislikes are critically authoritative, fine. You could also write an academic paper where you used survey results or some other set of criteria outside your personal tastes. Rhapsodizing why you enjoy coffee or beer better might make an enjoyable social media article, but it would not be an appropriate scholarly argument—unless you could find external reasons showing that one drink is healthier, or more people prefer one, or that there are social or historical grounds for one preference to be significant.

Summary: Does the Argument Hit the 'Sweet Spot'?

Putting these questions together so far, I am essentially advocating the undefinable: that your argument fall in the middle 'sweet spot' between being pedantically obvious and improvable or fantastic. This may be overthinking the matter entirely, or perhaps you see something stimulating here. What I am essentially recommending is that you generate an argument which has something interesting new to prove, but not too much so. If you are having a late-night conversation with friends, it would not be amusing for long to discuss whether rocks are hard; generally, they are. But it would also not do to discuss whether all the rocks have been microchipped to spy on us, or what size of rock is prettier. One topic is preposterous, the other is frivolous. It would be better to find something within these extremities where a dialogue is possible.

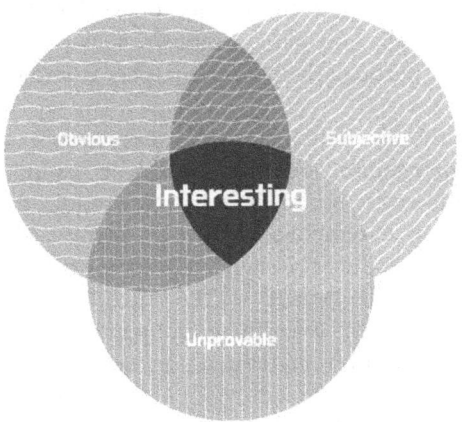

To concretize this differently, occasionally I encounter people who feel that literature means whatever anyone feels it does, and no one has a right to say they are wrong. But if anything can be anything without needing reasons, discussion is pointless—and sometimes this indeed is a cynical way for lazy people to end dialogue while appearing wise. I think there is a better middle ground. Literary texts may not often have binary correct/incorrect answers, but there may be a narrower range of better explanations that form a 'sweet spot' along a continuum. Some critics hold that not even the author's own opinion is the final one, but we may be able to show that x is a compellingly probable explanation and that y is unlikely, if it contributes to a discourse of ideas.

3.2 Thesis Statements

As mundane as it sounds, eventually your beautiful arguments need to be words. A thesis statement is the sentence or group of sentences which indicate the argument of the paper. An anchor is a small piece of metal relative to a ship, but even a giant cruise ship will be adrift without it—thus the icon for this chapter. An academic paper's thesis statement similarly is the least expendable element of the essay. Without one, the reader may be unable to see or contextualize the larger point of the paper or to follow the flow of ideas, particularly in longer papers where these ideas may be difficult ones.

Sometimes the word 'thesis' alone is used as a short form for an argument position, but this should be distinguished from a 'thesis' as the entire long research paper required for a graduate degree. A thesis statement is also not the same as a topic sentence, which often introduces a single body paragraph's subject—the thesis statement is usually in the introduction paragraph or section, and describes what the entire paper will be about.

An effective thesis statement generally does three things:

1. It specifies the subject of the paper to follow
2. It states the writer's position on the subject
3. It gives an indication of the major topics to follow

Bicycle paths are a good idea because they will promote fitness and reduce strain on roads.

The *subject* (1) is bicycle paths. The writer's *position* (2) is that they would be a good idea. The writer *indicates* (3) that the paper will discuss two reasons why, that bicycle paths would a) promote fitness and b) reduce strain on roads. By this sentence the reader knows the paper's subject, the writer's position, and the major claims which will follow.

To help illustrate these concepts I have used a simple thesis statement. For an actual paper it might be longer or more complex:

Ralph in *Lord of the Flies* is a better leader than Jack because he provides stable rules, looks to the future, and takes responsibility for problems.

In *Dubliners*, for Eveline, Mrs. Mooney, and Mrs. Kearney marriage is a means to an end and not love; their real concern is to escape a harsh life, to move up the social class ladder, and to avoid embarrassment.

These thesis statements are similarly organized, and I will of course discuss variations, but I write them to show examples where these same three elements are conveyed: in the first, the subject is *Lord of the Flies*, the position is that Ralph is a better leader than Jack, and the thesis indicates the reasons to be discussed. The second similarly has three characters in *Dubliners* as a subject, argues that they marry for personal goals and not love as its position, and states three reasons why.

Is it necessary that you write your thesis statement at the planning stage of the paper project, or at some certain point in writing, or as it appears in your paper? Of that I am less certain, and I suspect that so long as you have a reasonably specific idea of your paper's thesis argument, its actual phrasing is less time-critical. Optimally, I have my thesis statement ready at the planning stage because my structure and argumentation will be more focused. But I admit that sometimes I write an unpolished statement to get rolling and revise it later.

No Surprises

Novice writers and new learners of English may be tempted to approach an academic paper as they would a speech because it is a familiar process. There are admittedly likenesses between academic papers and speeches, in that in both you might be trying to persuade an audience. But there are moves in speaking that you can't or would not normally do in writing. One technique that people deploy in speeches is to build tension by keeping the audience in suspense: "I am going to tell you something that will change your life." An infomercial might similarly begin by building up to revealing the product, raising the audience's curiosity. This is similar to the 'clickbait' posts on social media which say "You won't believe what these supermodels did" in order to draw the viewer in.

Academic papers should generally not do this. They explain what the paper's goal is when it begins, so that the reader has a grounding and context for what will follow. Resist the temptation to be dramatic or coy with a title or introduction in order to entice. Some modes of speech making see a speech as a sort of story, and some TED-Talk type speeches are even described as such—they are the speaker's journey, or the like. But academic papers aren't stories. Our brains are wired to respond strongly to narratives, but this must again be resisted. Few people would want to view a movie where at the beginning the actors come onstage and say, "Hello, we are the characters in this film. This is the message we want to tell you, and to do it we are going to fall in love, argue over a misunderstanding and break apart, and later we'll get back together and marry." But this is what academic papers do by declaring at the beginning what will be argued and how the paper will proceed.

Why can't the reader just pick up the arguments as they appear? I mentioned in the previous chapter that planning can be minimal with a brief essay, but it becomes vital as the work becomes longer. Similarly here, making finding your paper's argument the reader's problem is not a good habit, for in a short paper with a simple claim, this should not be difficult; but as writing projects lengthen and information becomes more complex, the reader has enough cognitive burden understanding your information without trying to guess what you mean to show by it. As well, I will reiterate that your professor is grading you, but you are learning to model an imaginary and *voluntary* audience of readers, and such people are making a time investment in your paper. If they suspect you will never get around to a point, they may abandon it.

A last analogy I will use is dancing. Dancing is most enjoyable if you know the steps and you see their pattern and know where they will go. If you are dancing with someone and you don't know the steps, you may feel like you are being suddenly pulled and jolted, and unpleasantly surprised by random movements. An academic paper where I am unprepared to know what is coming, and why, also feels unpleasant, as though random information is flying at me that I can't expect or place within a framework. Your dance partner may be puzzled at your discomfort, as he or she knows the steps, and as a writer you may be puzzled at the reader's confusion, for you know the larger picture. The reader doesn't.

I realize some published papers and books in your field are not the best models for structural clarity. You may rightly object that some of the sources you read do not lucidly state their arguments. But I suspect they would have been easier to understand had they done so.

3.3 Being Clear

 **Tip**

Beware the *about*! Answer the question, "What is my paper trying to prove or show?" If you can't answer this, and all it does is talk 'about' something, you may have no clear thesis statement.

Usually thesis statements which only say the paper is "about" something is a red flag, for you have committed to nothing beside stating a topic, and that is not an argument. "This paper is about vaccine education" reveals no substantive position. Once more, a thesis statement has similarities to but is not a speech, where you might simply declare a subject via a statement or question: "Should shyness be treated with medicine?" and at best give an opinion at the end. That is not a helpful thesis statement to begin a paper with, because it does not answer the question (should it be?) and does not signal the subtopics or sub-arguments to follow. A better thesis statement might be, "Shyness should [not] be treated with medicine because x."

In the past, I admit that I have actually forbidden students to use the word 'about' and have mandated the word 'because' in thesis statements. 'About' is a word of evasion in this situation, and 'because' forces the writer to commit to specifics and/or reasons.

The Most Common Error: Being Vague

Assume your paper topic is sports cars. Yes, it is a juvenile subject, but intentionally so to avoid distracting you with the content and help you focus on the concepts. It would be fine to begin the paper and speak generally about them, but a poor way to climax the introduction would be to state "In this paper I am going to talk about sports cars." This tells the reader little other than your subject.

Your second draft states, "Sports cars are good for several reasons," or, better, "Sports cars are good for three important reasons." These thesis statements at least indicate your position (sports cars are good), but they still give no specifics: 'good' is a broad quality, and why are sports cars good? We are halfway there, but these can be improved to be more informative on what will follow in the paper.

This is not pedantry—I repeat that 'about' and 'for several important reasons [that you refuse to tell me]' is the most common error I see in undergraduate introductions, and even appears at the graduate level as well:

"The Boarding House" shows Mr. Doran as a victim, but I think Mrs. Mooney and Polly are the real victims. There are two reasons.

3 THESIS ARGUMENTS

Because of Higgins's characteristics in *Pygmalion*, he would be a bad husband for Eliza in the future.

People should not be afraid of artificial intelligence, for it has many valuable applications.

This is better than nothing. But I don't know how your paper will proceed. What are the two reasons? What are Higgins's characteristics? What are the valuable applications? The revised ones below are more informative:

"The Boarding House" shows Mr. Doran as a victim, but Mrs. Mooney and Polly are the real victims because no one makes Mr. Doran live there, and as women they will be hurt more by his actions if he runs away.

Because Higgins in *Pygmalion* is childish, narcissistic, and uninterested in personal feelings, he would be a bad husband for Eliza in the future.

People should not be afraid of artificial intelligence, for its ability to save lives in the medical and transportation fields outweighs its risks.

These thesis statements are not better merely because they're longer—don't fall into that trap, for I have read ones which rabbit on forever without ever actually telling me key information. They are better because they accomplish the three tasks I've laid out: the last one clarifies that the paper will be about AI, gives a position on it, and suggests that AI in medical and transportation fields can be expected subtopics to follow.

    A related problem is writers who list the literal category names of subtopics and actions that will follow without indicating what they *are*:

This paper will discuss whether English should be taught in other-language elementary schools, and in my body section I will discuss social and developmental issues, followed by a conclusion and appendix.

Bridget Jones is attracted to two men, but which one is better? I will analyze them objectively, describe how they treat Bridget, and conclude with who the better-matched person is for her.

These aren't bad, but they are chiefly lists of things the writer will do, without saying much about them. This would be better:

This paper will discuss whether English should be taught in other-language elementary schools, arguing that for socialization and developmental reasons it is a positive pedagogical choice.

Bridget Jones is attracted to two men, but which one is better? Because Mark Darcy is more respectful, reliable, and honest, he is the better-matched person is for her.

But occasionally brevity works. I admit this next one isn't great, but does make me curious. At least its direction is specific.

The study will focus on the effect of brightness on the path choice of people in exhibition spaces.

As with planning, thesis statement writing is not always a consciously separate or beginning-to-end process, as you might begin your project with a working thesis argument which you later return to for revision. For example, you might begin researching a paper on a historical matter and then find that the facts require you to modify your views. This is why having too settled or firm an opinion on a matter can be dangerous, as you may be tempted to reject opposing evidence.

3.4 Chunking and Phrasing

The Basic Frame

3 THESIS ARGUMENTS

I have said several times to beware of the word 'about.' If you are stuck and can't think of how to phrase your thesis statement, you might use this basic frame, containing the magic word 'because.'

Your opinion + "because" + reasons
People should do x because a, b, and c.
The novel means x because a, b, and c.
A, b, and c explain the meaning of x.

Using the basic frame, the sports car thesis statement becomes this:

Sports cars are good because they are fun, fast, and helpful for meeting people.

Or:

A large university is better than a small one because it has more varied course options, more campus facilities, and more potential alumni contacts.

Why Always Three Reasons?

There is no law. There is no thesis police, yet. You may notice that I use a 'three' here again in the number of sub-arguments in my examples of thesis statements. Yours of course don't have to have three. Throughout this book I may sometimes be over-prescriptive, or imply that things are rules when they're really practices. There are few things you could do in an academic paper that are actually illegal—other than perhaps plagiarism or threatening someone. But when I advise you to have 1-4 elements in your thesis statement, it is based on observation that most people can't recall much past this. In the same way, we invariably write telephone numbers in batches of 3's and 4's: 49-345-6789, because short series of numbers are easier to remember.

This is known in cognitive psychology as *chunking*, our trait of parsing concepts into small sets. We aren't crocodiles who can eat a whole pizza at once—we need to eat in bites—and our brains have similar limitations. The same applies to paragraph lengths and thesis statements, and so this is not a law, but a practical suggestion from experience that more than three elements may cause the reader to forget or confuse them. As I'll return to in a later chapter, this is also good practice for a PowerPoint table of contents slide.

Not all thesis statements have three elements. You can also have:

A is true because of x, y, and z.
Experts believe x but the truth is really y.
Result b happened because c and d.
This law should not be passed because it would x.

A thesis statement might also work well with four elements or reasons: "Sports cars are fun, fast, a good investment, and a helpful way to meet people"; as two ideas (fun and fast); or with one specific, strong idea that makes the position sufficiently clear: "Sports cars symbolize freedom in their owners and passengers." A crisply specific one-element thesis is far preferable to a vague, evasive three-element thesis: "Sports cars are excellent, fine, and wonderful" is a set of vague synonyms. In theory, you can have as many elements as you please.

But to demonstrate my point, read this following thesis statement and see if you still remember it all by the next page:

Sports cars are fun, fast, a helpful way to meet new friends, a safe financial investment, a safe way to rebel, beautiful, a symbol of freedom and prosperity, and an enjoyable way to learn auto mechanics. x

Now we have eight sub-arguments. In addition to soon forgetting them, the reader may get confused as to whether each of these elements is equal, or if some of them are subcategories of others. And this is a silly thesis statement about sports cars. If you have an eight-sub-argument thesis statement about robotics scripting or consubstantiation, imagine the reader trying to remember all of these elements while reading difficult content.

Parallel Construction

I will use the sports car example once more and then mercifully retire it. Notice that *fun, fast,* and *helpful* are adjectives. Yet even for this simple list if I start mixing up grammar phrasings and parts of speech randomly it becomes a confusing hodge-podge:

Sports cars are fun, I like them, there are pretty girls who will talk to you if they see one, once my brother had one and it was a good investment, and you can drive fast in one. **x**

And when we get into more abstract ideas we quickly get into trouble. We need to read this a few times, as it jumps between singular/plural, active/passive, and verb tenses:

A large university is better than a small one because it has more variety of courses, more campus facilities are available, and you will be benefiting from a larger number of alumni contacts. **x**

Thus when you design a thesis statement, or really any list, try to ensure that its list elements are parallel in phrasing:

All adjectives: The law is unworkable because it would result in a situation that is unpredictable and inefficient.

All nouns: Macbeth is seduced by ambition, pride, and fear, and the witches play on these emotions to corrupt him.

All verbs: The government should fund, advertise, and expand this important program.

All adverbs: Tom's robbery in *Hard Times* is not a sudden act of passion but planned slowly and deliberately.

Advanced Thesis Statements

You may be annoyed with me here, if you weren't already, feeling that you are an adult writing about serious things, and I am childishly proscribing 'about' and prescribing sets of three, and discussing sentences about sports cars. I am illustrating the principles underneath. I will also counter that I've read doctoral-candidate papers which are at an extremely high *content* level, but still fail to have a few sentences which would tell me what the paper is trying to do. It reads like the author lacks writing competence, which is bad, or that the author is too impatient or haughty to worry about 'the little details,' which is worse.

Students who read scholarly articles might also object that the writers of published articles or books in their field don't always follow the conventions I describe. The article you read might not have an overt thesis, but the author may be skilled enough to carry the reader through the discussion without confusion. But sometimes experts in a field are not good writers, and sadly, again, ego and pride can come into play—I have encountered established authorities who seem not to care whether people understand them (French critical theorists are infamous for their impenetrability and opacity). Not all published works are well-written from a compositional standpoint, even if the content and author are respected.

When you reach a certain proficiency and experience level, you will be able to follow the spirit and not the letter of the rules. So long as the reader is well-prepared to know what the paper is doing, and sees the big picture of your flow of ideas, my examples can be modified or abandoned for more refined or subtle thesis statements. I will only insist: do not be too proud to encapsulate your paper's arguments in a mere set of sentences.

The following are workable thesis statements which well-indicate the paper's point and direction. They are my own or from student papers. Note that the thesis statements with more precisely described sub-arguments tend to have fewer of them, down to two or even one. Note also that there is a pattern of parallel phrasing and verb tenses, such as *seeing/taking/sharing*.

3 THESIS ARGUMENTS

Bridget's mother Pam is a selfish person who causes others to have conflicts: between Bridget and her, between Bridget and Mark, and between Julio and Bridget's father.

Food is important in *Lucky Jim* because Margaret's fussiness about food and Christine's large appetite reflect their personalities and emotional problems.

In *The Hitchhiker's Guide to the Galaxy* and *White Teeth* the authors use the characteristics and meanings of mice to symbolize meaning for the readers.

The purpose of this paper is to demonstrate a workflow solution does exist that makes flatbed scanning feasible for the small-budget archivist, by using a Canon 9000F Mark II flatbed scanner with a transparency adapter, along with Adobe Photoshop scripting, to successfully scan and render optimum-quality digitized 8mm/Super 8 silent film.

The introduction of digital textbooks will help students motivate their learning by utilizing the advantages of multimedia and effectively cultivate concrete and practical curriculum, and provide flexible learning activities based on learner autonomy.

So far all most our thesis statements have been one sentence. Sometimes you might need more in a more complex or longer paper:

Hagrid acts as a father figure to Harry. Seeing Hagrid helping Harry to buy what is needed, taking care of Harry's feelings, and sharing a deep emotional relationship with Harry, it can be claimed that Hagrid has the qualities of both a friend and reliable father.

First, this research will show that authentic science picture books will highly affect learners' affective domains such as children's interest, motivation, and confidence through the experiment.

Second, meaningful learning through the books has a positive influence on vocabulary memory capacity.

It is believed that concrete deterioration due to deicing chemicals may start with physical reactions, which generate micro and macro cracks in concrete. Because the acquired cracks make concrete more permeable and more susceptible to the ingress of deicing chemical ions, chemical deterioration is then generated.

I give these examples reluctantly, for it is inevitable that someone will conclude, the complexity and sophistication of my paper will be shown by having multiple sentences. That is not how it works. More is not better; any more than two or three sentences is pushing your luck, as the energy of the thesis statement starts to dissipate. As with our eight-sub-argument example, the reader may have difficulty determining whether all of these sentences form your thesis statement or if one sentence is the main one and the others are sub-ones in some hierarchy. If in any doubt, this is not a bad place to do some hand-holding and ensure the thesis statement is recognized by explicitly writing "The thesis of this paper is" or something similar.

I've had students tell me that their argument is so complex and profound that it can't be condensed into one sentence, and I don't buy it. My doctoral dissertation was 630 pages and I can distill its central argument into one sentence (granted, a long sentence). Albert Einstein said something to the effect of "if you cannot explain it simply, you don't understand it." There may be exceptions, but usually a sprawling paragraph-length thesis statement reflects unclear thinking.

3.5 Thesis Statement Placement

In the next chapter we will return to the larger structural framework of an academic paper. For now, after we have derived and phrased a thesis statement, where does it go? The simple answer is: really—anywhere in the introduction. It may seem frustrating (or liberating) that I should suddenly *not* have a *do* and *don't* here, but there is no convention where a thesis statement goes in an introduction. It usually tends to be placed near the beginning *or* near the end, but it could be placed at any point.

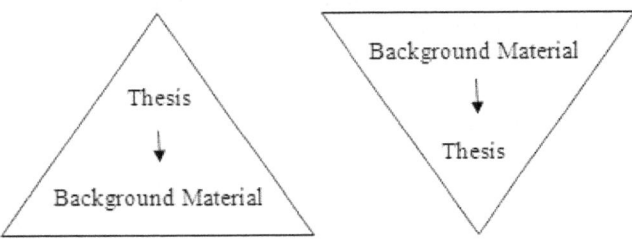

Some people put their thesis statement at the beginning of the introduction, even as the first sentence, to give a dramatic and journalistic effect: "Mr. Bennet in *Pride and Prejudice* is a bad father because x." The introduction would then continue into background information explaining and contextualizing the thesis. Or, in a paper about modern war and drones: "Tanks are no longer the queen of the battlefield. Why do we still fight wars pretending they are?" I find this move works well when little initial explanation is required. Most readers will recognize Mr. Bennet and know what tanks are.

Other writers turn this pyramid upside down and talk about necessary background information before coming to the point. They might discuss World War II generally and its destructiveness, giving some key dates, before coming to the climax: "One of the determining factors in the war's victory was the invention of radar. Radar was a, b, and c." Here is an example introduction of the latter (thesis at the end), about Terry Pratchett's *Guards! Guards!*

In *Guards! Guards!*, one of the interesting factors Pratchett uses in the novel is that he makes heroes from characters who are somewhat 'below average.' For example, the Watchmen were commonly seen as "total whittles, every one of them" (121). However, they manage to defeat Wonse, who is the secretary of the patrician and also a magician powerful enough to summon a dragon. A similar case also applies to Errol. At first, no one cared about Errol. He was just a little, scrubby-looking swamp dragon who seemed weak and useless. However, by carefully looking into the story, we can find that it is Errol who takes an important role throughout the plot.

In this second example from my own writing the thesis statement is explicitly indicated:

A comparison of satire in the American presidential elections of 1980 and 2008 seems at first an arbitrary choice. The former resulted in a Republican landslide under Ronald Reagan and the latter a Democrat victory under Barack Obama. Nevertheless, the two elections have historical parallels. The 1980 campaign featured a president with dismal approval ratings, and whose policies had given rise to stagflation and an energy crisis; the description could as easily apply to George W. Bush in 2008.

Slate pundit Troy Patterson wrote in April 2008 about "the Satire Recession," arguing that modern news satire has declined into nothing more than "personality jokes" that rarely rise above cutesy ad-hominem gags. Yet satire in the 1980 election also rarely rose above one-liners, and if anything was safer and less partisan than that of the 2008 campaign. I would like to, in fact, make the opposite argument: In comparison to the 1980 American presidential election, the 2008 campaign featured satire which was more biting, more partisan, and was used by a media more aware of its political influence.

A third example is from a paper I co-wrote:

Wikipedia authoring has been deployed in several academic institutions worldwide, but little research has been done on the pedagogy of creating or editing Wikipedia entries in the liberal arts, especially for second language (L2) speakers of English. The purpose of this research is to assess the feasibility of incorporating Wikipedia content authoring into the liberal arts curriculum, using a case study of Korean postsecondary coursework in English. The argument concluded here is that Wikipedia writing is a useful learning tool for improving communication and digital literacy skills, subject knowledge, and language fluency.

Placement or signaling of thesis statements depends on your personal style, and is another aspect of writing which is more art than science. Yet often the thesis will "feel" better at the beginning or end of the paragraph based on the topic and its immediacy or complexity, and my experience is that the placement will usually come naturally without overthinking it. You do not need an extensive definition of what a bad father is, but radar and satire are more obscure or complex subjects requiring some explanation.

It is possible to put your thesis statement elsewhere in your introduction such as directly in the middle—in effect, a diamond shape). If you do so, be clear to the reader about what you are doing, as such a placement might confuse the reader otherwise. This might also be a situation where you write "The thesis of this paper is" or some variation. Note the Wikipedia introduction did this in the last sentence with a "The argument concluded here is x" phrasing.

Alternative 1: The Linked 'Hypothesis' Thesis

A hypothesis thesis is an example of intelligently breaking the rules. I suggested earlier that a thesis statement should not normally be a question, as questions usually do not indicate the arguments to follow. There are exceptions. You might state a central research question as the thesis statement of your paper and then organize the paper around answering it, in effect finalizing your position in your conclusion rather than in your introduction, like a detective: "Through examining the evidence we can find out who killed Sir Butters in the lounge." This approach is one commonly used in social sciences papers. For example, you might pose the question:

European presidential elections nearly always tend to be very close. This paper intends to analyze why this is so.

You might then state how your paper will investigate the matter and proceed with evidence, examples, and surveys, ending with a conclusion in which you explain and summarize the answers derived: "Therefore, we can conclude that European elections are usually close because of x." The initial thesis statement in the introduction does not actually indicate the answer, but it is so specific that the reader understands the paper's direction.

This thesis structure might also pose a hypothesis which you intend to test. The hypothesis style is often common in social sciences papers and in science or engineering fields, where a controversial idea or solution to a problem might be under investigation:

Is Speckle's experiment replicable? Using modern methods and big data realization, it should be possible to find out by remodeling its parameters.

Or, an engineering paper could posit a hypothesis that some chemical process might make better metals for bridge building. The paper could then lay out the experiments and tests carried out to evaluate the hypothesis. The end section of the paper is where the author asserts that the hypothesis is shown to be true or false. It may happen that the hypothesis is falsified. This does not make the paper a failure. The knowledge obtained from recognizing the failure may help others in learning from the results and moving closer towards other solutions which do work.

Alternative 2: Mini-Thesis "Guide" Paragraph

Something else I will throw out here which may help you is a maneuver I've experimented with myself in a few recent papers which I am liking more and more. In a long paper of 20-some pages, the introduction section can get quite long, and if you choose to place your thesis statement at the end, the readers may be slogging through 3-4 pages to read it—at which point you may be seriously trying their patience. What I do is begin the paper with a short guide or mini-anchor paragraph where I lay out the main argument in brief. This better situates the reader to understand the rest of the introduction, and at its end I write a fuller explanation. In effect, I state the thesis statement twice:

Near the end of Chaucer's *Tale of Sir Thopas* something interesting happens when the narrator pauses to interject an intertextual comparison between his tale and others 'of bataille and of chivalry' (VII.894). Chaucer is no greenhorn to metafictional comments, imploring 'Go, litel bok, go' (V.1786) to his *Troilus*, and depicting himself in *The Legend of Good Women* being scolded by the god of love for writing the earlier poem (265). Nor is a chivalric story referring to another fictional hero exceptional. But this degree of awareness, where a tale's speaker lists other romances as narrative artefacts, calling attention to the fact that the text is another narrative performance, is unusual. More than other tales, *Thopas* responds to other texts, both outside ones and intra-textually within the *Canterbury Tales*.

This synopsis optimally allows the reader to relax and better contextualize what follows, until the thesis statement is restated in more expanded form at the end of the introduction section. I see no reason why a thesis statement can't be repeated. Do note that writing about your claims in your paper's abstract (more on this later) does not replace laying them out in your introduction.

Cultural Styles

I've had Asian students tell me that "our culture isn't so confrontational, and we value fitting in" as a way of explaining their introduction-writing habits. While I think this can sometimes be a lazy student's excuse for sloppiness, there may also be legitimate culturally-bound tendencies in designing introductions, or even paper sections. In my time in Korea, I notice it is influenced by Chinese rather than Greco-Roman models in how scholars arrange and argue ideas. Some cultures prefer early or roundabout thesis statements—or subtle/discreet or blunt/frank ones. I am not judging or mocking these values, although they don't mean that a writer can't learn another culture's conventions or employ multiple styles for particular audiences.

I remarked before that whether it is the way the universe hums or human nature, how people conceptualize the arrangement of sections in academic writing is similar in most cultures. Nevertheless, in newspaper essays or academic writing Koreans often have a characteristically distinct rhetorical practice for developing an argument, known as *ki-sung-jon-gyul* (기승전결).

Contrastive rhetoric is a branch of applied linguistics pioneered by American linguist Robert Kaplan in the late 1960's. This subject concerns how writers are affected by their own cultural and L1 linguistic rhetorical conventions. Thus a Korean writer, brought up in a society traditionally valuing harmony and tact, might write in a non-committal manner which indirectly states the argument and gradually moves toward a conclusion. In much English-language journalism written by Koreans, I will see the author begin with an anecdote or appeal to a piece of folk wisdom before segueing into an opinion: "Something my teacher taught me as a child was x."

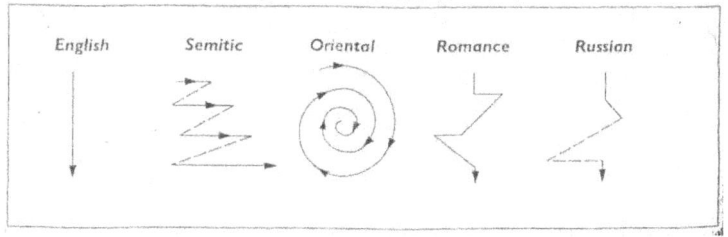

Figure 17.1. Patterns of Written Discourse (Kaplan, 1966:14).

The predominant rhetorical style of North American academic writing tends toward straight-as-an-arrow directness (First line: "Taxation is theft!"), although I see a slight difference between Canadian and American writing, with the former a little more indirect in comparison, reflecting the country's stereotypical civility. Other cultures have their own conventions. A Latinate writer from Europe or Central America might have a style which makes arguments with zigzag detours and diversions from the main subject. Middle Eastern writers might tend towards a strongly narrative style. One of my students from India took half his paper to come to the subject.

This is a delicate point because I again don't wish to imply that one culture's writing practices are bad or inferior. It's all quite relative; an Indian writer could argue with justice that a poetic, reflective progression toward a central idea is more scholarly and elegant than rushed "New-York-minute" American impatience. It's also silly to argue that millions of people are all governed by the same conventions, or that they can't change or adjust for the situation—I would not say I have a culturally Canadian style that is inescapable for me. Maybe I do. But I will gently reiterate, "when in Rome"; a paper written in English should have some awareness of its audience's cultural and disciplinary expectations, just as a paper written in any language would. I have by now learned that British and American journals have different preferences on how quickly or slowly they wish me to go.

Hedging

It is essential to be clear in a thesis statement. And yet no one likes a writer who declares with finality that x is y, and that is the end of the matter. Particularly with a scientific topic, a future finding may discover that this viewpoint is incorrect. In the chapter on editing I will discuss eliminating useless modifiers; yet sometimes, particularly with a subject that is contentious or quickly evolving, hedging is prudent.

Hedging means padding some arguments or statements with qualifiers to either appear more diplomatic or to protect yourself. In this book I have used direct phrasings where I feel confident about an idea and wish to be clear: x is/are y. But at other times I use words like *probably*, *may*, *likely*, or *perhaps* where I am less sure or where I don't want to offend readers by sounding like the academic writing-führer ordering people around.

Here are examples of conciliatory or hedging wordings:

x suggests / indicates a relationship with y
The evidence points to a likely / possible / probable conclusion that x causes y
We can assume / conclude that x seems to cause y

Again, this should not be confused with vagueness or coyness in conveying a position. Hedging means conceding, implicitly or explicitly, that your arguments are offered within a context of still-developing opinions which may add to, modify, or challenge your paper's findings in future.

3.6 Titles

Why is a discussion on essay titles here? In a way, titles and thesis statements are friends—they both indicate in brief what the subsequent paper is going to be about, guiding the reader to contextualize and follow your arguments. Titles are a form of meta-commentary, the signposting language directing you within the paper.

I use examples from my undergraduates not to make fun of them, for they are learning as I once was, but they tend to write short, vague titles that sound like Broadway musical names ("Cats!"), either because they don't know what to write, or are influenced by speech modes of wanting to build suspense. Thus I receive papers titled, "The Big Problem." Great. This tells the reader little. It is hardly better than essays literally titled "Assignment #1." A paper named, "Why Does Alison Leave?" is better, but I don't know which Alison is meant in a course with several texts and characters named Alison.

Research papers and scholarly books tend to have long titles, perhaps of two or even three lines. Adam Smith's *Wealth of Nations* was originally titled *An Inquiry into the Nature and Causes of the Wealth of Nations*. Having an expansive and descriptive title tends to give the paper a professional air, though overdoing it can admittedly be pretentious. Again, the field you are writing in may make a difference, as science and engineering tends to prefer pithier titles and the humanities tends to like longer ones.

But more practically, an informative title makes indexing and finding the paper easier in online search engines. Academics want their papers to be read and cited by others, raising its impact factor or other evaluation metrics. A paper titled "School uniforms" will be lost in searches, but one called "A longitudinal study of church, cultural, and gender trends in 1980s secondary public school uniforms in the Philippines" might be found by people who used any combination of the search terms *public school*, *church*, *gender*, *1980s*, or *Philippines*.

As with thesis statements, I'm not sure you need a fully-formed title when you begin writing, although it probably helps; I usually write whatever comes to mind to give the file a title and end up changing it multiple times anyway.

To colon or not to colon? A popular trend lately seems to be two or more clauses linked with colons. I have frequently titled papers using a memorable idea or quote from the text with a description of the essay after the colon.

Exodus Inverted: A New Look at the *Grapes of Wrath*

"How Strange Life is!": The Performative Narrator in Steven Leacock's *Sunshine Sketches of a Little Town*

As I get older, I find the colon business feeling increasingly tired and twee, and my titles are becoming shorter. Interestingly, other theorists note this is common, that younger scholars prefer multipart titles and more established ones like the power move of a brief but confident phrasing. The second is my own.

Can You Tickle Yourself if You Swap Bodies With Someone Else?

Mr. Collins's Secret Sermon in *Pride and Prejudice*

Some writers also enjoy writing provocative or humorous titles to enliven a serious topic or attract readers. There is a surprising amount of swear words or playful pop culture references in the titles of professors' papers, especially conference papers. I have done this, and it can work, but discretion is needed. Tolerance of cheeky titles probably varies between disciplines; I see it in my field of literature, although it likely would be less acceptable in linguistics or the sciences or more conservative subjects. A more chic journal might enjoy a catchy title, whereas a stodgier or more senior journal would reject it as childishly unprofessional.

I have mixed feelings on this practice. Trendy or attention-grabbing titles can be easily overdone; the succinct and blunt name of the 1986 academic paper "On Bullshit" by Harry Frankfurt has helped make the essay famous, but obscenities for their own sake might misfire and appear sophomoric, or even offend. A further danger is that a cutesy pop reference can become quickly dated. Around 2016 I tried to publish a paper on a medieval poem with the pre-title "Bad Romance" and the editors asked me to change it. Looking back, I'm glad they did so. You may have recognized the allusion, but a paper title with a Lady Gaga lyric that feels cool and edgy now might be read by a researcher in 2078 with bafflement.

4 STRUCTURE

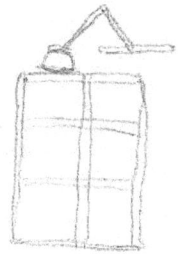

This chapter returns to discussing the overall arrangement and sectioning of a paper, within which the thesis statement and introduction sit. Structure is the second construction block of academic writing, between grammar and content. Structure again involves the arrangement of the parts of your essay into sentences, paragraph units, and sections or chapters. Just as buildings have steel frames and wooden beams to hold them together, an effective paper is built on a solid, rational organization. Without structure, the building may collapse, and a paper is also in danger of failing to convey its contents if the reader is distracted by the disorder of its sections.

4.1 Paragraphs

Informal writing tends to be less paragraph-bound, and short bits of writing in English such as e-mails or notices may not use them at all. But they are a basic structural unit of academic and serious writing, although it is of course possible to go deeper into sentences, clauses, words, phonemes, and other linguistic units. For our purposes we will start with paragraphs, and we can define one as a group of sentences which stand separate as a connected and complete unit of thought.

When I discuss paragraphs a common student query will be how long they should be. There is no rule or convention on paragraph length, although as a rule of thumb I write paragraphs of between a quarter to half a page, and I rarely let a paragraph go longer than one page or write one shorter than three sentences.

Paragraphs were not common in western typography until about the seventeenth century. Before then, in medieval manuscripts there are sometimes divisions between sections, but often there is nothing. The ancient Greeks used horizontal lines called *paragraphos* to divide sections or point to important lines, thus the modern word. Some late medieval texts used an elegantly-shaped "C" (for *capitulum*, chapter), later called a pilcrow (¶).

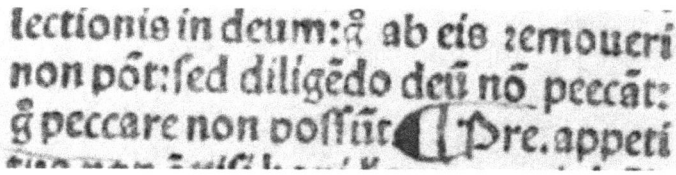

The basic function of the paragraph is to divide long stretches of writing into bites, making the text easier to 'digest.' Recall the discussion about chunking; just as humans are not built to eat a full meal in one bite, our brains prefer to take text in pieces. This is one reason medieval manuscripts are tiring to read, as there are few visual breaks in the text that allow one to stop. Conversely, just as eating one pea at a time would be frustrating, endless tiny paragraphs make for continuously interrupted reading as the eye scans for the beginning of the new one.

To sum, paragraphs are both content and visual units that allow you to stop and process the information read, and then easily find where you left off and continue. Paragraphs signal to the reader that you are finished talking about one idea, indicating that you can stop, momentarily think or look away, and then continue.

For typographical reasons, sometimes paragraph length may be affected by the requirements of your audience or the print or online presentation format. Writing for academic journals or newspapers may call for shorter paragraphs as the page size might be narrow and the text may run in narrow vertical columns (as do some formatting styles such as IEEE; more on this later). The same might apply to websites. For papers printed on conventional letter-size or A4 paper, however, the practices of the discipline might favor longer paragraphs as a mark of professional tone.

A two-column layout

Your paper's content is of course more important than its visual appearance, and as much as I natter you to think about everything, you normally needn't overthink this. I tend to think variety is good, and so I have shorter and longer paragraphs, but I do avoid paragraphs lengths at either extreme. Again, having endless multi-page paragraphs fatigues the reader's concentration, just as beginning new paragraphs every few sentences can be tiresome, as the reader's eye constantly needs to scan the line for the next one.

Developing a sense for paragraph division takes practice.

Making a well-crafted and unified paragraph involves balancing cohesion, making sure that every sentence has a logical connection to each other, and having the discipline to divide your blocks of thought into functional pieces. One useful skill in editing is the ability to re-read your text and realize that a paragraph is too long or drifts from one idea to another. Often the solution is to find a suitable place where the topic shifts and the remainder can be separated into a new paragraph, with some additional text to smooth over the break where necessary.

A technical question: Should writers indent or skip a line between paragraphs? Your professors or department may have a convention or rule. Otherwise I favor indentation in academic writing and believe it is a more efficient use of the page, although I have noticed that more writers in the last decade are skipping a space, perhaps because of the influence of internet text. For some reason html code does not handle indentation well. Indenting may begin to disappear from English writing in your lifetime, but for now it is dominant in journals and monographs. You may prefer or be directed to skip lines in your course paper, and that's fine. But I advise you to not do both; this always looks like paper-padding to fill space to me.

4.2 The Five-Paragraph Model

English rhetoric has shifted over the centuries toward more awareness of the reader's needs regarding structure and clarity. In the medieval era, literacy was usually an indication that one was gentry or aristocratic, and had time to luxuriate over words. Early modern essays written in the 1700's or 1800's seem to have less concern about the reader's ability to understand; comprehension was thought to be the audience's problem, particularly in a period where reading was still a more elite pastime and leisure time was plentiful. This remains typical of some European and particularly French discourse even to this day, where some scholars seem to pride themselves on being difficult, or at least have a more idiosyncratic or cavalier attitude toward their writing style that may not prioritize clarity.

But since the Hemingway-esque directness of the twentieth century there is greater emphasis in English culture on making things simple, or at least understandable. This is perhaps partly a response to a far more varied readership, and partly due to modern distractions such as television, internet, and social media, which have severely diminished attention spans. We can philosophize whether this trend is good or if it just panders to the reader, but if we want to be read, post-classroom academia isn't a democracy—we have to make accommodations to the expectations of readers who have other choices.

Thus once we have paragraphs we need to arrange them into a meaningful sequence recognizable to a community of readers. Most students in English-speaking countries are taught in middle or high school about the five-paragraph essay formula:

Introduction
Three body paragraphs
Conclusion

Koreans may notice that this looks similar to their school model of introduction, body, and conclusion (서론 본론 결론). No one seems to know where the five-paragraph model originates, and some trace it to the modern theme essay taught in Harvard in the 1880s, and others to ancient Greco-Roman treatises on rhetoric. But I suspect the five-paragraph model is pretty obvious, for countries everywhere have some equivalent—how can you conclude something that you haven't introduced yet?

It has become fashionable in the last few years for teachers and composition theorists to hate the five-paragraph model, and to denounce it as stuffy and artificial, much like Robin Williams's teacher in *Dead Poet's Society* who sarcastically charts a poem on the chalkboard as a mathematical formula. You may again also be dismissing it as childish when you are planning a dissertation. I discuss it only as a place to start and a means to address rhetorical concepts. You may already have intuited that the model can refer to either five actual paragraphs for a high school student, or abstractly to five sections or conceptual divisions.

When I was a graduate student instructor in Las Vegas my students in engineering or the sciences sometimes viewed writing courses with skepticism, dismissing them as subjective or impractical. The irony is that engineers often excel in applying structural concepts to writing because they understand flowcharts and sequences, and they quickly apprehend its recursive steps and organizational logic. Academic papers are admittedly more structure-bound than other forms of writing, and particularly so in the sciences. But again, the five-paragraph model I will cover here is intended to be a conceptual springboard, not a straightjacket.

Introductions

We have briefly discussed introductions insofar as how thesis statements are placed in them, but not the overall purposes of and techniques for introductions. The introduction paragraph or section really does in large what your thesis statement does in short: It states your paper's subject, gives your thesis statement and some background information, and optimally signals how you are going to discuss the content in the paper so that the reader understands the sequence of what will follow.

I struggled with introductions as an undergraduate. What seemed to help was to type whatever came to mind just to fill a space, which gave me confidence to begin the subsequent paper sections. Later on, I would discard or improve the introduction. If you are writing in a group, you can leverage each other's strengths, but if you write alone, don't feel bad if you are better at some sections than others. As I age and gain more experience, I now find conclusions harder to write.

As I mentioned, don't confuse thesis statements and topic sentences. Thesis statements go inside introduction paragraphs and they introduce the position of the entire paper. Topic sentences begin body paragraphs or sections, and state what the subject of that paragraph or group will be about. They typically restate the sub-arguments of the thesis statement, or at least link back to it.

- Thesis statement (in introduction): A large university is better than a small one because it has more course variety, more facilities, and larger numbers of alumni contacts.
- Topic sentence 1 (in body section 1): A large university has more course variety.
- Topic sentence 2 (in body section 2): A large university has more facilities.
- Topic sentence 3 (in body section 3): A large university has larger numbers of alumni contacts.

If we display this graphically, we see the five parts of: introduction, 3x body, and conclusion. This is another reason I have used thesis statements with three sub-arguments as examples, as they fit into this schema nicely. I will discuss later what happens when they *don't* fit.

Notice also that these three reasons are fairly equal in difficulty or abstraction (course variety, facilities, alumni). As we look at more advanced examples, you might see that often the thesis subtopics build in complexity, using previous ones as a springboard to cover something harder, or more theoretical or speculative.

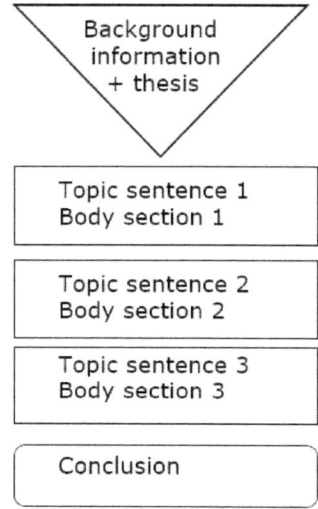

For a fuller example, I am going to reprint two paragraphs of a student paper on Kingsley Amis's *Lucky Jim*. If I were to recreate her outline for the paper it would look like this:

1. Introduction paragraph
   a. Background information
   b. Thesis: Amis emphasizes Jim's happy ending by contrasting it against unhappy things in his life: the people around him, his work, and his careless actions.
2. Body paragraph one
   a. Topic sentence: Jim's coworkers/friends
   b. Reasons and examples why they make him unhappy
3. Body paragraph two
   a. Topic sentence: Jim's job tasks
   b. Reasons and examples why they make him unhappy
4. Body paragraph three
   a. Topic sentence: Jim's careless actions
   b. Reasons and examples why they make him unhappy
5. Conclusion

4 STRUCTURE

So as not to confuse you, I will give only her introduction and first body paragraph. In the introduction you can see how she states the novel's name, gives background and context, and ends with a classic three-point thesis:

In the beginning of Kingsley Amis' *Lucky Jim*, Jim is a sad and miserable person who has lots of troubles in his life. He has awful people around him who take advantage of him or are mean or manipulative. Even in his work his job is unstable and does not pay him much. Moreover, his careless actions drag him into more trouble. But eventually he overcomes all of his unhappiness and gets all that he wishes for. Amis cleverly makes unhappy things seem unhappier to emphasize a dramatic happy ending later. There are three elements which contrast to the happy ending: the people around him, his work, and his careless actions.

Here we have the first body paragraph. I know that the content may not make much sense if you haven't read the novel, but look at what the writer does at a structural level by listing the first sub-argument as a topic sentence and then giving quotations and reasons to support it:

The first piece of evidence is the people around him. Margaret especially wants to take advantage of Jim's good nature and continually threatens fake suicides. It highlights how manipulative and fraudulent she is when Jim and Catchpole meet and talk about Margaret. "There were two bottles," says Catchpole, who adds, "She forgot to tell a lie there... but she wasn't taking any risks" (Amis 238). From these lines about Margaret, who "battens neurotically on Jim's pity" (Allen), it shows how unlucky it is for Jim to be associated with her, as she is only interested in getting attention. Additionally, as Gwen Cassidy says, "People who regularly spend about a quarter of their hours each day with family and friends are 12 times as likely to report feeling joyful." Because of Margaret, it clearly shows that Jim is not happy with his life because he has few good people around him.

The next example is from a student paper in the social sciences. Again, it begins with a statement of the subject; it provides some background and identifies a gap or problem; and it moves toward a thesis argument.

This paper studies the effect of political participation from the potential of social network sites utilized during the U.S. presidential campaign in 2016, with the result from current research that the size of support networks in social network sites has an impact on voting and political participation. Worldwide, the number of social network services users is increasing rapidly. This study aims to examine effective political participation of SNS use through survey analysis using Pew Internet and American Life Project survey data. This study found out that SNS users were positively influenced to participate in the election.

If this feels too dry, it is certainly possible to begin a paper with a short quotation, or an interesting fact or anecdote. I even began one of my MA thesis chapters with a comic strip to illustrate popular ideas regarding Vikings. But more on these advanced moves later on.

Variations

We will need to complicate our five-paragraph model a great deal later on with such things as literature review and methodology sections. Before we get there, the first variation or addition I'll give—and often the first one undergraduates need—is a background information paragraph after the introduction and before the body section begins. If our paper is a hamburger, we are adding a pickle or slice of cheese.

The reason background information paragraphs become helpful or inevitable is that as subjects become more complex, more detail is necessary for the paper's discussion to make sense, and one introduction paragraph becomes overlong and sprawling, as it tries to explain and define *and* give a thesis argument. Splitting this into two paragraphs will allow a leaner, clearer introduction while giving the reader necessary explanatory information in a subsequent paragraph.

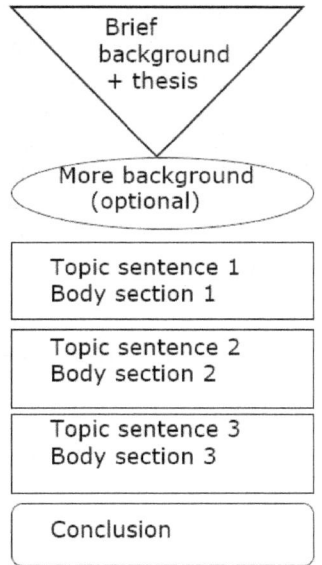

A good example of this is a paper I received on *Bridget Jones's Diary* where the introduction argued that Bridget's supposedly-humorous obsession with calorie-counting suggests that she has an eating disorder. Rather than overloading the introduction with medical terminology, the paper inserted a background information paragraph defining anorexia and other ailments, and provided information on symptoms and other features of the disorder, preparing the reader to understand the successive arguments made in the full body section.

Here as well, in a paper on farming co-operatives, a student inserts a background section to explain a United Nations policy, which will give enough historical context and statistical detail for the reader to understand the arguments made. Note that the tone of this paragraph is rather neutral, as its purpose is to inform before resuming the business of proving the thesis statement:

Faced with a world situation dominated by chronic hunger, food insecurity, and malnutrition, the member states of the United Nations in 2000 jointly declared in the Millennium Development Goals (MDGs) the target that each goal should be met by 2015. Of the eight MDGS, MDG 1 pledged to halve the proportion of hungry people from 20 to 10 percent by 2015. But by 2018 the proportion had only reached 16 percent. This continuing high global hunger level makes extreme difficulties in achieving the first MDG, but the devastating world hunger issue is also the underlying factor standing between pursuing other MDGs. For instance, hunger and malnutrition lead to poor maternal health (Goal 5), as well as low birth weight.

I suppose there is no correct length for such introductory/background paragraphs or sections, but they probably should be brief. The real meat of the paper is its body, where arguments are discussed. No one wants a hamburger which is one-half giant pickles—and this leads to the concept of section proportionality.

4.3 Proportionality

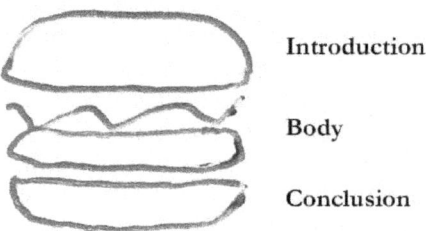

Introduction

Body

Conclusion

It may seem kiddy to develop my hamburger model further, but follow the analogy. A hamburger which was mostly bread or tomatoes, or even patties, would not be so palatable. An enjoyable hamburger has a range of proportions in its components, and if we were to imagine a perfect Platonic hamburger, it would have a certain percentage of bun, burger, and condiments. We might say our ideal hamburger is 25% upper bun, 10% cheese, 45% burger, and 20% lower bread.

This concept fits academic papers as a whole: A readable paper has a certain percentage ratio of introduction, body, and conclusion. In fact, I think we could use the same ranges for our ideal paper:

25% introduction
10% background information
45% body sections
20% conclusion

I am not being totally serious, and these numbers should be seen as approximations, but I do recommend you think about achieving a sense of proportion in your paper sections, as a paper in which one section is almost missing or which overwhelms the paper may also feel amiss or unpersuasive to the reader. For example, with introductions:

A *too-short* introduction which jumps immediately to the thesis statement without giving adequate context or background explanation may feel abrupt, and does not prepare the reader.

A *too-long* introduction with an excess of detail or information may frustrate the reader, who is waiting for you to get on with the main business of the paper. Or worse, the introduction may start discussing content which really should be in the body—leaving your paper with little left to do when you finally get to it.

There are no rules for this, for papers and writing situations will differ. Every writer has to develop an intuition for balance here, and as discussed earlier, some of this is culturally-specific. As well, if decisions come down to content versus structure, the latter should probably take priority. But I suppose that for a course paper I would advise these lengths or ratios for introductions:

For a 3-page paper: About ½-¾ of a page

For a 5-page paper: About ¾-1 page
For a 10-page paper: About 1-1½ pages
For a 20-page paper: About 2-3 pages

That is about 15%-25% of the paper total—though as I will discuss in later chapters, published papers often have introduction sections upwards of a third of the paper, for different reasons: your reader usually does not know you and must be convinced your paper and topic are important. Here is a student sample which strikes a good sense of proportion in being about 20% of an 800-word paper:

In Shakespeare's *The Tempest*, Caliban is described as "a freckl'd whelp, hag-born, not hounour'd with a human shape" (I.2.283). All the characters in the play who come across Caliban think he is savage and inferior. Prospero addresses Caliban as the "most lying slave" (I.2.344), and his daughter, Miranda, describes Caliban as an "abhorrèd slave" (I.2.352). Their attitudes towards Caliban imply that the relationship between Caliban and them is not equal, but rather hierarchical, and it seems that they consider themselves superior to Caliban. These kinds of remarks about Caliban may mislead the audience into believing that Caliban is indeed uncivilized. However, when carefully analyzing the characteristics of Caliban, he is not as savage as Prospero and other characters think. His ability to use language, to reason, and to understand moral ideas suggests that we are meant to see he is more civilized than what the others think.

This next example is *okay*, but not quite as well done:

Mr. Collins is a foolish character, but he is partly sympathetic because he is trapped. He can't achieve happiness because his whole life is trapped in a dilemma between pleasing himself and pleasing Lady Catherine and the people he depends on for a living.

The writer tried—and this isn't *bad*, in that it does give a thesis statement. But this is the entire introduction paragraph, and it feels too rushed. Worse, and this may be a pet peeve of mine—

who is Mr. Collins? The introduction never indicates the name of the novel or author. It would be improved with more detail:

In Jane Austen's *Pride and Prejudice*, most people see Mr. Collins as comically stupid, but even he has some tragic qualities worth noticing.
+
[background information on the novel and characters.]
+
Mr. Collins is a foolish character, but he is partly sympathetic because he is trapped. He cannot achieve happiness because his life is trapped in a dilemma between pleasing himself, and pleasing Lady Catherine and the people he depends on for a living.
+
[end of introduction—or, place the background information here instead.]

 **Tip**

It may seem obvious, but in a literature essay, be sure to state the name and author of the text or novel you're discussing, typically in the introduction—and ideally, in the paper's title as well. The reader may not know which 'John' you mean!

4.4 Transitions and Signposting

Transitions are meta-language, language about other language. They are the direction signs or traffic lights of your paper when ideas, paragraphs, or sections change. Words and phrases with *first*, *moreover*, or *finally* do not actually communicate content—rather, they tell the reader how to read the essay. Just as a good public speaker will give verbal cues to the audience, such as "the last thing I'll discuss is," transition terms such as *first*, *next*, or *in conclusion* tell readers where they are within the paper or indicate new subtopics. Apparently, *first, second, third* are correct and *firstly, secondly, thirdly* are not, but I still see the latter more often.

I don't have a great deal of advice on transitions. Some people like tea, or zombie movies, or baseball, and some people like transitions. I use them sparingly, as you may have noticed, for they feel obvious to me. The reader can usually tell that you are moving to a new idea with a new paragraph, and often an entire transition sentence is redundant: "There is a second reason why Stevens is rude to Miss Kenton." It would be just as informative to shorten this to a phrase or word: "Stevens is also rude to Miss Kenton because" or simply "Additionally." But if you feel a transition is necessary as hand-holding to help the reader understand what you are doing and how your arguments form a structure, or it's the general convention of your field to have few or many, it's your decision.

4.5 Conclusions

 **Tip**

Remember that your readers don't know the end of your paper; you wrote it, and they didn't. One method I use to begin a conclusion is to ask, now that the reader knows as much as I do—so what? Why is what I wrote important?

The conclusion restates the main arguments of the paper and draws up any remaining threads. It is the last major section of the paper, excepting possible reference or appendix sections or the like.

In STEM fields, the conclusion may be easier as there is a more standardized practice: the paper summarizes arguments, admits limitations, and suggests future research directions. Nevertheless, one gets no points for being extra boring, and social sciences and humanities papers generally don't follow this format. This may not be the best pedagogy to teach conclusion writing, but I would like to begin by recommending some things *not* to do in one.

Bad Move 1: A Micro-Conclusion Because You Have Nothing Left to Say.

I occasionally do get papers with two-sentence conclusions, because the well has run dry. The claims are proven; what is left to do? Yet the paper visually looks wrong when there are two lines of conclusion, and it rhetorically feels like something is absent. There is no feeling of making the paper's contents meaningful, of looking back at it differently, or summing it up somehow. It is the textual equivalent of a balloon fizzling out.

Another variation is papers where the writer literally copies and pastes sentences from the introduction into the conclusion. This is, as pundit Dorothy Parker used to say, terrible with raisins in it. It not only adds no new content, but insults the readers, who can see that you are trying to trick them by simply parroting from your introduction. If you don't seem to care about your paper, why should they? Almost as bad is doing no more than recycling sentences from your introduction with synonyms, for it also looks as though you are cynically filling a space rather than adding something of value.

Bad Move 2: Shoveling in Bad Poetry to Fill Space.

Ever since I was small, in my heart I wanted to soar on the wind like an eagle. A sports car is like the smile on a young child's face. Never compromise; taste the passion and follow your dreams.

I'm exaggerating for comic effect, but I do see this—and for some reason, invariably with American or L1 speakers of English. This sort of emotional informality would be ridiculous in a technical or scientific paper, but is little better in any academic subject, for it also insults the reader by obviously being shoveled-in fluff to fill space.

Bad Move 3: Overdoing it by Shocking the Reader with Important New Information.

It may also be that Polly is pregnant at the end of "The Boarding House."

Yikes. Boom! Although you may not know this story by James Joyce, the idea that the main character is pregnant is a hugely important claim or piece of information which would retroactively change the entire paper's meaning, and to drop this bomb on the reader at the end without warning is disproportional. The reader may feel you have withheld something crucial in bad faith.

It is again difficult to quantify what I am describing, for establishing this balance will be unique to each paper. Adding a new idea or small twist to your paper in the conclusion to help the reader see your content in a new and interesting way can be an effective strategy, but it also needs to be proportionate to the overall paper. In other words, do not introduce anything so large in your conclusion that it upsets the basis of your essay.

Advice for Conclusions

Alas, these are only things not to do in a conclusion. What are good things to do? I confess I find conclusions troublesome. But one epiphany that has helped me is to think of my paper as a time-based act for the reader. I know all the parts of the paper, because I wrote it, but the reader knows none of your content at the beginning and all of it at the end.

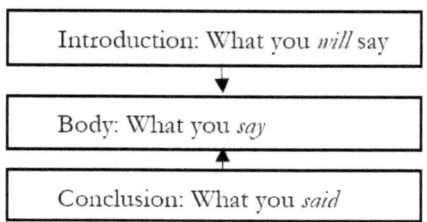

There are two implications to this. One, you might approach your introduction as things you will discuss, looking forward; and approach your conclusion as things you did discuss, looking back. In doing so, you will see your content from different perspectives. Two, you might rhetorically speak to your reader differently at the end of the paper, as a sort of near-equal. In short, you might imagine yourself asking the reader, now that you know what I know—what does it mean, or why? Or, in rougher language, now that I've explained myself, who cares?

Who Cares?

Now that I've proven x to you, so what? Again, you don't have to do this in your conclusion, but it might be a useful locomotive to get you started. Some science and social science papers explicitly have a brief synopsis defending why the paper is useful or important at their close by placing it within a continuing practice:

Further research on data usage in future may help in improved understanding of how the search process advocated here can most efficiently reduce wait times.

Further studies considering the economic benefit and lifetime of ETE treatment should be done, and detailed estimation of shrinkage rates should be accompanied with clear observations.

Your approach might be less formulaic, but you might discuss the consequences or importance of the topic or your paper. Why should the reader care about what you have written?

Thus although animal testing is presently regrettably necessary, computer modeling has been shown to be increasingly effective, and will likely become more so in the coming years.

While these conclusions are promising, more research will be necessary to provide a clearer picture of the relationship between Stein's earlier and later poems.

Note that my examples are not written in past tense, although they rhetorically look back on the paper, attempting to reflect on its information and make it somehow relevant to the reader.

But how can some topics be made relevant to the reader? In a scientific or business field, the information may have obvious real-life consequences. It may be harder to relate your arguments about the French Revolution, turtle depopulation, or *Paradise Lost* to people's lives, but you might observe how a clearer understanding of the topic will help those interested in it. How we interpret a line of *Henry V*, or whether Shakespeare wrote it in his greenhouse or in his bathtub, may not seem relevant to most readers' lives, but you might argue that seeing such small details more accurately will help scholars to better understand the play or apply this information to related problems.

Here is an attempt I made of this in a conclusion to a paper arguing that learners of English might better learn to use the articles *a/the* by being taught their etymological roots in Old English. You need not agree with the claim; what I am hoping you will pay attention to is how I've attempted to give the research a relevant application:

For high-level learners of English, particularly those concerned with research papers or thesis projects for possible publication or entry to western graduate programs, functional or near-native grasp of articles yields an immediate index of the writer's perceived competence or credibility. At present, more is needed for these students than photocopies listing examples of articles and exceptions for lakes and rivers. Ferris and Hedgcock (1998) lament that "we have seen English reference grammars that present over 40 different rules for the use of the definite article" (p. 206). What is better is the fostering of a reasonably workable intuition for article usage, and teachers might best model replication of this native instinct by themselves understanding their etymological origins and development.

4 STRUCTURE

I will add a few more well-done student examples, the first from the *Guards! Guards!* paper I mentioned in the discussion on thesis statement placement. This conclusion looks back at the paper's thesis statement defending the mini-dragon Errol, and nicely sums up its arguments:

By looking at Errol, we now can get a second thought about this little creature. Errol reminded Vimes of himself and the police watch for being disgraced and "always dealing off the bottom of the pack" (121). However, just like the watchmen save the city and become heroes, Errol had the potential to be qualified enough to be treated as a main character in this novel. He was a good helper to Captain Vimes with the dragon, and he also was a vector between Vimes and Sybil. Also, he finally got rid of the dragon from Ankh-Morpork at the time everyone thought it was hopeless. We should give a higher appraisal to Errol for all of these good factors.

This next conclusion regards Zadie Smith's *White Teeth*, and it dexterously widens the paper's frame at its close to touch on the real-life social issues the novel discusses.

In conclusion, as part of a second generation, Millat represents the migrants who mentally wander, not having a sense of belonging anywhere. As this novel is involved in such complicated situations with many religions, ethnicities, and personal backgrounds, almost everything is about hybridity, and so is Millat. He decides to take part in KEVIN because he is desperate to find out what he is and where he needs to be. His struggle throughout the whole book is not a rare case. In this intercultural society, people look for their own identity. Some people may end up assimilating in their new culture, and others may refuse to do so and confront their own future or fate like Millat, or may give up on ideas of belonging, like Samad. As the narrator says, "Because this is the other thing about immigrants... they cannot escape their history any more than you yourself can lose your shadow" (*Teeth* 385), every person traces back his or her history for roots, looking forward to discovering what he or she is.

A final example is from the social sciences.

It will take substantial money to develop the high technology which is needed in next-generation cars. To protect the environment and activate alternative energy car markets, the effort of private corporations will not be enough. Government support is needed for such development to lessen the financial burdens of automobile corporations. The cost of specific parts such as 7,000 cell batteries or hydrogen container is relatively high. The corporations' first rule is maximizing profits; so to develop market conditions, more investments from the private and public sectors are needed. When the government voluntarily jumps into the alternative energy market, buyers will see more cars with more rational prices on their catalogues.

Some conclusions will flow easily, and others can be difficult to write. The writer must again balance creating some sense of significance in the paper's subject while avoiding introducing too much new or unrelated material. But conclusions are usually, naturally, the last thing the reader sees. If most of the paper is fluidly argued but the conclusion is weak or anticlimactic, that may be what the reader remembers in forming an impression of the writer and essay.

4.6 Beyond Five Paragraphs

As noted, the five-paragraph model seems to create strong feelings for and against it. I have read social media articles calling it childish or even harmful, and arguments that writers should organically sequence their ideas in the logical steps of explaining or solving a problem, rather than being concerned with artificial components. Fair enough. It is simply a template to help you plan your text, and if a writing situation occurs where it is a hindrance, alter or discard it. When we discuss more complex sections within a thesis or dissertation, we will need a fuller schema.

As well, young learners understand the five-paragraph model as a frame for five actual paragraphs, but hopefully you have already discerned that it is merely an abstraction which can be expanded. You can't practically write a 100-page master's thesis with five paragraphs in it, or even a 20-page seminar paper. More likely, such papers might have hundreds or dozens of paragraphs. This might be perfectly obvious to you, in which case, go on—but at an abstract level, I would like to discuss two ways how you might plan or conceptualize such a structure.

Let's as usual take a simple thesis statement as an example to help focus on the ideas at play:

The government should not institute a sales tax because it would increase bureaucracy, stifle consumer spending, and reduce foreign investment.

To write a ten-page paper, we might need about twelve paragraphs. With two paragraphs for an introduction and one for a conclusion, we need nine body paragraphs. It would look quite awkward to have nine thesis sub-arguments—it would make more sense to subdivide the three sub-arguments into sections:

Introduction (x2)

Body 1: **Bureaucracy**	Bod 1 Para 1: Sales bureaucracy
	Bod 1 Para 2: Industrial bureaucracy
	Bod 1 Para 3: State bureaucracy
Body 2: **Spending**	Bod 2 Para 1: Luxury items
	Bod 2 Para 2: Food purchases
	Bod 2 Para 3: Job losses
Body 3: **Investment**	Bod 3 Para 1: Import costs
	Bod 3 Para 2: Industrial costs
	Bod 3 Para 3: Legal costs

Conclusion

We now have a clear plan for a twelve-paragraph paper. For an honors thesis or seminar paper of 25 pages, we could again subdivide each topic into a further three, so that *Bod 1 Para 1: Sales bureaucracy* would be split into a, b, and c (different *ways* in which sales taxes produce bureaucracy in shops and stores), to produce 27 different body paragraphs.

I suppose another way of doing this would be to take a five-paragraph outline and then write separate papers for each part—say a five-page "introduction" paper, three "body section" papers of 3 x 5 pages, and a "conclusion" paper of 5 pages, collected to make a 25-page paper, with some editing and smoothing. At a structural level it might look like this:

Paper 1: Master introduction
Thesis: x is true because of a, b, and c
In the following sections I'm going to prove it.

Paper 2	Paper 3	Paper 4
Introduction	Introduction	Introduction
Sub-thesis: a is true because of a1, a2, a3	Sub-thesis: b is true because of b1, b2, b3	Sub-thesis: c is true because of c1, c2, c3
Body section 1 (a1)	Body section 1 (b1)	Body section 1 (c1)
Body section 2 (a2)	Body section 2 (b2)	Body section 2 (c2)
Body section 3 (a3)	Body section 3 (b3)	Body section 3 (c3)
Conclusion	Conclusion	Conclusion

Paper 5: Master conclusion
Therefore, we can see that because
a, b, and c are true, x is true.
Who cares? What does this mean for future studies?

Perhaps this feels overcomplicated. Perhaps there are too many redundancies. But this is what I did in writing my own master's thesis. I found myself frozen, unable to begin a 100-page paper, when my advisor suggested I write several shorter papers and then smooth them together. I generated a five-paragraph model outline, and then I wrote a 20-page "introduction" paper, three 20-page "body section" papers, and a final 20-page "conclusion" paper. This was certainly less intimidating and stressful, as it helped me break up the task into more easily remembered pieces—and who would know or care how you completed the final product?

My doctorate dissertation was also not planned as such. Rather, I decided on a common topic or argument and then wrote 22 successive papers, consisting of an introduction paper, 20 "body" papers, and a conclusion paper. Twice I remember copy-and-pasting these essays into a master word processor file, and finding it a distinctly peculiar mental shift to suddenly stop seeing these texts as papers and begin seeing them as chapters.

If you are thinking, "Why can't I just do it without thinking about some clumsy system"—then go ahead. These two methods are not prescriptions—they are suggestions. Stratagems like these, however sophomoric or contrived, made writing these texts less frightening for me, and the emotional tricks we develop to confront problems may be benign and helpful ones, just as there's nothing wrong with drinking coffee to put yourself in a happy mood to write, if that's the case. And although having this sort of system seems to overcomplicate it, some means of dividing the portions of a long paper is preferable to attempting to keep a large and complex group of ideas ordered in your head.

Example of a Comparison Paper Structure

For now let's step back down to something easier, by taking the comparison-style frame to exemplify planning out a longer paper's structure. Imagine that you are writing a paper comparing big companies to small companies. We can do better than "both have benefits and downsides, and everyone has to decide in the end." That is not a thesis; that is an evasive and tired cliché. Everyone smarter than a protozoon knows that most things have benefits and downsides. Rather, for example's sake I advise, "small companies are more flexible, exciting, and profitable." There are two ways we might lay out our arguments: subject-by-subject or point-by-point:

Subject-by-Subject
1. Introduction
2. Big companies are
   a. Less flexible; b. Less dynamic; c. Less profitable
3. Small companies are
   a. More flexible; b. More dynamic; c. More profitable
4. Conclusion

Point-by-Point
1. Introduction
2. Flexibility
   a. Big companies; b. Small companies
3. Dynamism
   a. Big companies; b. Small companies
4. Profitability
   a. Big companies; b. Small companies
5. Conclusion

Or, as a literature example, a paper I wrote as an undergraduate compared Jordan, Myrtle, and Daisy in *The Great Gatsby*. The layout I used was subject-by-subject, that is, by character:

1. Thesis: Many personal problems in the novel are the result of the socioeconomic dependence of Jordan, Myrtle, and Daisy on their husbands.
2. Body 1: Jordan is independent, but this is seen as temporary until she 'matures'
3. Body 2: Myrtle dresses independently, but it's just an act to attract Tom's support
4. Body 3: Daisy pretends to be independent, but relies on Tom, whom she doesn't love
5. Conclusion

Because Jordan, Myrtle, and Daisy are the main female characters in the novel it is easy to create this triplet structure—also notice that I arrange the sub-arguments in ascending order of importance: Jordan is a minor character, Myrtle is more central, and Daisy is the most important. Again, to me papers flow better when there is some rationale to the sequencing of thesis parts, and I like to go from easier/concrete to harder/abstract. That is one nice thing about a paper on an experiment, as typically the sequence is chronological—the writer simply reports the steps.

I discuss this because sometimes I see in literature papers and presentations a pair or set of characters chosen or ordered randomly. There are many characters in *The Great Gatsby*, and a paper haphazardly choosing three of them for paragraph sections (Tom? Owl Eyes?) without some sort of rationale connecting them may be a difficult paper to understand. The reader or an editor might well ask, why those three?

If I were to write a point-by-point paper about the same thing, it could be divided by b1: "displays of independence that are real, but temporary" and b2: "displays of independence that are pretended, but permanent." And that's fine. An outline could also be hybrid, combining both formats.

The last pages have been examples to illustrate ways to solve a problem: how to expand structural modules in longer papers, and how to scale up planning concepts to address them. They are suggestions, and you may not need them. But a research paper does need evidence, and to that we turn.

5 EVIDENCE & RHETORIC

Writing is so complex an activity, so closely tied to a person's intellectual development, that it must be nurtured and practiced over all the years of a student's schooling and in every curricular area. – Barbara Walvoord

I have talked about three different building blocks of academic writing—grammar, structure, and content—and this chapter focuses on the third. To repeat the discussion in chapter one, all three are necessary to good writing. A paper that is grammatically perfect, with a fluid arrangement of ideas, may still be worthless if its content is nonsense or it lacks a position and evidence. Again, there are genres of professional writing intended solely to inform the reader, such as journalism or technical reports, but most academic papers deal with expanding knowledge via proposing and supporting thesis arguments.

Earlier chapters examined how to construct arguments and thesis statements, but also how to arrange or present your thesis in a structured way that prepares the reader to understand and be persuaded by your ideas. These *are* also rhetorical concerns—but in this chapter I will address rhetoric more formally and in more detail. Like the word *argument*, rhetoric also has a rather pejorative common nuance, meaning something like "pretty or dishonest words that mean nothing." But I will use it in its more academic and original sense: rhetoric is the study of persuasion, of saying or writing the right things in the right way to persuade others. This chapter will explain it at a more theoretical level so that we can apply it more proficiently and exactly to writing.

5.1 Aristotelian Rhetoric

Many of the ancient Greco-Roman traditions of thought came from the sequence of Socrates, his student Plato, and his student Aristotle. They did not likely invent such concepts, but their influence on western civilization is spectacular. Many academic subjects, and the university institution of the west to an extent originate from the academy they founded. Aristotle (384-322 BC), who was in his day a polymath responsible for fostering numerous fields of inquiry, from science, engineering, physics, literary theory, and philosophy, to psychology, can also be said to be one of the fathers of rhetoric.

Aristotle's titanic influence continued through the European middle ages, in the scholastic debate of tradition which underlay medieval university classes. Although a pre-Christian, he was esteemed by both the European church and in the Muslim world—some of his scientific treatises only survive because they were preserved and esteemed by Arab scholars. Twenty-three centuries later, composition theorists still work on the foundation laid by Aristotle and the ancient Greco-Roman thinkers.

Rhetoric is again the art and technique of persuasion, and Aristotle believed it to be so important that he viewed it as one of the three branches of philosophy, along with logic and dialectic (discussion practices). Aristotle was chiefly interested in spoken rhetoric, the tools for convincing a jury or a group of voters or policy-makers. I keep emphasizing that speeches and academic papers are different, but much of what Aristotle asserts about making a successful speech equally applies to writing. His methodology breaks down into yet another group of three components, which he calls modes of persuasion: logos, pathos, and ethos.

Rhetoric is about effective persuasion of a position, and is technically agnostic on whether the position is actually true or ethical, and this is one reason that in common usage the word can have a negative meaning. Essentially rhetoric is audience-oriented—another Greek term in the discipline is *kairos* (καιρός), which simply refers to choosing the right moment or situation to persuade. As I mentioned in the planning chapter, it is tempting to think of your paper's audience as the instructor and go no further, but you should be visualizing a readership of academic peers who may not know you, and who may even be initially opposed to your arguments. So that we may have a toolset for describing evidentiary strategies, how do Aristotle's three forms operate?

5.2 Appeal to Logic (Logos)

Logos is easily recognized from its etymological descendant, 'logic,' λόγος, which is what it means. Going back to Ancient Greek, logos had the broader meaning of truth or reason, and thus the names of many academic disciplines end with *-ology*. But in modern usage logos/logic has the more restricted sense of seeing concepts with an almost mathematical mindset, as groups of principles bound by necessary relationships. Thus logos asks, is the argument logically sound? Does it make reasoned sense? Does it consist of principles that support a conclusion and do not contradict each other? Does it derive a conclusion from factual or statistical evidence?

Remember that rhetoric is concerned with persuasion, and is neutral on whether the position actually *is* logical. Nevertheless, Aristotle probably wasn't a sociopath, and likely assumed the claim to be advocated is ideally actually sound, and isn't trying to trick the audience. Moreover, all things being equal, it ought to be easier to logically persuade the reader if you believe yourself that the argument is really true.

Facts, whether empirical observations, statistics, or conclusions, are obvious forms of logos, as are relationships of facts—although facts are not always logos-relevant and not all logos arguments use facts. What makes an evidentiary strategy logos is the reliance on rational or reasoned proofs, and for the

Greeks a favorite rhetorical device was the syllogism, made of a major premise, minor premise, and a conclusion made necessary by their relationship:

Major: Only people wear glasses.
Minor: Larissa wears glasses.
Conclusion: Therefore, Larissa is a person.

Mr. Kim claims he saw an owl at the time of the crime.
The crime happened in daytime, and owls are nocturnal.
Therefore, Mr. Kim can't be correct.

It is the relationship between the statements which compels the conclusion. Garbage in, garbage out, of course—if any part is faulty, the entire syllogism is faulty:

Only people wear glasses.
Mary doesn't wear glasses.
Therefore, Mary is not a person. **x**

Everyone wants to live to old age.
Exercise and diet are key to longevity.
Therefore, everyone should exercise and eat well. **x**

The first one is obviously silly. But the second one is trickier, for it seems reasonable; yet the first premise isn't true. Many people aren't really concerned with living to old age and would rather enjoy themselves, and this invalidates the conclusion. Or, a famous flawed syllogism is the promise the weird witches make to Macbeth in Shakespeare's play:

(Macbeth thinks)
The witches said, no man born from a woman can hurt me.
Every man is born from a woman.
Therefore, Macduff can't hurt me. **x**

The climax of the play is where Macduff reveals that he was

delivered by caesarian section, thus he was never 'born,' and he slays Macbeth. The syllogism is strictly true, but misleads the play's antihero. Does your syllogism actually prove what you believe it is proving, or fail to limit other possibilities—for example, what if a woman were to kill Macbeth?

Solid logos is nearly bulletproof argumentation. As a Victorian professor might write, QED: *Quod erat demonstrandum*, "what was to be demonstrated is done," loosely. A correct or firm logos argument can be very compelling, as cold, hard reason is difficult to refute. Such a paper can be straightforward to write because you are again dealing with ideas that fit like mathematical concepts and are sometimes even represented as such. This is no accident, for the Greeks thought of logic in such terms, seeing mathematics as the purest subject. It is no surprise that Aristotle esteemed logos above other forms of persuasion.

The chief problem is that just as logos is generally binary logic, its effectiveness in academic writing is also binary: it works or it doesn't. It is all-or-nothing. If you have *any* faulty logic or contradiction in the chain or set of claims, the entire paper may collapse spectacularly.

5.3 Faulty Logic

These arguments display flawed logic or are otherwise suspect as evidence. I will anticipate two objections—one is that these mistakes are obvious. But they are intentionally easily recognizable errors so that you are not distracted by the content of the claims, but by the logical error committed—why are they erroneous? The second response I receive from students is that they would never do this, and they know better. But the forms of flawed logic I list here do show up in student writing, and even in professional writing or journalism.

1. *False Analogy or Comparison.* "Why do people need to wear clothes at work when they don't in the bathtub?" These of course aren't the same situations. False comparison claims sometimes also happen in literature papers when students

compare dissimilar time periods: "The women in *Pride and Prejudice* are foolish to want husbands so much when they can just be happy on their own." This applies the socioeconomic rules of 1813 to ours, which are different. The women in the novel can't work in an office.

2. *False Equivalence.* "There are many opinions about the moon. Scientists believe it is made of rock. Some people believe it is made of cheese." The fact that there are opposing opinions on a topic does not mean both deserve equal respect or space. A variation on this is the *Middle Ground* error, where the writer tries to seem reasonable and open-minded by finding the middle point between two arguments. It's commendable to consider an opposing viewpoint, but not always a virtue to compromise—stating that the moon may consist of extremely hard cheese to mollify both sides and appear statesmanlike would be silly.

3. *Either / Or Fallacy.* "Either you are on our side, or you are on the side of Al Qaeda"—or ISIS or the Russians or Fijians or whoever this week. The statement pretends only two choices exist, whereas the world is messy: many nations are somewhat aligned either way, or are neutral. Or, your mother may have scolded you as a child, "do you want your room to be clean, or a pig-pen?" This again assumes only one possibility or the other, and no gradations between fastidiously spotless and filthy are possible. Sometimes binaries help make sense of ideas—"Is Macbeth insane or not?" But they can also prevent us from seeing other nuances. It is more likely that Macbeth's sanity varies throughout the play.

4. *Ad Hominem* ('against the man'). "Dr. Jones can't be believed. He has a strange nose and a creepy mustache." Dr. Jones's appearance has no relevance to the truth of his claims. Or to be less obvious, one might attack someone's view based on their prior actions, such as scorning Bill

Clinton's comments on foreign relations because he had a sexual scandal. This ought to be irrelevant, although a student did point out to me that his morality could affect his judgments. That's a fair claim. But to me the burden of evidence falls on showing that Bill Clinton's statements should be rejected because of his conduct.

5. *Bandwagon.* "In a recent study, 87% of respondents indicated that Martians will cause crime; this is why the proposed law restricting them should be passed." This is again tricky. Surveys suggesting a popular view should probably be seriously considered, but do not prove it. A popular belief may be supplementary or contributory evidence, but it's not sufficient; claims are not true because a majority of people think they are. Gravity is real regardless of surveys asking the public whether it is. Martian crime might rise, but it would be better to quote statistics or experts in addition to surveys.

6. *Circular Reasoning.* "A Greek salad is healthier than pizza because it is better for you." The 'reason' simply rephrases the first argument. This error is also known as begging the question (*petitio principii*): "same-sex marriage is wrong because marriage is a bond between a man and a woman." This statement merely uses itself to prove itself. Note that begging the question does *not* mean "invite the question," as it is often misused.

7. *Coincidence Fallacy.* "More wars in the twentieth century started in even-numbered years. Why is this so?" This may be true but pure coincidence, and there may be no connection at all. Or similarly, two events may follow each other with no relationship, which is called a *non sequitur*. If a new iPhone is released and then it rains more that month, it is unlikely that one action caused the other.

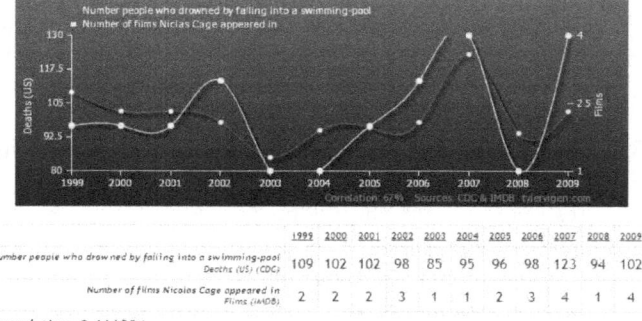

An internet image showing silly but statistically true correlations between different phenomena.

8. *Causation Fallacy.* A related error to the coincidence fallacy is confusing cause-and-effect relationships. A recent example is a *New York Times* blog post reporting a British study claiming that people who attend operas live longer. The commenters correctly wrote that the people who have the leisure affluence to attend operas are already likely to be in better health, and that the operas were not the cause.

This error is a difficult one to diagnose. A common statistic is that 20-40% of affairs end in divorce. It is probably partly true that affairs cause divorces; it is likely also partly true that the marriages where affairs happened were already bad ones. To what extent are the affairs the cause, or the symptom? It would be a mistake to assume either the simplest (one is true) or the most complex (it must be both) explanation.

9. *Cherry-Picking.* "Hitler was an excellent leader and a good person. Under his government, Germany built the autobahn and promoted the Volkswagen. Hitler loved dogs and was kind to his pets." These things are true, but they are highly

selective facts ignoring the larger picture. A variation of cherry-picking in literature papers is quote mining, where a single incidence or small number of words from a text are used to endorse a disproportionately large claim: "Shakespeare uses the word 'grapes' five times in his plays. What does this mean?" To argue that grapes are vital to understanding his plays would be outlandish. Unfortunately, because quote mining is a matter of judgment (if the plays mentioned grapes *36* times, is it significant?), it is a depressingly common facet of Shakespearean criticism. I am not even sure a paper on the grapes claim would be immediately rejected.

10. *No True Scotsman.* "None of our classmates is an author" (but Barb Scott wrote a novel)—"but it wasn't published, so she isn't a real author" (yes, it was, by Harley Press)—"okay, but it wasn't a bestseller, so she isn't a real author" (but it was a bestseller, in England)—"well… it wasn't a bestseller in America, so she isn't a real author." Here evidence contradicting the position is discounted by making the requirements so restrictive that no example can meet it. This error is also called *special pleading*, where you rule out examples that don't support your bias: A nation without religion would be better, but North Korea, Soviet Russia, Communist Bulgaria, and revolutionary France don't count.

11. *Ad Snarkium.* "Only an idiot would argue that smoking should be abolished, or a virtue-signaling woke grouch who hates freedom." Insults and sarcasm are not proof. Here the opposing position is phrased in a mocking way to poison it, rather than discussing it. Sadly, this is a practice endemic on social media. A variation on *ad snarkium* is the "scarecrow" argument, where you misrepresent the opposing argument or those holding it to discredit it: "Gun supporters, who believe that mistaking their pets for burglars and marrying their cousins is better than learning to read…" Of course you can criticize gun owners, but the statement above does

not fairly describe them; it only mocks them.

12. *Selection Bias.* "The survey we conducted in the campus cafés show that 68% like jazz music." But people who relax with coffee in campus cafés are more likely to like jazz music than the general public. The survey erred in only questioning those people. A variation on selection bias is sample error: "the four engineers we surveyed prove that 75% of experts have confidence in city water supplies." Sometimes the sample set is necessarily small, and you may not be able to survey many Nobel laureates; but there are many engineers, and the tiny number surveyed may not be fairly representative of them.

    It isn't quite the same, but recall at the beginning of the book where I mentioned *extrapolation error*—wrongly assuming that a chart line or some pattern or arc over a period will always be the case. In a way, this is akin to selection bias, for a smaller set of data is given too much predictive power over an unknown future.

13. *Slippery Slope.* "If people are allowed to pirate software files, they will gradually lose respect for all laws, and they will try to do whatever they want, including cannibalism." It is not necessarily true that people will do this. Or: "if small children are allowed to stay up an hour later, they will continually beg to stay up later." This is likely partly true, but children can't stay up 24 hours a day—eventually this will stop. Note that these logic errors are becoming more subtle. Whereas a false premise argument is nearly always wrong, an argument which warns of precedents might not be a slippery slope one. Some people believe marijuana use is a gateway to using heavier drugs, but some activists dispute this claim with statistics or other arguments.

14. *Moving the Goalposts.* This error refers to holding positions to different standards based on your sympathies toward them. If one Martian commits a crime and you conclude "those

dirty Martians can't be trusted," but a hundred Neptunians commit crimes and you rationalize, "but that's different" or "they're just exceptions, as most Neptunians are honest," you are judging two things differently based on your biases. Similarly, in academic argumentation, evidence for the opposing side of your argument is held to harsher standards than your own. A variation is the 'Kafka Trap':

"Those Martians set the fire!"
Situation A: The Martians confess.
"I knew those Martians were no good!"
Situation B: The Martians deny it.
"This proves the Martians did it, for denying it is exactly what a guilty party would do!"

But all this is doing is of course rearranging any opposing evidence to re-fit prior prejudices. In your 'logic' there is no possible outcome where the Martians can be innocent.

'Grey' Evidence

But you probably know that real life is not so simple, and that logical errors are more likely when things aren't nicely labeled for demonstration, as they are here. I make them too; recall that I mentioned toward the end of this list that the logical flaws are becoming more subtle and partial. A false analogy argument may be fairly cut-and-dried, but an ad hominem argument may be less binary—now we are dealing with degrees to which someone's behavior informs their judgment; and a slippery slope argument might be true, or true to a certain degree or in a certain situation. Perhaps increased production of new iPhones causes air pollution in cities with factories. Perhaps those few mentions of grapes in Shakespeare is really significant. How do we know?

This is part of the reason academic papers are written—because the interpretation of facts and ideas, such as their connections and causations, is disputed. These questions could be paper topics themselves, where you argue how a phenomenon should be understood, or whether the grapes or air pollution are relevant, or whether celebrity x's affair caused the divorce. Some of the hardest thinking involves reasoning out degrees of error, or judging the relative value of claims. If you are in favor of a piece of legislation, it would be completely appropriate to cite an authoritative survey stating that the public agrees with you; you would simply need the discipline and balance to understand that this supports your argument but is not sufficient—more is needed.

5.4 Appeal to Emotion (Pathos)

A pathos strategy (πάθος) asks: Does the argument move people's hearts to care? Does it have an emotional appeal to bring the audience to agree?

You might be objecting, come now, when would I use an emotional claim to support an argument in a serious paper? I should advocate this dairy testing method or this reading of *Animal Farm* using my feelings? Surely logic should be the only thing which counts. Aristotle might have agreed with you. He held that logos is the purest form of rhetoric, and that other forms of persuasion are useful but less respectable means of pursuing an argument. Perhaps a little arrogantly, he saw pathos as an unfortunate necessity for an ignorant public which requires spoon-feeding—in a perfect world logic would be enough! Yet Aristotle was practical enough to see that emotion and the power of a dramatic delivery can sway an audience's feelings. Again, he was talking about oral speech, which implies other means of moving people's hearts, such as diction and body language, but many pathos techniques apply equally to text.

We greatly underestimate how powerful pathos strategies are. They are fundamental to propaganda and advertising. For example, when I was a boy it was far more acceptable to ride in a car on the highway eating fast food and then throw the paper wrappers out the window. Littering is now much less socially acceptable in the west, partly because of the campaigns of the 1970's which stigmatized people who litter as irresponsible and selfish. Similarly, it was once regrettably amusing to joke about driving drunk or domestic violence in old movie comedies or in popular culture. Most people would find such humor offensive or tasteless now, and much of this societal change is because of government-sponsored promotions relying on pathos arguments.

For example, the USA had a public service commercial which depicted no more than someone throwing trash out of their car window, ending with a native Indian seeing this and weeping as the car drove away. A logos-based commercial based on statistics and facts about animal deaths or auto injuries might have convinced the public in their heads, but not their hearts. In a country where people remain sensitive about the fraught history of first nations relations, this emotional strategy was far more effective in changing behaviors.

Keep America Beautiful ad campaign, 1971

In the 1980s, Michelin Tires had a series of commercials where babies play on their tires. A series of tepid statistics showing that certain tires perform better in emergency situations could be effective, but the image of the babies raised powerful protective emotions in parents that made them equate the tires with safety. Advertisers are psychological experts at guiding people to identify with a product based on primal emotions of sex, prestige, adventure, or security. Note when observing commercials for alcoholic beverages or other products how the objects are held, what body gestures the models have, and what colors and fonts are employed. These features are often carefully calculated to suggest sexual meanings or other semi-conscious emotional responses.

These emotional messages can and have been powerful enough to make people follow dictators. The Greeks recognized but were wary of pathos for its potential to mislead people, to manipulate them into accepting positions that would be recognized as false using reason. For this reason, again, rhetoric has a bad connotation in popular usage—a politician's speech might be criticized as "mere rhetoric," beautiful words that obscure lies or disguise inaction. Aristotle's forebear Plato saw such rhetoric as the dangerous and seductive sophistry which unfairly condemned Socrates to death. Perhaps at some time in your life you felt offended after watching a movie or TV show which tried to move your emotions to endorse behaviors or ideas you disapproved of. A classic example is the Nazi propaganda film *Triumph of the Will* (1935), which used stirring music and imagery to corrupt viewers into its agenda.

Why Use Pathos, Then?

How does this relate to academic writing, and again, why would you use pathos appeals as evidence, particularly when I have stressed how it can be easily abused? I agree they are seldom appropriate or convincing, but not never. They are the perhaps the dessert of rhetoric; a dinner of pie would make people nauseated and unsatisfied, but a small amount might complement a meal. If you were writing a biology paper on dairy testing, it would be reasonable to occasionally mention that people *not* dying from bacterial infections might be a good thing. In an essay on *Grapes of Wrath*, it would be acceptable to concede that in judging the Joads' moral actions, they are starving and homeless. A paper analyzing a particular war could be offensively cold and unpersuasive if it never mentioned its human costs.

Personal examples, where appropriate, are also occasionally

an effective use of pathos. If you were to write a paper about campus alcoholism, for example, you could detail statistics about fatalities, expulsions, broken relationships, or academic problems that result from binge drinking. All this could be convincing as evidence. But if you included a short anecdote about a roommate who had a drinking problem which resulted in sexual assault or failing out, that sort of personal story is not only relevant but effective in capping your other arguments. To do this you will have to use 'I' or 'we' in your paper, and I know the use of personal pronouns in academic writing is controversial—but to me it is justified here. I will return to that issue later.

Yes, of course pathos can be quickly overdone. One danger is that it can look childish, such as the insipid claim politicians make that "we're not just talking about statistics here, these are real people!"—did others imply we were speaking about tomatoes? Pathos requires judicious use to avoid a text full of unpersuasive melodrama. You might oppose hunting—but the plaint, "this innocent dead giraffe is a reason to prohibit hunting" relies on an extreme example (much hunting is not of inedible and rare animals for fun, but for food); but more problematically, the approach may be suspected of attempting to maneuver readers into feeling guilty, so that they will accept a specious argument. An "appeal to emotion" is sometimes in fact categorized as a logical fallacy.

I only repeat: seldom, but not never. There may be occasions where a small amount of pathos works. A social science paper may add a personal touch to a social issue; a literature paper might sympathize with a fictional character. Engineering students are likely to object here again, there is hardly a place to discuss emotions when analyzing a chemical reagent or gas sequestration technique. Perhaps not. But there may be moments in an introduction or conclusion to state that a process has human implications. It's not maudlin or irrelevant to note that a finding might make people's lives safer, or to quote the widow of someone who drowned before discussing an electrolytic process for improving shipbuilding. Why else are papers written if they make no personal difference to anyone?

5.5 Appeal to Authority (Ethos)

Ethos (ἦθος) is Greek for one's nature, or collectively for a people's customs, but in rhetoric it more specifically refers to the speaker's credibility. Ethos asks: do I trust you? Does your argument seem to have authority or give the impression that you are knowledgeable and competent? Ethos speaks to the aura of credibility created in the paper and the writer, which hopes to persuade readers. Whether it is there is their decision.

Do not confuse ethos with ethics. There is an etymological connection in Greek in that one of good moral character is more likely to inspire trust, but Aristotle concedes that expertise may be a more important and persuasive factor than personal morality. U.S. President Richard Nixon may not have been an ethical politician, but as an educated and important man his writing would certainly have ethos. Morally dubious figures such as ex-dictators and spies might not be moral paragons, but they may have credibility in discussing the historical events they witnessed. There are of course limits; a scholar who committed a horrendous crime might be a gifted public intellect but his or her ideas would nevertheless be tainted and viewed with distrust. Nazi architect and inner party member Albert Speer might be authoritative as a source of historical information, but might be a dubious choice to quote in a paper on architecture.

Aristotle, again, discussed ethos as a vocal and not textual act. He would have observed with reluctance that how one speaks and appears can be as important in persuading an audience as the content. Someone who has a look of gravitas, a commanding voice and clear elocution, and a mastery of the rhythms of speech will be more persuasive than a subject expert with an untidy appearance and feeble, shaky voice—thus the CNN station break has James Earl Jones, the sonorous voice of Darth Vader, say "this is CNN" and not a child. In English we say "gold in the pockets of fools is still gold," meaning that the truth is so regardless of who says it, but reality does not support these beautiful aspirations. People pay attention to the impression of the person speaking and how they are perceived by others in a social context—to an equal or even greater extent than they pay attention to what is said. This is also true with text.

Trust is as well somewhat personal, and textual ethos reflects a certain intimacy between the writer and the reader. There is a feeling of closeness in the written word not found in a speech to a group of people: you are privately holding a text face to face, virtually if not physically, and there is a kind of bond between you and the reader, who is trusting you with his or her time. You will never put your heart on the line the way you will in writing someone a love letter, committing yourself in a piece of paper! The recipient may not accept you, but will probably keep that letter forever.

Logos, pathos, and ethos personified.

5.6 Two Types of Ethos

Visual Ethos

I will break the sort of ethos applied in academic writing into visual and textual forms. Visual credibility is straightforward—it comes from having a professional presentation, correct text formatting and layout, and a clean, readable appearance. This is partly why composition instructors teach citation systems such as MLA and APA; applying them correctly gives the impression that the paper is serious and has the authorizing marks of belonging within a community of scholars.

Even where no actual citation system is specified, the paper's typography and appearance evoke ethos (or don't). Using clean paper with Times New Roman in clear, black ink gives an impression of authority and academic gravity which Hello Kitty paper and Comic Sans does not. This ought to be obvious. But I have received undergraduate papers with interesting content that visually looked amateurish or careless. I have had papers that were dirty, crumpled, smeared with ink or rain, on pink paper, or smelling of marijuana. Such details are going to detract from the paper and your reader's confidence in your ideas, even where the reader knows this should not be a factor in judging content.

I sometimes have students who triple-space or sneak in larger margins. They are asked to use 11-12 Times New Roman or Ariel fonts, generally the standard for academia, and they use a script font or some ridiculous giant typeface. They do this because they were asked to write ten pages and they finish seven and run out of ideas or effort, and believe that they can stretch the text over more pages via tricks. The result looks lazy and childish, and you diminish trust in your reader, who can see what you are trying to do.

 **Tip**

The cheapest investment you can make in your education is a box of paper clips. Crinkling the paper edges together to bind them looks childish, and at some point will make a difference in the reception or grade given to your essay.

Perhaps this is not the case and you have written ten pages, and good ones, but you still object in principle that the reader should make rushed judgments based on the surface look of your paper. But whether you feel this is fair or not will change little—people cannot help making such valuations, even if they are aware they are doing so. The impression of competence and authority will have an effect in convincing your reader that your arguments are strong ones, and lacking this, the reader may have the option to not bother evaluating your ideas at all.

Textual Ethos

The other means of building ethos, and perhaps a more genuine one because it is difficult to forge, is the trust evoked in your paper's content. A simple way of doing this is to use a more professional vocabulary, a topic I will return to in the editing chapter. Another vital way to build ethos is using external sources. An e-mail written to a friend endorsing an action requires little secondary support: you should go to Mexico because I had fun there, and you can trust my testimony. But an academic paper can't rely on this relationship, and you don't have first-hand familiarity with Victorian England or Linus Pauling to give yourself personal authority with. You need to build this authority second-hand by referring to or quoting the people who do, or who have more expertise on the subject.

There is a cliché that U.S. president Ronald Reagan was not a strong intellect but was astute enough to surround himself with gifted advisors. In the same way, leveraging the knowledge of specialists will make your ideas more persuasive by association. This is one of many reasons why papers quote from external sources; using them may serve multiple rhetorical strategies, in that the quotations and facts may be logos or pathos based evidence, but they will also help situate you as a member of a scholarly discourse. Deploying external sources is such an important aspect of academic writing that it requires a new chapter.

6 EXTERNAL SOURCES

Doveryai, no proveryai [Trust, but verify!] – Russian Proverb

The last chapter discussed using the rhetorical techniques of logos, pathos, and ethos, in a *kairos* situation of timeliness, in supporting arguments. A paper might use any or all of these modes in arranging evidence, bearing in mind that some modes may fit some subjects and writing situations better than others. But there's no rule, and some forms of evidence are multiform, anyway—a statistic or quotation might be simultaneously a logos and ethos strategy, or even pathos. A piece of data might be both logos, in that it presents a fact leading to a logical conclusion, and ethos, in that it is given by an authority figure on the subject.

This chapter expands on using external sources for these various strategies. Using sources will suggest a convincing sense of credibility and professionalism in your paper, and may help explain or support a logical claim, or may move sympathies. That doesn't mean what you already know is of no value. Your prior knowledge, or what you gather directly through surveys, experiments, or reasoning is certainly important; but much of a research paper's evidence is normally external and will take the form of quotations and information from books, journals, websites and other texts written by people who can reinforce and attest to your arguments.

Thus one of your first steps in writing a paper should

reflexively be to find books or sources about the issues. This helps to establish and narrow a thesis argument at the planning stage, but will also provide helpful evidentiary material. Subject disciplines may have a culture which emphasizes certain genres of documents. In social sciences, case studies and survey data are important in establishing credibility for an argument, whereas in the humanities close readings of texts and expert quotations about interpretation are likely to carry more weight. A science or engineering paper might favor mathematical equations or first-hand experiment results.

You may or have encountered the terms primary, secondary, and tertiary sources in doing research. They overlap, but we can basically define them as this:

Primary source: The text your paper is about, or accounts of something made by eyewitnesses. Examples are the novel or poem your paper is about, or contemporary historical writings such as diaries or accounts. Primary sources also include information you created or collected, such as laboratory or survey results.

Secondary source: Texts that discuss the primary sources or ideas in them. Examples are journal articles, monographs, or documentaries that talk about and analyze the novel, diary, notes, or similar experiments or surveys.

Tertiary source: Resource materials that give overviews and list primary or secondary sources. Examples are encyclopedias, textbooks, indexes, or Wikipedia.

In a very short paper, you may not have the space for anything but primary texts. Generally, the closer to the original phenomena the better, and researchers generally seek out primary sources first. Someone who was on the Titanic will have authoritative and detailed first-hand perspectives that a scholar a century later will not. A paper on Sylvia Plath would benefit by having her personal notes, just as a science paper on atomic fission would try to obtain first-hand reports from the Los Alamos scientists.

But this is not always so; sometimes primary sources are too close to events to be objective, or are written by people who don't understand them (the person on the Titanic may have been a child, and the Los Alamos scientists didn't know then about the arms races of later decades), and an expert far removed may have a more informed perspective. An author's later biography might color an earlier text's understanding. Your experimental or survey results may be flawed or nonreplicable. I can't tell you what the balance in your paper should be between primary and secondary sources, as this will differ between projects—although it's mostly the case that tertiary sources are less important. They are chiefly to help you find the first two types.

In an academic paper you list the sources you have read, referenced, or quoted at end. You probably know this, but why? This is done partly to assure the reader that you have read widely and deeply and are trustworthy on the subject, but also to help the reader find these sources for their own further use, and partly to protect yourself from possible accusations that you have plagiarized without crediting the authors of the sources. The elements in such a list are called end-text references, but normally we refer to them by the title given to the list, such as works cited or references.

To finalize this—again, realizing that you may know this—I should summarize and clarify the terms used so that they are not confusing:

In-Text References: References to outside sources within your paper (the introduction, body, or conclusion).

Watts and Zhan (2016) estimate that the European public sector is missing out on combined cost savings of around 100 billion euro per annum by failing to maximize the potential of big data for operational efficiency.

Teachers know by experience that "motivation is a star player in second language learning" (Brown 207).

The first example has only a citation (Watts and Zhan), and the second has a citation (Brown) and a quotation ("motivation is a star player") in quotation marks.

End-Text References: References to outside sources outside your paper text (that is, at the end of the paper, or sometimes in footnotes at the bottom of the page).

Ishiguro, Kazuo. *Klara and the Sun*. Knopf, 2021.

Vayena, E (2015). Ethical challenges of big data in public health. *PLoS Computational Biology 11*(2), e1003904.

6.1 Something's Missing

How can we know if an essay has enough external sources? That will be specific to your project. Often it is evident that the paper's content feels thin and unpersuasive. Occasionally I read a paper which is overlong and plodding and perhaps has too much external evidence, but that's rarely the case—if the quantity (not quality) of sources is problematic, it's nearly always for being not enough.

A typical red flag for not having enough external information or sources, particularly for undergraduate papers with a length specification, is that they are too short in length, and that the student ran out of things to say. I've given examples of the typographical tricks students use to bloat the paper's appearance, but subtler writers may resort to piling on more claims as opposed to proof, resulting in papers which end up feeling like lists.

Typically, such essays assume too much, because writers may feel that their ideas are so self-evident that no further support is necessary: "sex education will not change quickly in this country because Koreans are conservative." Like the false premise error discussed earlier, here the claim is taken for granted and the writer moves on to implications, but it was never proven. You need to first demonstrate that Koreans are generally conservative regarding sex education. The formation "most people" is nearly always a bad sign: most people believe Shylock is wrong / don't like paying taxes / want to drive electric cars. Assuming these statements and then moving on is unpersuasive to the reader, as well as imprecise. It would be better to prove that most people are x with evidence, quotations, or statistics.

 **Tip**

Very often, if you have run out of things to write, it is not because you have too few ideas but because you have not provided enough examples or proof regarding the ones you have.

In the following examples, b is better than a. This isn't merely because b is longer, and your goal should not be to fill space; the paper being too short is a symptom of the essay's deeper problem, not the problem itself. But b is more interesting and persuasive by incorporating external sources.

A: Many people nowadays believe…
B: In a recent Pew survey, 36% of respondents believe…

A: There was a case where a girl was assaulted by a teacher and the principal didn't help.
B: In October 2017 a 13-year-old girl in a middle school in the Daegu region was assaulted by a male teacher and the principal did not intervene.

A: In some countries divorce is still difficult to obtain.
B: In some countries, especially those with deeply Catholic traditions such as Ireland, France, and Italy, divorce is still

difficult to obtain.

A: Polly seems aware of how she is trapping Mr. Doran into marriage.
B: Polly's theatrical tears and the ending where she sits dreamily in her room and "waited on patiently, almost cheerfully, without alarm" (6) suggest that she is fully aware of how she is trapping Mr. Doran into marriage.

A: Lots of people are addicted to the internet nowadays.
B: A 2019 study claimed that 64% of U.S. female and 55% of male internet users are internet addicts, with higher percentages exhibited among Generation X users (born 1965-79). One of the few researchers studying the problem, Dr. Lee Bayard, notes that "it is far less of a socioeconomic problem and more of a generational problem than we first assumed."

A: Computer research has changed over the years, but some things remain the same.
B: Even by 1984, observers noted the shift in research towards "developing programs that write programs" (Shallis 121). Nevertheless, Shallis was prescient in noting that a computer is distinct from a human in terms of purpose, that a human wants to read a thermometer out of curiosity and a computer's aim "can only be that of its designer" (12).

One of my disappointments as a young(er) professor was while teaching in the United States during a national debate on lowering the drinking age from 21 to 18. This was an argument essay topic students were interested in. Despite my advice that there was a country next to theirs with a drinking age of 18 or 19, and to do some research to find out whether Canada's laws work or not!—or look at how other countries deal with this—there wasn't the slightest interest in seeing the controversy outside American concerns. This is only an example, and not meant to single out Americans; students everywhere fail to look at how a social issue applies in the 190 countries outside their own, or to take advantage of all the sources of information coming from them. I know that young writers have a narrower experience, but the insularity of these papers can make them depressing to read.

6.2 Judging Sources

I also find teaching the judging of sources in class frustrating, because my undergraduate students usually do not take the task seriously. Many simply cite from the nearest thing found on a popular search engine, which is usually a homework help site or Wikipedia. Whether out of naiveté or laziness, many writers assume that any secondary source is basically as good as another. It is perhaps not a glamorous part of writing. But critically evaluating sources is, if we refer to Bloom's taxonomy again, one of the hardest and most valuable cognitive skills a university education can teach.

While I am not *that* old, perhaps the biggest difference between me and my present students—even more than most of them being L2 or from a different culture—is that they grew up with the internet and I didn't, as I only began to use it in my late twenties. As a Gen-X'er I am a 'digital settler,' and they are 'digital natives.' I have seen the progression from my undergraduate days in the '80s when there was little online, and where the difficulty with research was locating enough sources, to the '90s when the internet was beginning to be taken seriously in academia, to now, where we are drowning in online sources and many are unhelpful or unreliable. I have just typed the search string *Pride and Prejudice* and Google gave me 91,300,000 hits—who could sift through them all? For this reason, an essential research skill in the twenty-first century is not finding sources, but evaluating them and winnowing out the chaos and rubbish that is out there. AI search engines can help you find things, but no AI yet can tell you the academic quality of a source or judge its veracity.

Source: Wikipedia Commons, https://commons.wikimedia.org

You may or may not be familiar with these titles, but that is partly intentional so that you are not distracted by recognizing them. You probably know that the *New York Times* or *Nature* are reputable, but what happens when you encounter an unfamiliar source? Yet there are fairly easy visual cues to judging printed materials from the graphics, topics, and fonts. You can readily see that a bound book or journal with small print, a list of professors, and a university sponsor is likely more reputable than a folded tabloid newspaper with giant fonts and pictures of soccer players and bikini girls.

This doesn't make tabloid newspapers bad, for they serve their audiences; some people want to read about celebrities and athletes, or they want something easy and fun for a subway or airplane trip. Such outlets might also be of interest as primary materials, if you were writing a paper about the perceptions of bikini girls or celebrity gossip, for example, as a sociological or cultural issue. In this excerpt here, note that I am referencing a pop song and TV commercial for examples but not using it as a direct source of expert criticism:

The UK profanity *bloody* had lost some of its offensive bite by 1954, so much that in the 1964 film adaptation of *Pygmalion* Eliza says "move your bloomin' arse" to comically expose her veneer of refinement. Yet the 1967 Royal Guardsmen novelty song "Snoopy and the Red Baron" had the line "the bloody Red Baron of Germany" bleeped out in the UK and Australia, and as late as 2007 an Australian tourism commercial asking "So where the bloody hell are you?" was banned in England (qtd. in Dialect Blog).

With this exception in mind, I turn back to using serious primary and secondary sources not to illustrate but to support your argument. As said, there are fairly obvious visual cues to evaluating reliability in print sources. But these visual or genre cues may not exist online, where you may not be able to see a document's cover or print form. You may still be able to critically judge a text's reliability or quality from its writer, or from the text's origins—the publisher, organization, or website name. An article from *Annual Review of Immunology* written by a physician, an editorial from the *Economist* written by a recognized expert, and a blog posting from your roommate are all textual sources, but obviously the first two have more weight in convincing your reader, just as they would in a real-life conversation.

Sometimes even this is missing, and there is little to tell you about the authority or credibility of your source. Perhaps a source which doesn't give you this information ought to tell you not to use it, but for argument's sake, is there anything else that can guide our evaluation? One remaining clue is whether the source itself refers to and quotes other sources that you can verify and judge. Another is the vocabulary choices and level of discourse. If you see the phrases "LOL awesome cat vid bro" and

"Melbourne has begun to process primary clearances for its UN human rights initiative," it's not hard to grasp that one text feels like a clickbait social media posting and the other resembles a news article. Partly this is because the subject matter is different, but also the higher level of vocabulary and sentence complexity in the second text elicits clues to its origins and reliability.

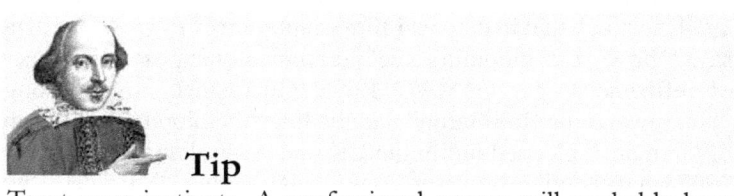

Tip

Trust your instincts. A professional source will probably have smaller print, will use a more complex vocabulary, and is more likely to be affiliated with an organization you have heard of.

The Food Chain of Academic Publications

Scholarly sources include journal articles, conference papers and proceedings, monographs, and edited books, as well as websites, newspapers, and podcasts. Which of these forms is valued most or has the highest trustworthiness or credibility slightly differs between disciplines, but is somewhat consistent. The larger issue is determining what is of academic reliability or not within these types.

Broadly, sources that are peer reviewed are more credible. Peer review means that a group of academics or experts with a background in the paper's field reads and critiques a submission and disputes its information or findings before it is accepted. A second and more quantitative metric for gauging source quality is impact factor (IF), which is a calculated number measuring how many citations a journal's output received elsewhere. IF is influential in STEM (science, technology, engineering, and medicine) disciplines and even affects hiring and tenure decisions. But it is less prevalent in the social sciences and humanities, it only measures journals, and as a purely objective formula IF has come under considerable criticism.

6 EXTERNAL SOURCES

It would be nice if academia had some recognized hierarchy of source reputation, and in a sense it does. As I'll expand on, academic journals endeavor to belong to scholarly databases and indexes disseminated by academic foundations, and books also have different levels of perceived authority and quality based on their publisher. For papers and journals, the present 'gold standard' is to be listed in the Thomson-Reuters/Clarivate "Web of Science" index of SCI (sciences), SSCI (social sciences), and A&HCI (arts and humanities), with their expanded index (SCI-E) and other foundations like Scopus a close second. For books there is less of a formal reputational standard, but the university the press belongs to is a key determinant—a book from Oxford, Stanford, or Harvard will have a stronger guarantee of reliability and eminence than one from a minor university press.

The following tree or hierarchy, from best to least good or worthless, is not written in stone—it may change—and is only my assessment, but I think it gives a fairly accurate guide to what is perceived within academia to be the highest quality and most reliable secondary scholarly sources. This can also get confusing because articles and other sources are often available in multiple databases in different 'tiers.'

The Best: Most Authoritative
Type: Web of Science journals (SCI, SSCI, A&HCI); top university-associated presses; conference proceedings from top organizations (IEEE)
Authors: Written and reviewed by the top and best-known scholars in the field
Features: Likely at the very highest subject level of discourse, and written for the most experienced specialists

Second Best: Highly Authoritative
Type: Scopus journals; well-known index databases (e.g. JSTOR, EBSCO, ProQuest; national (e.g. Korea's National Research Foundation, NRF) or field-specific ones (ERIC, PubMed); books from prestige university or scholarly presses; conference proceedings from well-known organizations

Authors: Written and reviewed by scholars in the field
Features: At a high subject level of discourse, and written for field-specific professionals

Third Best: Somewhat Authoritative
Type: Journals or proceedings in unfamiliar or minor indexes; online-only journals; books from minor presses; journalism from respected newspapers or disciplinary organizations
Authors: Graduate students, some professors, journalists with professional experience or credentials
Features: Likely written for students, or for non-research academics or educated readers

Grey Sources: Limited Authority
Type: Non-indexed articles in newspapers or websites; social media journalism websites; YouTube videos; podcasts; TV broadcasts or documentaries; Wikipedia; self-published books (more on this later)
Authors: Journalists or amateurs without subject credentials; little or no fact-checking or peer review
Features: Written for a general audience to inform and amuse at an easier or entry-level complexity level

Junk Sources: Dubious Authority
Type: Tabloid newspapers, pop media sites, personal blogs and videos, social media posts, predatory journals
Authors: Anyone, informed/sane or not; no oversight
Features: Unpredictable. The text might be expertly written, or may be an ideological rant, a joke, a commercial, or a paid publication with little or no peer review

I will discuss predatory journals in more detail later. They are not an explicit category, but are a blanket term for pay-to-publish journals listed only by bogus or frivolous indexes—there's nothing wrong with Google Scholar, but it's not some exclusive academic index; its *goal* is to list everything. Typically, such journals operate by flattering and enticing gullible or desperate authors into publishing papers with them for hefty fees. As a result, often anything gets published regardless of quality. These journals should not be cited. It is not always easy to recognize them, but as stated, they are almost never included on prestige indexes, and they often have suspicious factual, spelling, and grammar errors.

Let me add two qualifications to what I've written here before the pitchforks come out. The first is to address the question, why wouldn't I just consult the top-tier sources and forget everything else? Optimally, the top *is* where you should begin—but there may be situations where little has been published on your topic by such journals and presses, such as a subject seen as insufficiently academic (e.g. a comic book), or something so recent that it has not been discussed yet in print (e.g. a new social media meme). In that case you will need to work your way down the food chain until you find sufficient materials. You may also seek a variety of viewpoints from lesser or more marginalized academic outlets.

The second qualification is to address the charge that I'm an elitist snob to say some source outlets are better and others just don't *belong*. I am not saying that Facebook posts are bad; they serve the purposes they are intended for. Someone may also counter that if Jane Goodall or Timothy Berners-Lee writes an essay for a social media site, it's certainly reputable. If your uncle went to college with Steven Pinker and he writes you a personal Facebook message, well and good. As well, an older high-tier article may be of less credibility than a newer lower-tier one on a very recent issue. The distinction I am making is that all things being equal, these outlets are less safe or reliably reputable. There is little gatekeeping on social media, and the chances of reading text by unqualified or unserious people, or ones with an agenda, are high; whereas you are less likely to read accidentally or deliberately false information in an SCI journal.

Moreover, lest the lawyers at Scopus or elsewhere eye me up, I am not saying these tiers are necessarily or generally lower in source quality, but the present academic *perception* is that they are typically not of the caliber of a Web of Science journal. And things change—a time will likely soon come when it's unimportant whether a journal is print or online only. But some outlets are assumed to be the best in their field, and your readers will act on these presumptions when evaluating your paper's secondary evidence. Your readers don't know that your Aunt Nicole really is brilliant and is deeply read on your subject; they only see that her discussion originates from a personal WordPress site and not *Paris Review*.

6.3 Protecting Yourself

The internet, as well as many forms of electronic media, are still very recent in origin. For some readers 1994 is long ago or before their lifetime, but compared to the centuries of printed books there are few established standards for how to evaluate all of the sources available online. In a generation this may be different, but for now the online world is still the wild west for academia. My recommendations are drawn only from my experience as both a writer and reader of writing at undergraduate, graduate, and professorial levels, as a guide to better selection and evaluation of online textual sources.

Safety in Numbers

One way to protect yourself from faulty or dubious sources in your writing is to have many of them. If the paper has eight secondary sources and one is seen as questionable, this is a serious percentage; but one dubious text might not be fatal if you have sixty sources in your reference list. More is generally better—and you might also aim at a variety of print and online formats, such as monographs, edited collections, journal articles, magazines, internet sources, newspapers, interviews, videos, and so on, where you feel assured that they are at least upper-tier in content and reputational quality.

Variety also means more than the text's format. It also includes chronological sweep. Where appropriate, try to include sources from a wide swath of years or periods, as this will make the paper look more well-rounded and credible. This may not always be possible or workable, for the topic or event may be a local or recent one. You can locate sources about pandemics, but you obviously can't find pre-2020 articles about Covid-19—it didn't exist. As well, disciplinary fields vary in how authoritative older sources are. In my field, W. W. Skeat's analyses of medieval texts from 150 years ago are perfectly valid, but a paper from 2006 discussing social media might be only marginally useful. As I'll return to later, this may be why citation systems in the social sciences, such as APA, cite the publication year.

Geographical variety may also be greatly authoritative, as I mentioned in my anecdote about drinking age essays in the US. I once sat on a thesis committee for a student defending an honors thesis comparing deforestation in Korea and Germany. She had about twenty sources, but all were Korean authors. I am not implying that a Korean source is less valid, but this felt like lazy work to the committee, for there were no insights at all from German experts to ensure that country's issues were accurately represented.

Opposing Viewpoints

Having a variety of sources includes documenting a variety of opinions. What if some contradict or challenge your paper's thesis statement? They should also be included. There is really no choice, for a reader who observes that your paper has conspicuously avoided a major authority in the field, or fails to account for what seems an obvious objection to your position, is closer to distrusting you. If your paper is about postwar economics and you leave out Milton Freedman because you disagree with his views, your reader will notice and may dismiss your paper as one-sided. You cannot whistle past a known authority on your topic whom you disagree with.

If you are paying attention, you will object that this contradicts my statements in chapter one that an argument research paper argues its thesis statement consistently, without a false sense of 'fairness.' But acknowledging conflicting viewpoints does not mean your essay agrees with them. There are various ways you might finesse this, but I will recommend three moves here:

1. *Easy Level.* State the opposing source as a minority opinion among the larger community of experts. "While Friedman asserted x, most scholars disagree."

2. *Harder Level.* State the opposing source and, instead of challenging it, explain that it is not relevant here, or is no longer relevant. "Friedman's argument that x perhaps held then but was not meant to describe the internet economy of the twenty-first century."

3. *Ninja Level.* State the opposing source, and show why it is incorrect or unpersuasive. "Friedman argued x, but this does not account for y." This is a risky move, for you may not convince anyone that you know better than Friedman did, but you may earn massive respect for showing you do, or for being brave enough to try.

I am not saying I've always handled this masterfully—I'm not excerpting many of my undergraduate papers! But in this snippet from my paper on *Murder on the Orient Express* I tried to respectfully disagree with other authors, while explaining why I do so.

Hall and Plain argue that muscular heroism became taboo in postwar England, and if so, perhaps Hercule Poirot's vitality is retroactively minimized by readers and critics. At best there is the defense that his too-cute fastidiousness lures others into underestimating him as a detective (Heilbrun 4). Yet such readings are unpersuasive, for looking down on Poirot as a sexless outsider making safe jokes on the British implies we should also look down on the equally non-British Orient Express train line that he is so closely associated with. If it is true that Poirot is so anemic and harmless, then why is everyone inevitably awed by him?

Any of these three moves require that you present opposing ideas in good faith, especially if you then qualify or critique them. Few academics (hopefully) are going to write you nasty e-mails if you civilly disagree with them, but the reader will certainly perceive you as making an unfair cheap shot if you maliciously defame other authorities—particularly ones who aren't alive and can't defend themselves. This means avoiding an over-simplistic or demeaning summary—"Keynes thought money will fall from heaven when needed"—or making an ad hominem attack— "Heidegger's points should be read in light of his affair with his graduate student Arendt." Presenting an opposing view accurately and with collegiality is a power move which shows you are capable of maturely defending your ideas among experts.

Another lazy habit I would like to discourage is conceding opposing ideas you anticipate, but without bothering to research them—the "some may say" scarecrow strategy:

By only judging Millat's public persona in *White Teeth*, some may say he is a successful character. But Millat is actually deeply conflicted and unhappy because of his absentee father and lack of identity.

Who are the some who say this? This isn't persuasive. It isn't *wrong*—in a brief exam essay the "some may say" facade is sufficient in order to state an opposing viewpoint before rhetorically addressing it. But in research paper or one with more serious goals, the claim will be more compelling by reporting an actual opposing source and then responding:

By only judging Millat's public persona in *White Teeth*, some critics say that he is "one of the more successful and unproblematic characters" (Cater 28). But such a view does not see that Millat is actually deeply conflicted and unhappy because of his absentee father and lack of identity.

Use Some Physical Sources

Don't get everything from the internet. As I mentioned, when I was an undergraduate the internet was not yet in common use. As a graduate student in the 90's I used internet sources in my papers, but sparingly, as my older professors were skeptical of the internet as a serious platform. They mostly saw it as a geeky adolescent forum for pixelated pinup girls and *Star Trek* chats.

In two decades the internet has grown to become an essential academic tool, and anyone entirely refusing to use it would be seen as a dinosaur or relic. Conferences and meetings are held online, search engines for publications and primary texts are increasingly powerful, and a wider breadth of sources is now in electronic form. Some journals and e-books are no longer ever published on paper. The outbreak of Covid-19 has accelerated this shift to online academic life in ways that will take decades to trace, and which may be permanent.

Yet I hope I am not the last generation to genuinely value libraries. I feel more serious as a researcher in one, and I find neighboring books and journals in the stacks which I probably would not find online. As well, there is still a respectability and gravitas in having a reference list with printed sources. If a reference list consists entirely of online sources, there is a part of many older readers' minds which interprets this as laziness, that the writer could not be bothered to travel to an actual library and do the physical work necessary to locate real books. Many of your older professors and readers began to use the internet as adults and have less trust in online sources than younger ones do.

Another, and perhaps the most important reason to use some non-electronic sources, is that print inevitably involves more rigorous peer review. When you write an article for a print journal or a book, the publisher will normally have a more careful evaluation process because printing is expensive, and far more difficult to correct or delete than digital files are, and no publisher wants to risk a monetary loss or injure its reputation by publishing poor-quality work.

6 EXTERNAL SOURCES

The best and worst thing about the internet is that it has few gatekeepers, allowing anyone to 'publish' anything near-instantly without much oversight. However, you can also write nonsense or hate speech and make it resemble a serious text written by an authority. There may be consequences for doing so, but they are likely to come after the fact. In the meantime, a teenager in Arizona may view your site and quote from it in a high school essay. The internet is simply too new to have reliable mechanisms to prevent either benign or malevolent misinformation, though again these may develop as it matures.

There are exceptions in both directions. As mentioned, there are scam print journals and vanity presses which publish any rubbish for a fee. Conversely, there are beginning to be online-only academic journals where peer review and quality control is nurtured. I'm still wary of online-only journals, as their critical reputations tend to be lower. When there are no print costs, there is little brake on accepting everything. But as I noted, this may change; some online-only journals in emerging or rapidly-moving fields are solid. Increasingly, citation systems do not differentiate between the print and online version of an article, and the distinction may disappear someday with print-on-demand (POD) technologies.

Be Careful About Joke News Websites

Reliability is often a problem when non-westerners unknowingly read or quote from websites that have fictional and humorous articles, such as *The Onion* or *Babylon Bee*. In 2009 a Korean newspaper reprinted an article from the American parody newspaper *Weekly World News* claiming that archeologists had found a space alien gravesite in Rwanda. The newspaper carelessly ran the ridiculous story without fact-checking. In 2012 the same happened when Chinese media reprinted a joke article from the *Onion* claiming that Americans had voted Kim Jong-Un the sexiest man of the year.

In fairness, someone who grows up in the west knows the tradition of parody newspapers and websites, and can recognize the imbedded clues that the article is not real, such as the presence of slang and obscenities. An outsider or L2 speaker is less adept at seeing that the article is meant in fun because he or she comes from a different culture and standards of humor.

Tip

How to recognize a comedy website:
1. Parody websites often have swear words and slang
2. Google it. Does another website or Wikipedia describe it as a comedy site?

Devil's Advocate Papers

This won't happen often in academia, but you may encounter a text with an outrageous or humorous position presented seriously. This is known as a devil's advocate or counterfactual paper, where a position the author probably does not agree with is taken for rhetorical effect. The classic example is Jonathan Swift's essay "A Modest Proposal" (1729) where he sarcastically suggests that the Irish famine can be solved by buying children to eat, as a way of shaming people into action.

There are still readers who misunderstand Swift's essay and believe he is truly advocating we eat children. Yet essays where the writer experiments with an unorthodox position can be thought-provoking. There is an entire semi-scholarly subgenre of counterfactual history where scholars make arguments based on hypothetical events, for example "how would Russia be different if Stalin died in a 1944 coup?"

Wikipedia

In 2009 I was a graduate student writing an article analyzing media satire about U.S. president Barack Obama's election, and I made use of quotes from Wikipedia as primary and secondary evidence. One reviewer wrote angrily, "I am shocked to see someone citing it here." Wikipedia still has a troubled reputation among academics, with some rejecting it as a valid scholarly source and others supporting it or even writing for it. As anybody can edit a Wikipedia page, the site has ongoing problems with hackers creating false or vandalized content. Having said this, Wikipedia's 'peer review,' such as it is, can be lightning-fast, correcting or removing inaccurate information in seconds via its army of editors and AI watch-bots.

Because of its 'gray' status, at present I would use Wikipedia sparingly as a direct secondary source, unless there is a special purpose in doing more. This may change in future as the site matures. As well, if your paper is about Wikipedia, or its entries are somehow a primary source, that might be a justified reason to cite it. Further, there is nothing wrong with using Wikipedia as a tertiary source, to find other sources in its entry reference lists. I admit to using Wikipedia for general overviews of a subject or to rapidly find simple facts or data, and often find useful links to reputable sources at the bottom of entries.

Experts aren't Experts in Everything

It's risky to assume an expert in one discipline is an expert in all others. If Bill Gates were to write an essay claiming that grasshoppers evolved from tigers, his authority as a computer entrepreneur does not give him reliability on evolutionary biology. If I wanted financial advice, I would trust Warren Buffet's words. If Buffet wrote an analysis of jazz music, I would justly feel that he is no more credible than another informed fan. It would be unethical for him to write on the basis of a reputation earned through unrelated credentials. To me a classic example is Sigmund Freud, who is the father of modern psychology, but in his late years wrote treatises on topics that he was unqualified in, and which are of minimal worth.

6.4 Scholarly Search Engines

Try not to rely entirely on popular internet search engines such as Google, Yahoo, or Naver or similar. They are not likely to point you to scholarly journals written by professors, but rather to television or newspaper sites. I am not insulting journalists or other content creators—but they are not trained or expected to be subject experts in rarified and complex fields. Their job normally is to report and explain events to a wide readership.

Similarly, popular search engines are not designed for the small proportion of people doing academic research. They will turn up popular sites such as media or gossip ones, rather than books or scholarly sources, because such sites vastly outnumber academic ones. Worse, some search engines accept payment to push links; news 'stories' reporting that "Flirt-E's new too-spicy music video is sparking outrage" may be paid for by promoters, who have manufactured the clickbait 'controversy' in order to get readers to follow a link. The article somehow never specifies who the critics are, and they may not exist.

There are exceptions, such as Google Scholar, which is more likely to link to useful sites and articles. There are also the free Project Gutenberg and Open Library sites for books. But in general, because access to journal articles is unfortunately typically paid for, university students may need to use their library websites as portals to journal search engines. Google Scholar does try to recognize if your computer is on campus. Young writers who complain about logging in to their campus library websites deserve to be hit on the head with the telephone-book sized periodical indexes I used in libraries in the 1980's. It sounds square to say so, but try to have some gratitude for the comparative ease of accessing online sources.

Google Scholar and most university library portals work like search engines in that they allow you to type in key words, and then hits are displayed in the form of books or articles—or a list of source databases is given for you to search individually in. Sometimes the hyperlink only leads to another website, or to someone's book or paper which merely cites that title. But optimally a pdf link is listed, allowing you to open and view or save the file directly.

[BOOK] **Lord** of the **Flies**　　　　　　　　　　　　　　　　　　　　[PDF] jkhs.org.uk
W Golding - 1983 - books.google.com
In addition to the full text of Lord of the Flies, this volume contains statements by Golding about the novel, reminiscences of Golding by his brother, an appreciation of the novel by EM Forster, and a number of critical essays from various points of view. Included are
Cited by 1500　Related articles　All 91 versions　Cite　Save

Below is Hanyang University library's search page, which allows you to access an article database relevant to your field. Upon connecting to the database you can enter search terms and display and download journal articles in pdf format. Some hits will display as .html sites and not .pdfs, but I can usually just print them to .pdfs.

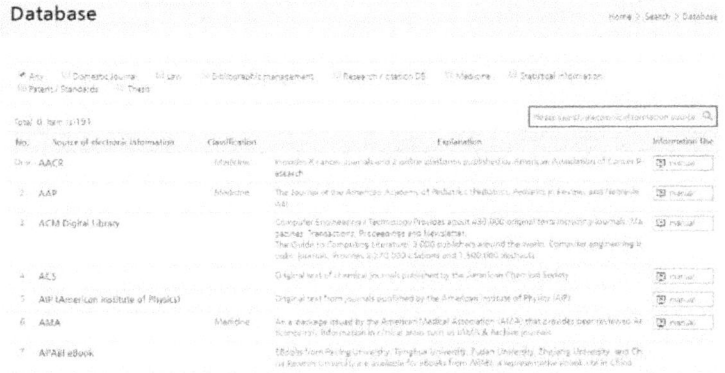

You may already know or have heard of the usual suspects in terms of article database providers: Web of Science, Scopus, JSTOR, Wiley, IEEE, and so on. This can get confusing for several reasons.

1. I earlier discussed article indexes as reputational sources, such as WoS/Clarivate and Scopus. These organizations also operate their own article databases. Articles may be on only

one database, but more often are cross-linked across many of them.
2. Some article databases are only *citation* indexes, meaning they list the article's title and particulars, but not the actual article full-text.
3. Some article sites, such as Google Scholar, aren't really databases and don't host anything—they're just search engines which link you to other article databases or the entry's host website.
4. Some publishing companies (such as Wiley) and field-specific organizations (such as IEEE) have their own article databases, and only host their own journals.
5. Some article databases are disciplinary and only have, for example, medical, educational, law, or engineering materials.

If this all seems confusing, you are not alone. As an example, Hanyang's library website has over 230 databases to wade through. But an academic journal article is often the best quality academic source you are going to find, and in many fields is preferred to print books. It's well worth learning how to use a scholarly search portal, particularly for those papers which you can instantly view and download, for your university tuition is helping to pay for it anyway.

It's no surprise that article database subscriptions are expensive—so much so for institutional access that there are periodic backlashes and boycotts against access companies in the scholarly community. Some top-tier U.S. libraries might pay in the region of $6 million a year for journal packages. There is a growing movement of open-access journals where research is free to anyone, often called green publishing. Sometimes this merely a euphemism for authors paying additional fees to make a single article open-access within a paid journal, but some journals now are indeed entirely free online. This may be an ethical idea you want to support—and I would not say that green access has any usual correlation to article or journal quality or reputation.

6 EXTERNAL SOURCES

When You Can't Find What You Need

My standard modus operandi is to hammer every index and search engine I can find and download everything. I then eliminate duplicates, standardize file names (Author(s), Brief Title), and do a triage—I categorize articles that are helpful, ones that aren't, and ones that *might* be useful for this or a future project.

Inevitably, there is a reference to a tantalizing article or book I can't find online or in a library. A perennial problem for researchers is sources behind paywalls your institution does not have access to, and in Korea, where English-language books are sparse in libraries, this can be frustrating. In my field of medieval literature this is less a problem for older sources, where works from WWII or earlier are probably public domain. But for newer literature or faster-moving fields, that is not an option. Sometimes articles and scanned books are available on (I have mentioned some of these earlier):

Open Library
Internet Archive
Project Gutenberg
Google Books or Google Scholar

If that doesn't work, if your institution doesn't subscribe to JSTOR, the site does allow limited access with free memberships. A shadier way is to piece together pages from the free samples that Google Books, Amazon, or Hathi Trust might provide, but this isn't terribly ethical and often doesn't work—pagination and issues may differ, and sometimes only very tiny snippets of text are displayed. It would probably be better to ask a colleague in a different institution to help—or to look up the author on ResearchGate and send a private message asking for the .pdf. I find most authors are flattered to share; at least I am when I am occasionally asked.

6.5 Search Terms

Another ninja-level skill in using search engines is learning how to more precisely use Boolean search terms. This will vary between platforms, but often the use of +, -, and quotation marks " " will help eliminate false hits.

The string *metal fatigue* will result in all pages with *metal* or *fatigue* in them, giving you possibly millions of hits which include any sense of the word *metal*, such as websites about heavy metal music, as well as sites with any mention of *fatigue*, including human tiredness.

"metal fatigue" forces the search engine to look for only that exact string, reducing the number of false hits.

Similarly, *merchant of venice* results in 164 million hits because Google looks for any page with *merchant* or *venice* in it, but "merchant of venice" gives (only) 12 million.

jane austen + *zombies* asks the search engine to look only for pages with both of these terms—that is, only those sites about Jane Austen which also discuss the 1989 postmodern novel combining *Pride and Prejudice* with zombies.

anne hathaway – *shakespeare* asks the search engine to look only for sites about the movie actress Anne Hathaway, and not Shakespeare's wife Anne Hathaway. Where you have terms which have multiple meanings, you can use a minus sign with a selected term to flag what you don't want, in order to remove those hits from the search.

These formatting rules might be forgotten in the future, as it's now possible to just type what you want in an AI-enabled search engine. I obtained good results by simply asking ChatGPT, "tell me about Anne Hathaway, but the one married to Shakespeare, not the actress." Still, these shortcuts are: faster.

6.6 Fine Tuning: Avoiding Bias

"In a corporate statement, Dale Rand, spokesperson for Quisling Pulp & Paper, explained that forests are actually healthier without trees." The 'expert' quoted here has an obvious interest in protecting his employer. The example is ridiculous, but some sources *will* have a bias or agenda at play. This is going to be less the case with a top journal article, but with lesser or 'grey' sources the text may not have been written for benign purposes.

For example, if I am writing on economics or taxation, I want to be careful about using sources sponsored by a political or advocacy group. A controversial issue such as abortion or Tibet may also turn up materials with a partisan program. A website which seemingly discusses a novel might be doing so to advance an outside agenda—a human rights website might talk about Melville's *Benito Cereno* or Conrad's *Heart of Darkness* negatively because of its period racism. Conversely, a novelist's fan website which only has gushing praise of the books is of dubious reliability. This is a common problem with Jane Austen criticism, where there are numerous websites written by adoring 'Janeite' fans. Movie company websites which feature film adaptations of literature may also be questionable, as they want you to see the movie and are unlikely to analyze the work candidly. A site about J. K. Rowling might be strongly positively biased about her *Harry Potter* novels, or it might be strongly critically biased against her political views.

This doesn't mean I can't ever use or quote from such sources, as these controversies may be worth addressing. But I may need to limit their influence on my position, and perhaps disclose the source's political or advocacy agendas to my reader if I include them. If the majority of your paper uses trustworthy scholarly texts, it is not a serious problem to have a small number of partisan opinions which are noted as such.

You may also be thinking, isn't the point of argument writing to have some claim that the reader is to be convinced of? Broadly, yes—but *cui bono*—in whose interests? These are subjective qualities; but ideally academia seeks to further the truth for the reader's intellectual benefit. A political or commercial source often has different goals from the reader's.

Everyone says they would not be fooled by a biased source. But they are. When I taught international relations students I received many corporate case study papers, and coffee chains are a popular topic, perhaps because students usually like coffee. There is nothing wrong with such a topic, but if your chief primary source is the café's website, you are unlikely to read anything negative or critical about that company, or praise for competing chains.

You may also see a great deal of 'water-is-wet' claims on a corporate website, legally equivocal statements which imply to the reader that something is unique which isn't. To use the coffee example, you may read that "our company uses only the best Arabic beans" (as does every coffee chain); "our company carefully trains our baristas" (as does every coffee chain); "our company provides baked goods and treats" (as do most coffee chains); "we provide a comfortable, European-styled environment" (as do most coffee chains). These are not exclusive qualities, and the chain is likely careful to not overtly state so. Or, consider the advertising claim of Ralph's Burgers:

Our Burgers are Made With 100% Real Beef!

This looks quotable. But on closer inspection, this only says the burgers are made *with* beef, not *of* beef. The prepositional phrasing does not rule out including other ingredients: the burger may also be made with other things, such as 100% real corn or bread filler. I am not saying all commercial sources are exercises in sneaky legalese. But to write a paper relying uncritically on a corporate website without balancing its information with other views gives the impression of shoddy research, and may be presenting misleading claims.

Korea Fighting!

6 EXTERNAL SOURCES

Are you inclined to believe a source's arguments because it says nice things about your country, or because it praises left-handed turnip farmers, and your uncle is one? I don't wish to offend Koreans, but I use them as an example here because my experience is informed by teaching in Korea. Other cultures, and Canadians, do it too; their critical reading skills go out the window when the source shores up patriotic interests. In Korea there are still occasional newspaper articles or editorials asserting that Hangul is scientifically the best alphabet, or that kimchi has some miraculous medical property, and they periodically find their way into undergraduate papers.

Whether these claims are true or not, they are generally received with eye-rolling by non-Koreans, who can see the references for these claims are Parks, Chois, and Kims. The same would be true of an online report stating that Arabic is proven to be the best language, written by Cairo specialists, or a Canadian news article reporting that ice hockey and donuts cure cancer. These are seductive claims for a citizen of these nations, but are met with skepticism by foreigners.

I'm not advising that you avoid writing about issues which have national resonance for you. You may have valid and persuasive first-hand perspectives that others don't. I only indicate warnings on this matter, because they have proven to be blind spots among my students:

1. As noted, sources which praise or endorse your country's interests are always going to look much more credible to you than to a reader of another country. For years I simply refused the paper topic of the Korean Wave or K-Pop, because the sources quoted were invariably government and promotional ad-copy stuffed with overblown praise and trendy buzzwords.
2. If your argument is about your country's interests, can you reasonably guarantee that you are portraying any opposing country's interests fairly? As I mentioned earlier, the readers see that the other country can't fight back, because you are writing the paper—and their sympathies may run against you quickly if they feel you are loading the dice for your personal

interests, not theirs. Your paper must take a position; but this is a situation where you must honestly concede and describe facts and claims that counter your own before challenging them.
3. Are you reasonably sure that the source regarding your country's culture or issues is relevant to your topic, or are you allowing your enthusiasm for the source to pad or run away with the paper? I once had a student who asked to compare the school system in *Hard Times* to theirs. The resulting paper discussed *Hard Times* for a few rote sentences, and then the remainder was a criticism of his country's school system. Some of my U.S. students in Las Vegas did the same—how they could begin a paper on the *Ramayana* and still make the rest about America was a rhetorical wonder. This is like tiresome people who can take any conversational topic and bring it back to their children or their health problems, wasting the time of any captive listener.

The Bible and Other Sacred Texts

Religious bias is another sensitive issue. A text originating from a religious advocacy group should immediately alert a researcher to possible bias. But it would also show bias to rule out such sources. There are certainly religious websites created by cranks or fanatics, but there are also Christian universities with centuries of academic scholarship, with respected press imprints and journals. Not many people would dispute the authority of a journal or expert from the University of Notre Dame. The same would apply with top-ranked Islamic scholarship or other faith systems.

I have had students ask if they can use the Bible as a primary or secondary source. My simple answer is, certainly, as long as it is not the only source in the paper. Strictly speaking (and respectfully, as a Christian) the Bible is not intended to be an objective text, and needs to be used in conjunction with other materials. How would you feel if you read a paper and all the argument claims were supported by Upanishads or Surahs, or another set of sacred writings, with no other sources?

Thus I would write a paper on first-century Rome using scriptural accounts as evidence, but I would include Greco-Roman texts for balance where they exist. In a social issues paper you might note that Southern U.S. Baptists believe x because of verse y; but it is not prudent to use scripture *alone* to prove your argument— "my thesis is correct because Acts 2:17 says so"— unless the discipline specifically calls for such an approach, such as in a theology or Biblical history paper. As with any essay, your audience will impact your methods, and a certain line is crossed if readers perceive you are using scripture to evangelize them and not to pursue an academic thesis.

To review, having a compelling wealth of external materials gives you both more information and greater credibility. The unfortunate reality is that, especially in the online world, there are a great deal of dubious sources mixed in with reputable ones. Your task is to evaluate those sources as best you can. As in real life, your reader will judge you by the company you keep.

7 MLA & APA FORMAT

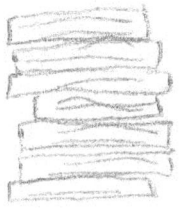

I once asked a young dissertation writer whether her suddenly grayed hair was due to ill health or personal tragedy; she answered: "It was the footnotes." — Joanna Russ

Ideally, I would make this chapter sexy and fun, but it's difficult to describe citation systems in a stimulating manner. There is going to have to be some eat-your-peas information for the next few pages, as correct citation and formatting is going to be a burdensome but necessary task in thesis/diss and professional writing. Many journals and editors will return manuscripts unread if they are not formatted to requested specifications. The bad news is that there are going to be petty and arbitrary rules. The good news is that they are fairly consistent and predictable.

In the pre-modern west there was no conventional grammar or typography for indicating another person's words. Ancient Greek authors would informally reference the source as in conversation: "Yesterday I heard a speech by Aspasia in the forum. If I remember rightly, she said..." Or, a Roman author might write "as wise Boethius says..." for a deceased authority. But by the middle ages a Greek character called a *diple*, looking much like a modern apostrophe, was used to indicate each line of cited words, and double quotation marks in their more familiar form appeared around 1520 in German printing, soon spreading across Europe.

In early printed books, quoted material would sometimes be set in a different or smaller font. Texts often also had wide margins for notes to be added by readers or authors. By the 1600s the space had moved to the page bottom, giving us our modern footnotes. Gradually the practice of adding some symbol to quoted material in order to match it to the footnote or endnote developed, and the writer Edward Gibbon, who wrote *The Decline and Fall of the Roman Empire* (1776) was influential in popularizing a consistent typographical system for notes using numbers, although authors or printers continued to use various conventions, such as asterisks (*) and daggers (†) to indicate notes.

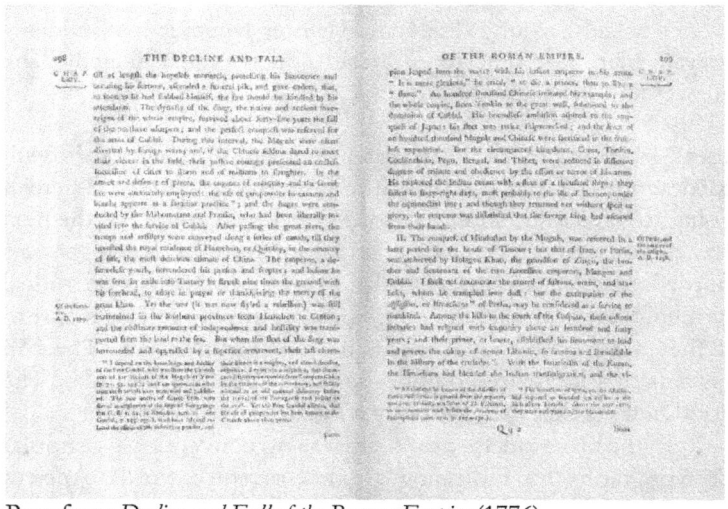

Page from *Decline and Fall of the Roman Empire* (1776)

This history may not be terribly compelling, but it should telegraph that citation systems are more or less arbitrary inventions, as for centuries authors and publishers did as they wished. In 1891 this changed when the University of Chicago Press began and issued a brief style guide for manuscripts. In 1906 this was published as the *Chicago Manual of Style*, which evolved into becoming the dominant template for manuscript formatting and typography.

Throughout the twentieth century other systems followed

7 MLA & APA FORMAT

to meet the preferences of different communities and disciplines. MLA style (Modern Languages Association, first printed in 1985) dominates in the humanities, and APA style (American Psychological Association, first printed in 1929) is normally used in the social sciences. Chicago format still has adherents in history and linguistics—and IEEE style, for the Institute of Electrical and Electronics Engineers, is actually based on Chicago.

There is now a miscellany of other systems such as Turabian, Harvard, AMA, IEEE, and England's MHRA, for specialized disciplines, different countries, or even individual universities. To make things more complicated, there are even variations or in-house standards for particular journals or presses, and your university department may also have special rules for thesis or dissertation formatting. I will mostly discuss the 'big four' of MLA and APA, with some Chicago and IEEE in this book, because I can't cover them all—and even with these standards, they keep changing over the years as new technologies such as text messages and tweets appear. MLA's most recent release is version 9, although its updates are smaller than the significant modifications of MLA 8 in 2016.

Why does there need to be so many systems, and why can't we just use hyperlinks now? This may be the case in future. But for now, not every source is online, and not everyone reads papers on electronic devices. Some of these style systems suspiciously look like vanity projects, but many legitimately reflect different disciplinary priorities. For example, APA citation is primarily used in disciplines where information changes rapidly. Perhaps for this reason, APA emphasizes dates rather than names. As I noted in the previous chapter, if you are writing a literature paper on James Joyce, a source from 30 years ago is probably as valid as one from this year. In the social sciences this likely wouldn't be the case—the reader should know that your source on solar panels is from 1989 and reflects a 'historical' viewpoint.

Both MLA and APA citation standards have their own formats for title pages (or lack thereof), references, and citations, which I'll discuss in that order. I will also tend to cover MLA first, not because it's necessarily better, but because it's often simpler in format, and from there we can move up slightly in prescriptiveness to APA, with a detour in Chicago and IEEE.

7.1 Title Pages

Universal Rules for MLA and APA
- Use 1 inch (2.54 cm) margins on all sides except for the top header (1/2 inch).
- Use A4 size formatting for Europe/Asia and Letter for North America, if not specified.
- Again, nothing looks as amateurish as bending the pages into a crinkle to fasten them because "sorry, professor, I forgot a paperclip." Graders also prefer paperclips to staples because many like to lay out the pages side by side to read them.
- Everything on the title page uses the same font and size as the rest of the paper. Do not use a giant font in your title to 'make it stand out.' Most citation systems, however, allow boldface or italics if preferred.

Tip on Making Headers

In Microsoft Word I find it easiest to insert page numbers first in a header and then click on a number, move the cursor left, and type the header text next to it.

MLA 'Title Pages'

Like *Fight Club*, the first rule of making an MLA title page is to not make an MLA title page. MLA does not require them. Some universities have custom rules, but normally you put the particulars in the upper left of the first page.

Top right: Writer's last name, page number
Top left: Writer's name; professor's name; course name; date
Centered: Paper title

> Bennett 1
>
> Elizabeth Bennett
> Dr. Ken Eckert
> English 348
> May 5, 2020
>
> Pride and Pastiche: Humor and Intertextual
> Parody in *Bridget Jones's Diary*
>
> Helen Fielding's *Bridget Jones's Diary* came out in 1996, and some two decades later its scholarly treatment has remained about as thin as the novel's protagonist endeavors to be. BJD criticism has ranged from superficial to a small but hopeful number of instructive readings, and might be usefully parsed into four schools. The first is more fan service than criticism, largely gushing over 'how hot Mark Darcy/Colin Firth is.' The second interrogates its disreputable genre affiliation. Part of the difficulty in establishing a critical context for BJD is that whether it deserves to be seriously read at all is contested, with some calling it

In earlier versions of this book I used to have fun with silly names, such as having Elizabeth Bennet write the paper for Professor Darcy. I then began receiving papers 'written' by Shakespeare and J. K. Rowling, where students mistakenly assumed the *novel* author's name goes at the top. Elizabeth Bennett/Bennet should of course be replaced by your name.

APA Title Pages

APA title pages can be confusing because titles have long and short versions. The short version is called the running head, and it includes a few keywords from the title in ALL CAPS. Whereas MLA uses last names, APA uses the running head to identify pages in case they are separated.

Running head: BUSINESS MODELS   1

Differences in Business Models Between
Jet Airways and Air Asia
Peter Frank
English 27791
University of Bali

Top left: Running head and page number
Horizontally centered: Title, name, course, university

The actual words "running head" go on the title page but are omitted on following pages. Thus the title page would show in its header:

Running head: BUSINESS MODELS   1

But successive pages would look like this:

BUSINESS MODELS   2

For example, page two would look like this. Note that the title is repeated on the first page of text.

BUSINESS MODELS   2

Differences in Business Models Between
Jet Airways and Air Asia

In 1989, Jet Airways was introduced as a budget addition to the Quantas fleet in Australia. At the time the decision was viewed by business experts

---

What if your running head is so long that it crowds into the page number? The simple answer is that it shouldn't be so long. A running head is a shortened version of your title which allows readers or a machine scanner to identify which paper the page belongs to, or to index the paper within a search engine. As I mentioned, some professors like to lay out the pages side by side, and running heads allow mixed up sheets of paper to be rematched. Two or three key words is usually sufficient, and the APA manual suggests a 40-character limit.

The running head uses key words from your title. It may confuse readers to write a running head with totally different text:

Title: Demographic Issues in China after the One Child Policy

Running head: CHINESE BIRTHRATES **x**
A better running head might be ONE CHILD POLICY.

 **Tip**

You only have to make or download one perfect APA title page and save it as a blank file. You can then load it every time you need to and change the text.

Different Headers

If using Microsoft Word, like MLA, I find it easiest to insert page numbers first in a header and then add the header text to it. Pressing the tab key once or twice should left-align your header text.

Your APA title page header needs to be different from the successive pages, as only this page contains the string "Running Head." In Word, under the menu item "Header & Footer Tools," check the option "Different First Page."

Institutional Standards

I should qualify that these are general style standards, and individual university departments or institutions may have their own in-house rules for thesis or dissertation title pages which override these. Hanyang University's looks like this:

```
Thesis for the degree of Doctor of Philosophy


Some Fancy Name that Everyone is Going to
                    WOW




                    Lorem Lipsum



                   Graduate School
                  Hanyang Univeristy


                   February 2015
```

As well, theses and dissertations often have narrower margins for some reason, perhaps very conservatively preserving the nineteenth-century printing technologies of such documents.

7.2 End-Text References

End-text references refer to entries documenting the external sources which you studied or quoted in your paper. This list usually goes at the end of your paper and typically begins on a separate sheet of paper, although sometimes authors continue them on the same sheet after the end of the text if the list is short. Both MLA and APA publish hefty guidebooks, but there are also good online sources for detailed usage rules. Among the best are Diana Hacker's and the Purdue OWL, but many universities have guides on their library websites.

Here is a typical MLA reference entry. Again, keep in mind that if you consult a website or source still referring to MLA 7 or an older style it will differ. MLA 9 no longer normally indicates the city of publication for books by major publishers, for increasingly such books are printed anywhere by regional printers. APA is also increasingly mandating the same.

Fay, J. Michael. "Land of the Surfing Hippos." *National Geographic,* Aug. 2004, pp. 100-3, http://www.ngeog.com/surfhipsampleurl1833620. Accessed 8 Jun. 2023.

Spark, Muriel. *The Prime of Miss Jean Brodie.* MacMillan, 1961.

Here are two APA entries. APA doesn't capitalize key words like MLA does, and only lists author initials.

Fiala, D. (2012). Time-aware PageRank for bibliographic networks. *Journal of Informetrics, 6*(3), 370-388.

Knoke, D., & Yang, S. (2008). *Social network analysis.* Los Angeles, CA: Sage Publications.

Notice that lines after the first one are indented. This is called using "hanging indents." These can be formatted in most word processing programs. In Microsoft Word you can type ctrl + tab to do this, but the better way is to format hanging indents (spacing, line spacing options, indentation, hanging indents). Word also has an easy alphabetization function on the home tab.

Making a reference list isn't terribly fun for most people. The formatting rules, especially in APA, are meticulous and inflexible. But it is important to do this correctly, because a faulty list of references will reduce the reader's respect for your paper, and again may be summarily rejected by a department or editors. The good news is that there are citation websites and software plug-ins for word processors which can automate some of this drudgery, generating a near-perfect citation which you can paste into your document. Websites such as Citation Machine will even automate a correct title page.

There's nothing criminal or unethical with using citation software or some reference manager or AI-powered checker to make your work easier, but you might still familiarize yourself with the standards and the logic behind them so that you can recognize situations where the software creates an incorrect entry. People who have some knowledge of how a car engine works will be better drivers, and the same applies here. For example, a reference generator may not understand where names or proper nouns need to be capitalized:

Abrams, S. (1998, July 30). We're no james bonds, say spy chiefs. *Daily Record*, 8. **x**

Also, if you copy and paste text such as a generated reference into your paper, be careful that it doesn't look like this:

Experts say that "roses are red" (Smith 46). **x**

If you look closely, you can see that both the quotation and the citation are in different fonts, sizes, and colors. A good habit is to select all text and make sure everything is unified with the same typography.

MLA Works Cited

MLA lists used to be called a bibliography, but the term is disappearing, as this literally means a list of books, whereas a works cited list includes all formats of texts, physical and electronic. Here's an example of MLA.

Works Cited

Duggan, Stephen, and Betty Drury. *The Rescue of Science and Learning*. Macmillan, 1968.

McGonagall, Jane. "Gaming and Productivity." *YouTube*, uploaded by Big Think, 3 July 2012, www.youtube.com/watch?v=mkdzy9bWW3E.

Patterson, Troy. "The Satire Recession: How Political Satire Got So Flabby." *Slate*, 8 Apr. 2008, http://www.slate.com/id/2188472/pagenum/all/#p2.

The following is a partial list of the more familiar types of source formats in MLA, with semi-fictional names, although MLA also has standards for unusual sources such as e-mails, songs, or social media tweets and posts. Again, be warned that standards periodically change.

In MLA, the names of books and longer works are italicized in italics, and short articles and chapters are in quotation marks. You can also underline (which is now rather old-school) rather than *italicizing*, but don't do both. Also do not literally write the format of the text in your list, e.g. 'book' or 'academic journal with doi' in your list. I know this may sound patronizing, but I have had students reproduce these headings in their papers.

Book
Jameson, Fredric. *The Political Unconscious*. Cornell UP, 1981. (*University Press* is often abbreviated as UP).

Edited book with multiple authors
McDonald, Nicola, editor. *Pulp Fictions of Medieval England*. Manchester UP, 2004.

Chapter or article in an edited book
Foster, Mack. "Why It's Like Carrots." *Inquiry to Academic Writing: A Text and Reader*, edited by Stuart Greene and April Lidinsky, Bedford St. Martins, 2008, 2nd ed., pp. 344-49.

If you list another article in the same book later in your list, you can do this:

Timms, Siobhan. "Why Mice Actually Don't Like Cheese." Greene and Lidinsky, 358-71.

Kindle book
Fisher, Roger, and William Ury. *Getting to Yes*. Kindle ed., Penguin Books, 2011.

Book from a database
Austen, Jane. *Pride and Prejudice*. 1813. *Project Gutenberg*, http://www.gutenberg.org/ebooks/1342.

If you are citing one or multiple short stories from a complete work by one author such as Joyce's *Dubliners*, you need only the book once. You don't need to list each story separately.

Wikipedia article
"Plagiarism." *Wikipedia: The Free Encyclopedia*, http://en.wikipedia.org/wiki/Plagiarism. Accessed 16 May 2023.

Academic journal
Wood, Michael. "Broken Dates: Fiction and the Century." *Kenyon Review*, vol. 8, no. 3, 2004, pp. 2-33.

Academic journal, online
Corwin, Jay. "One Hundred Years of Solitude, Indigenous Myth, and Meaning." *Theory in Action*, 2013, pp. 112-26. http://scopus.net/literary-criticism/60307503.

Academic journal with doi (direct object identifier)
Peltonen, Kirsi, Helmer B. Larsen, and Karin Helweg. "Violence and Adolescent Mental Health." *Adolescent Psychiatry*, vol. 19, 2010, pp. 813-822. doi:10.1007/s00787-010-0130.

Newspaper, online version
"Lack of Direct Talks with N. Koreans Debated Barbs Traded in Messages." *Boston Globe*, 12 Oct. 2006, http://www.highbeam.com/doc/1P2-7980792.html.

YouTube video
McGonigal, Jane. "Gaming and Productivity." YouTube, uploaded by Big Think, 3 July 2012, www.youtube.com/watch?v=mkdzy9bWW3E.

Translated source
Try to translate the original title as faithfully as you can, if none is available. Many writers also give the original language's script to help speakers of it to find it.

Sundberg-Weitman, Brita. "Svenska Journalister Ljuger Om Assange" [Swedish Journalists Lying about Assange]. *SVT Nyheter*, 17 Aug. 2012, http://www.svt.se/opinion/svenska-om-assange.

Pak, Wan-so. *Urŭm Sori* 울음소리 [The Sound of Crying]. Sol, 1996.

If you are citing a translation, particularly a literary one, you don't need to do this.

Kang, Han. *The Vegetarian*. Translated by Deborah Smith, Hogarth, 2016.

APA References

Here is a sample APA reference list page. The heading title "References" is centered and uppercased. Note that the entry "Oil price history and analysis" has no author, so the work is alphabetized under *O*.

APA does not seem to indicate how Korean names should be represented, as technically Koreans don't have first and middle names. The general practice is to print the family name and parse the first two as hyphenated syllables with periods. Thus Yu-Jong Choi is Choi, Y.-J. I find this hyphenation rule to be a drawback of APA. The ostensible reason is to avoid possibly prejudicing readers by revealing author genders, but the result can be lists with multiple S. J. Kims and H. G. Yangs (or J. Smiths and P. Browns), and it can be difficult to differentiate them.

REFERENCES

Daly, J. (2014, January 10). Russian energy sector 'Very successful' in 2013. *Oil Pricing*. Retrieved from http://oilprice.com/Energy/Energy-General/Russian-Energy-Successful-2013.html

Oil price history and analysis. (2019). *WTRG Economics*. Retrieved from http://www.wtrg.com/prices.htm

Park, C.-J. (1999). *Strategic planning of regional resources under the formation of market relations*. Amsterdam: Amstel.

Reference Formatting

The following is a partial list of reference styles, with again semi-fictional details. As with MLA, book names are italicized or underlined, but note that in APA short articles or chapter names are not placed in quotation marks. Again, whereas MLA capitalizes most words in a title, APA does not. Capitalize only initial words and those following a colon, as well as names, places, and proper terms (not everyone seems to agree whether 'the' is capitalized after a colon). As I noted, an automated citation generator might confuse these distinctions.

Book

Thatcher, M., & Cooke, A. (1989). *The revival of Britain: Speeches on home and European affairs, 1975-1988*. London: Aurum Press.

Edited book with multiple authors

Kramer, L. (Ed.). (1995). *Classical music and postmodern knowledge*. Faber & Faber.

Chapter in an edited volume

Lawrence, J. A., & Dodds, A. E. (2003). Goal-directed development. In J. Valines & K. Connolly (Eds.), *Handbook of developmental psychology* (pp. 51-58). London: Sage.

Kindle book
Gladwell, M. (2008). *Outliers: The story of success* [Kindle version]. Retrieved from Amazon.com.

Wikipedia article
Plagiarism. (n.d.). In *Wikipedia*. Retrieved from http://en.wikipedia.org/wiki/Plagiarism

Academic journal, online
Charney, J. (2004). North Koreans in China: A human rights analysis. *Journal of Korean Unification Studies, 13*(2), 75-97. http://www.refworld.org/47aea34520.pdf

Academic journal with doi
Linhares, A., & Brum, P. (2007). Strategic scenarios: What role do chunks play? *Cognitive Science, 31*(6), 98-107. http://dx.doi.org/doi:10.1080/03640210701703725

Online blog site
Miller, L. (2012, October 29). Early American horror show. *Salon.com*. Retrieved October 30, 2022, from http://www.salon.com/books/ 2012/102

Conference paper
Velden, E., Haque, A., & Lagoze, C. (2011). Resolving author name homonymy to improve resolution of structures in co-author networks. *Paper presented at the Proceedings of the 11th Annual ACM/IEEE Joint Conference on Digital Libraries.*

Published conference proceedings
Ranganathan, S. R. (1984). General classification: Papers presented to the second International Study Conference on Classification Research Elsinore, 1984. In P. A. Atherton (Ed.), *Classification research: Proceedings of the second International Conference, Elsinore, 14-18 Sept. 1985* (pp. 81-93). Copenhagen: Munksgaard, 1985.

Translated source
Similar to MLA, you might provide your own English translation if none is given. Some authors even list the title three times, in transliterated letters, in foreign script, and in translation, but APA isn't strict on this.

Murakami, H. 村上春樹. (1987). Noruwei no mori ノルウェイの森 [Norwegian Wood]. Tokyo: Kodansha.

APA format also doesn't seem consistent on whether the date of retrieval should be listed. In my own practice, I list retrieval dates for blog or media pages, as these sorts of sites are more likely to be changed. Scholarly texts and databases are typically more stable—or as stable as anything on the internet can be. If there isn't a directive given, perhaps this decision is also one the writer can make, with the usual advice to be consistent.

7.3 In-Text Citation

In-text citation refers to the quotations from other sources within your essay text. It is possible to have a paper with only a reference list and no quotations or citations from them inside your text. But normally, such a paper may not convince the reader that you have even read them: a dishonest writer could simply paste in a list of articles and books without ever looking at them. Here is an example of in-text quotations and citations:

The Joads in *The Grapes of Wrath* fare increasingly worse as they travel west. Their first meal of the journey is pork, "the very antithesis of the perfect Passover lamb" (Perkin 87), and their diet deteriorates, at one point consisting of biscuits.

Spahn and Watt (1983) were prescient in predicting that "developments in artificial intelligence will put a substantial share of employment at risk."

As expected, an increase in the curing age resulted in an increase in compressive strength, irrespective of binder [5].

Some people use these terms differently, but I will use 'quotation' to mean the words you are directly reproducing, and 'citation' to indicate where they are from. Many people also use 'quote' and 'quotation' interchangeably, although some grammarians classify 'quote' as a verb and 'quotation' as a noun. Applying these terms, a basic quotation sentence consists of some introductory words from the paper's writer (the signal phrase), the quotation, and the citation, although there will of course be variations on this.

Signal phrase   *Quotation*
Early theologians disagreed on whether "Christ was of one substance with the Father" (Dmitri 7).
                     Citation

Basic MLA citation: (Dmitri 7)
Basic APA citation: (Dimitri, 1982, p. 7)

North American writers usually use "double" quotation marks, and British ones prefer 'single' quotation marks. British English also places most punctuation after quotation marks rather than inside, as North Americans do. I allow my students to choose either convention so long as they are consistent in it, but if your department has a rule or practice, so be it.

Most sources have author names. If they don't, don't give up—do an online search for the names using the title of the source. If you can't find author names or the source is group-written or anonymous, there is a decision tree:

1. Best: Cite the author's last name: (McIlroy 73)
2. Second best: Cite the organization: (*Atlantic* 2-3)
3. OK: Cite key words in the title: ("Brain Matters" 4)

Literature papers often cite the work's name, not the author's —

(*Gatsby* 91)—I'll return to this later.

The two *worst* things I see students do in papers, apart from not citing at all, is to either cite a search engine or media agglomerator (Google)!—or to paste in an entire website URL. The first is inaccurate and useless, as it tells the reader nothing about the source's creators, and the second wastes space—or may imply an ulterior motive to pad word-count.

As for the correct way to cite, there are specific ways to cite different authorial forms in MLA and APA, with some common layouts here. The following is general practice whatever the source type (books, articles, videos), with certain exceptions.

Single Author

MLA
Experts say that "blueberries are blue" (Jones 6)
Klaus Jones notes that "blueberries are blue" (6)

APA
Experts say that "blueberries are blue" (Jones, 2012, p. 6)
According to Jones (2012), "blueberries are blue" (p. 6)

Multiple Authors
If there are multiple authors, list them all up to three or four, although practices vary.

MLA
(Drexler and Keshavarz 30)
(Graham, Jones, and Sully 6)

APA
(Drexler and Keshavarz, 1998, p. 30)
(Graham, Jones, & Sully, 2010, p. 6)

For a large list of authors you use "et al.," short for Latin *et alli*, "and others." Do not italicize this.

(Graham et al. 6)
(Graham et al., 2010, p. 6)

For some reason, APA uses ampersands (&) inside parentheses, but not outside of them:

Graham, Jones, and Sully (2010) have done similar work.

No Page Numbers

If it's an electronic source of a text with no page numbers, there's not much you can do—normally you just omit them. APA's culture is often to cite entire papers and to not indicate specific page ranges, anyway.

MLA
(McIlroy) (BBC) ("Brain Matters")

APA
(McIlroy, 1996) (BBC, 2020) ("Brain Matters," 2005)

Some writers of APA papers indicate position in a document by paragraph number:

(da Silva, 2014, para. 8)

As well, there are special conventions for literary works, with or without pagination, that I'll cover later.

No Date

This isn't an MLA problem, but in APA you indicate an undated source with *no date*, n. d.

(Ford, n. d.)

Corporate Authors
If the source was written by an organization, use its name instead of a last name. Do not confuse an organization's name (UNESCO) with a publisher's name (Penguin).

(Kaiser Foundation 18). (*Economist*).

If you have a long institutional name as a source, type it in full the first time with an abbreviation, and then in following citations use only the abbreviation:

First time
(National Institute of Mental and Social Health [NIMSH], 2002, p. 4)
Second time
(NIMSH, 2002, p. 28)

Using Keywords

If the source has no corporate or authorial information, again—why are you using it? But if you must, use some keywords from the source to refer the reader to the entry in your works cited list. Let's take as a theoretical example an anonymous and untitled social media thread that is extremely important as a primary source.

By 9 AM, an unnamed commenter added the explosive information of the senator's whereabouts ("Manila Folded").

Or, better, perhaps the source is reputable as a secondary 'gray' one, and simply has no identified creator. If the source's title is: "Binge Drinking a Recurring Problem in UCLA Dorms," you might cite: ("Binge Drinking" 3).

Which words you use are your decision, but using "a" or "problem" are likely poor choices as they are likely to appear in other titles, and may confuse readers. Also note that the key words are in quotation marks to ensure that the citation is not confused with a title or last name. In your end-text list, alphabetize by article name.

The deteriorating situation in Venezuela shows the same ominous possibilities ("Famine relief," 2020).

MLA Works Cited entry:
"Famine Relief: Not a Simple Matter of Supplying Food." *Nutrition Notes*, vol. 5, no. 1, 2002, pp. 70-80.
http://escholarship.org/uc/nutritionnoteworthy

APA References entry:
Famine relief: Not a simple matter of supplying food. (2002). *Nutrition Notes*, 5(1), 70-80.
http://escholarship.org/uc/nutritionnoteworthy

Two People with the Same Last Name

Add first initials in your in-text citation to differentiate multiple Smiths and Lees.

MLA
There are several precedents (G. Paulo 26). In a different context, N. Paulo (93) asserts x.

APA
There are several antecedents (G. Paulo, 1998, p. 26). In a different context, N. Paulo (1999, p. 93) asserts x.

Two Sources by the Same Author

If Prof. Nowak has written two books or articles, the reader will be confused as to which one is meant. Indicate the author, and then the work, using key words—or at least the text's short form:

MLA

A book: (Nowak, *Calculus* 28) [Or, minimally: *Calculus* 28]
An article: (Nowak, "Waveforms" 4-5)

APA
This is less likely to be an issue in APA, as the year will distinguish two works. But it could happen that the years are the same. At any rate, it is good to make sure.

A book: (Nowak, *Calculus*, 2000, p. 28)
An article: (Nowak, "Waveforms," 2002, pp. 4-5)

One Author with Multiple Texts in the Same Year

In MLA, add key words to the source as before.

In APA, add *A* and *B* and so on to differentiate the sources if an author has multiple publications in one year. These should correspond alphabetically to your reference list—that is, the first entry by that author for that year in your list is *A*.

The disaster was "shockingly expected" (Yu, 2003b). The Chinese had little experience with steam power and called it their "Titanic moment" (Yu, 2003a).

Quoting a Personal Interview

MLA
In-text: He replied, "I actually don't like baseball" (Ky).
End-text: Ky, Thao. Personal Interview. 6 Oct. 2021.

APA
In-text: The cellist doyenne claimed that "the weather keeps getting worse for outdoor concerts" (personal communication, April 4, 2017).

End-text: Personal interviews aren't listed in APA reference lists.

Timestamps

I didn't know this until very recently when a student pointed it out, but MLA and APA optionally allow timestamps where a quotation or piece of information is found in a specific time range in a video. Here we'll use a YouTube video as an example. As with the previous examples, we can cite by the creator's last name, or use a short form of the title in quotation marks.

MLA
(Maina 0:35-1:11)

APA
For some reason, APA tends to use the beginning of the timestamp only.

("Jackson 5," 2019, 4:13)

Repeated Use of the Same Source

If you have a series of sentences with quotations from the same author, if would be rather silly to repetitively give a full citation each time: (Donauschwaben-Machiavelli, 1982, p. 24). It is usually safe to cite the name once and then omit it:

Researchers see a link between headaches and sugar consumption (Alves 4). Furthermore, "cigarette smoking adds to the risks" (8).

If you feel there is a potential for confusion, you might explicitly signpost what you are doing, with something like "Donauschwaben-Machiavelichski's 1982 study deserves extended consideration."
 I also make a practice of re-stating full citations at the beginning of new paragraphs, as you might move the paragraph later during editing. For example, if para. 1 ends with a citation from Dr. x, and in para. 2 you begin with a quotation from the same source and cite only page numbers, if you move para. 2 to

a position before para. 1 later, the first-appearing citation will then have no referent.

There are of course situations requiring common sense. If your paper is discussing *Beloved* with few or no other sources, you don't need to incessantly cite (Morrison 64) or (*Beloved* 64). As the paper is about the novel, you might have the full citation a few times and then have only page numbers, trusting that the reader will distinguish when you quote from the text, and when you cite a secondary authority on it. This would apply with non-literary texts as well which are prominently discussed in the paper.

Translated Quotations

You may need to use a source written in a foreign language. An easier way to handle this is to paraphrase the quotation, which I'll expand on later. In some seminar papers it's taken for granted that the writer is translating, and the professor may not be strict. You probably don't need to translate terms such as *schadenfreude*, *laissez-faire*, or *pho*, and you may look patronizing to the reader if you do. In the example here, it's obvious that no one in ancient Sparta spoke English.

The Spartan king's defiant answer to the invaders to "come and take it" is sometimes used by modern U.S. gun rights advocates.

But in post-graduate academic practice, precision may perhaps still be better.

The Spartan king's defiant answer to the invaders to "come and take it" (μολὼν λαβέ) is sometimes used by modern U.S. gun rights advocates.

As well, there may be times where the original language's phrasing has a nuance or set of meanings that is lost in translation, and you wish to draw attention to this:

In Rulfo's *Pedro Páramo* (1955) Dorotea's spirit confesses that, while buried underground, she "forgot all about the sky" ("me olvidé del cielo"; 72), a more poetically ambiguous statement in Spanish where *cielo* can denote *sky* and *heaven*.

The delegates, unsurprisingly, called this proposal a choice "entre la peste et le choléra" (Herne, 2020)—"between the plague and cholera," or better translated as "between a rock and a hard place."

MLA
In MLA, if you wish to give both the translation and original, there doesn't seem to be a firm prescription. Some writers seem to use parentheses, and others don't.

The poet notes of Beowulf's father, "þæt wæs an cyning," "that was one peerless king" (Mitchell and Robinson 107).

Long ago his father told him that "clothes make the man" ("옷이 날개다," "clothes are your wings") when he began his first job.

APA
The practice in APA is to either provide both languages, or write your best translation and append "own translation."

Aveline sarcastically told the conspirators at their trial, "ne t'approche pas! Mes mains sont propres!" [don't come near me! My hands are clean!] (Rue, 1970).

According to Østerberg (1996), "Many of our actions involve changing the materials which surround us" (p. 136, own translation).

7.4 Citing Literature

Referencing literature is a special issue with some relevant exceptions. With some ancient texts the author is anonymous or disputed, and you need to cite the title—*Pearl*, *Gilgamesh*. Such citations are italicized so that no one confuses this reference with a research article written by Dr. Pearl. But you may have noticed that in this chapter, *Gatsby* was given as a citation for *The Great Gatsby*, instead of the author, who we do of course know—F. Scott Fitzgerald.

You can cite either, but the reason this exceptional practice is usually done is that you may be comparing different texts by the same author in your paper. If you cite *Gatsby* with (Fitzgerald 102) and then *Tender is the Night* with (Fitzgerald 61), the reader won't know which novel you mean. It would be better to use a short form of the titles: (*Gatsby* 102) and (*Tender* 61). Equally, in a paper on Robert Frost, you might shorten poem titles to ("Road not Taken") and ("Mending"), or something similar. I am only giving MLA form, but you can follow the logic.

Ordinarily, you can choose your own short forms or abbreviations which make sense.

(*Sun* 8) i.e. *The Sun Also Rises*
(*Catcher* 76) i.e. *Catcher in the Rye*
(HT 320) i.e. *Hard Times*
(GF 119) i.e. *Harry Potter and the Goblet of Fire*

But with some ancient or classic texts there is a conventional shorthand used, such as for Shakespeare. You might indicate the full title in first use—or not. Just as you might spell out UN or CERN for some audiences, but with a specialized audience it would look condescending, a readership of Shakespeareans would recognize MV where a more general one might not.

Ham.: Hamlet
H5: Henry V
Mac.: Macbeth
MV: Merchant of Venice
Rom.: Romeo & Juliet
Son.: Sonnets
Tmp: The Tempest
TN: Twelfth Night

When the Text Doesn't Have Page Numbers

Sometimes the work of literature you are writing on may not have page numbers, such as a .pdf file or an online version. If there are no numbers, again, just omit them.

(Wilde).

But this doesn't give the reader much help in locating the quotation. Where possible, try to give additional information, such as chapter headings:

The narrator says that a single man "in possession of a good fortune, must be in want of a wife" (P&P chap. 1).

In *Brave New World* Helmholtz muses that "words can be like X-rays, if you use them properly—they'll go through anything" (chap. 4).

For a short story with no given page numbers, usually the title of the story is enough. Note again that short stories are in quotation marks and not italics in MLA.

Joyce's young boy describes himself as "driven and derided by vanity" ("Araby").

For poems, cite the line number. Use a slash (/) to indicate line division.

The narrator intones, "And you, my father, there on that sad height / Curse, bless, me now with your fierce tears, I pray" (Thomas, lines 16-17).

Biblical scripture indicates book name, chapter, verse:

We are reassured, "Don't be afraid; you are worth more than many sparrows" (Matt. 10.31).

If you are citing a play, usually you don't cite the page number even if it is available. Plays are normally cited by act (Roman capitals), scene (Roman lowercase), and line numbers. The text below is from *All's Well that Ends Well*, Act one, Scene one, lines 61 to 62:

The countess pleads, "Love all, trust a few / Do wrong to none" (AWW I.i.61-62).

Some modern plays don't indicate line numbers. You may need to use what information you have.

Eliza shocks Freddy (and the audience) with her sudden vulgarity when she spouts, "Walk! Not bloody likely!" (*Pyg*. III).

7.5 Chicago, IEEE, and Footnotes

Footnotes in MLA and APA

Some citation systems, such as Chicago and IEEE, still preserve the logic of Gibbon's system. Rather than an in-text citation of author/short form and location reference or similar, these systems have a small number or symbol which links to the page bottom or paper end. Chicago style is now less popular, but remains prevalent in some fields such as history and linguistics, and in some subfields of English literature such as my own, medieval literature. One advantage is that it is perhaps the least "intrusive" standard, for it places no more than a small superscript number in the text, putting the details in footnotes or endnotes. My intuition is that the culture of Chicago/IEEE places more emphasis on the findings than on the authors.

However, many writers and editors find Chicago time-wastingly repetitive: sources are cited in full in footnotes/endnotes, and then again in a Notes or Bibliography list at the end, and the formatting is *different* between these sets. In some journals I have submitted to, they mercifully modify this so that only one or the other are printed, or the footnotes are at least set in a smaller font size to save space. Below is an example of in-text citation in Chicago format. Its specifics are easily found online, such as the *Chicago Manual of Style* website, presently in its 17th edition.

The word *brother* has a similar form in numerous languages: "broeder (Dutch), Bruder (German), phrater (Greek), brat (Russian), Brathair (Irish), and Bhratar (Sanskrit)."[1]

In the *Wife of Bath*'s tale the Knight is clearly in the wrong, with a ridiculous sense of snobbery in rejecting the woman who saves his life because of her social inequality.[2] The Wife later makes a joke at the Knight's expense,[3] asking him if all of Arthur's men are such boring bed-partners.

Notice that Chicago notes place the publication information of the source in parentheses ( ), and that there are few periods. Like other reference systems, the footnote number's placement is not fixed, and could come at the end of a clause or at the end of a sentence, depending on the writer's preference. Numbers normally come after end punctuation.

The Wife later makes a joke at the Knight's expense, asking him if all of Arthur's men are such boring bed-partners.[4]

As mentioned, Chicago normally forces you to re-list external sources in a Notes or Bibliography section—and in a different format!

---

[1] Robert McCrum, *The Story of English* (New York: Viking Penguin, 1986), 53.

[2] Robert P. Miller, "'Thy Gentillesse' in *Wife of Bath's Tale*, D 1159-62," *Modern Language Notes* 57:3 (1942): 102.

[3] Miller, 106.

[4] Miller, 106.

McCrum, Robert. *The Story of English*. New York: Viking Penguin, 1986.

Miller, Robert P. "'Thy Gentillesse' in *Wife of Bath's Tale*, D 1159-62." *Modern Language Notes* 57, no. 3 (1942): 173-76.

It's not surprising that Chicago is declining in use when it duplicates text so much. One small mercy is that in foot/endnotes, the full reference only needs to be given once, and then a short form is used, as you can see in footnote 4.

Another useful function of foot/endnotes is that you can create one for an extraneous detail or explanation which you feel is useful, but distracting or only partly relevant to the main text. An example is a minor explanatory note.[5] You might also make a helpful recommendation for a further source in the footnote.[6] This information may or may not need to be repeated in the Notes or Bibliography.

How would you give such a "for further reading" link in MLA or APA? One option is to add a "see" verb or something similar to the citation. Some writers use *c.f.* ("compare").

Celtic fairies are capable of fathering children and wear clothes, a marker of human self-consciousness (see Priest, 2008), but can still magically disappear.

But footnotes/endnotes *are* optionally used in MLA and APA for both "further reading" notes and expansion information. I have written them in my own work. Should *you* include optional notes, and how many? There is no rule. My advice is to use them, but sparingly. They can be helpful to give a minor expansion of detail,

---

[5] A notable exception to this issue is air traffic control, where standardized units of a and b have been c since the Reykjavik agreements.

[6] For more on the subject, see Jameson (1999), especially chapter x.

but constant expansion notes annoy journal editors and can look pretentious, as though you are showing off with arcane minutiae. Usually, if something is important it should be in your paper text—and if it is not important at all, why are you telling the reader about it? I average only a few notes per paper, writing them where there is a useful piece of trivia the reader might want to know about, or where I feel a book or paper is not crucially about my main topic but may be helpful for further reading.

IEEE

IEEE style, from the Institute of Electrical and Electronics Engineers, is a format also derived from Chicago style. IEEE uses same-font numbers in brackets after quotations:

Ordinary Portland cement (OPC) was decided on, but only after a lengthy cost dispute [8].

The vehicle was able to read the information of the process and use a Linux tool called *ptrace* [5] to maintain the transfer speed of the vehicle.

If the same source is referred to again, the citation number is repeated: [5]

If more than one source is mentioned at a sentence's end, they are separated by commas: [1], [7], [14]

IEEE's 'culture' is to infrequently list page numbers, but if you do:

[2, pp. 16] [7, pp. 4-5] [11, Fig. 2]

Where IEEE also significantly differs from most citation systems is that in the reference list, entries are not alphabetized, but appear in numerical order:

[12] A. Rezi and M. Allam, "Techniques in array processing by means of transformations," in *Control and Dynamic Systems*, Vol. 69, C. T. Leondes, Ed. San Diego: Academic Press, 1995, pp. 133-180.

[13] E. Guizzo, "Meet Pepper, Aldebaran's new personal robot," in Computers and You, R. S. Brake, Ed. New York: Spectrum, 2014, pp. 5-17.

It might be particularly wise to learn how to automate these lists in your word processor, as if you edit your text to insert a citation, you will otherwise have to re-number all the successive ones in your paper and reference list.

What happens if you are told to re-submit your paper with a different citation system? If you are using some reference managing system, much of the work will be done, bar some inspection and corrections. Without one, changing everything can be real drudgery. You can only do your best—and I can only promise you again that much of this becomes quicker and automatic after several years. I also predict that future word processor versions will have AI tools that do this conversion, with the caveat that it would again be wise to proofread.

7.6 Figures and Tables

Neither APA nor MLA seem totally clear on how to cite inserted graphical or tabular material. Try at least to be informative and consistent in your usage (but don't word-wrap text to the left or right of the insertion as you might in a magazine or website). It's your decision whether you place these materials within the text, or at the end of your paper in an appendix section. My advice is to put them in-text so that the reader can immediately see them, unless your table or survey section comes to multiple pages of information, which might be distracting. As ever, if a department or editor has a direction on this, it can be followed. Note my tables and figures have nonsense example data.

Figures and Tables Cited from Other Sources

MLA

For MLA, provide a reference below the graphic. For images in public domain, it might still be good practice to indicate this is the case, even if the images are not referenced in your end-text list.

Fig. 1. Image from Alice Leighton, *The Sweet Tale of Floris & Blanchefleur* (O'Connor, 1922).

Table 2
Household Pet Ownership 1996-2011

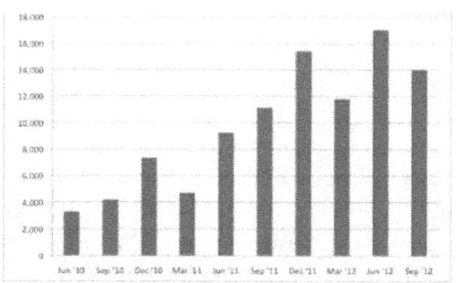

Source: Mohr, Andrea. "Family Variables Relating to Peer Victimization." *Swiss Journal of Psychology*, vol. 65, no. 2, 2006, pp. 107-116.

APA

For APA, to cite an image, place a reference below the graphic and provide an end-text citation.

Fig. 3. Vermeer, J. (c. 1665). *Girl with a pearl earring*. From Mauritshuis Royal Gallery, The Hague. Retrieved from http://www.mauritshuis.nl/index.aspx?Chapid=2295.

Tables and charts italicize titles, and note references (if any) appear below them. For some reason, APA capitalizes key words in table titles but not for figures.

Table 4. Internet Usage Growth, 1996-2018

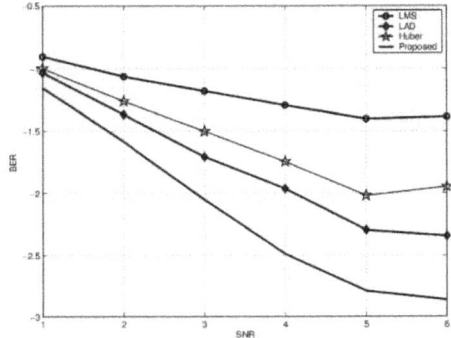

Note. From "Best management practices by period," by B. Adams and C. Matts, 2020, *Correlational Studies, 17*(1), 9-10.

Figures and Tables You Created

Your own tabular or chart information is labeled, but no citation is necessary—you made it.

APA

Table 5. *Company Fruit Shipments in Third Quarter (Crates)*

Product	Division A	Division B	Division C	Division D
Pears	152	178	121	143
Bananas	356	406	392	449
Oranges	729	830	784	722

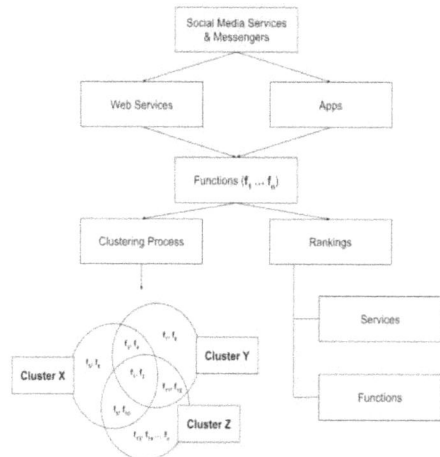

Fig. 6. Dendron clusters

You might still have an explanatory note even if there is no source to cite.

Note. N = 150 (n = 50 for each condition). Participants were on average 28.5 years old (SD = 10.1). p < .01.

7 MLA & APA FORMAT

MLA

Table 7
Google Ngram chart for "singleton," 1980-2008 (https://books.google.com/ngrams)

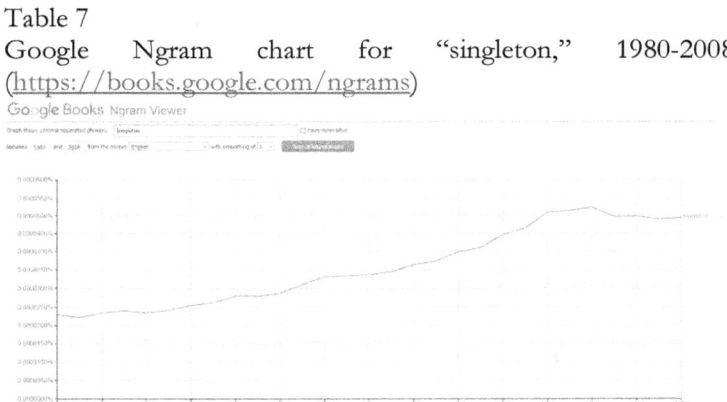

Correct labeling could get unclear with an online website which renders a mathematical or statistical calculation on the fly, such as this Ngram graph, which doesn't exist after the site makes it. In such cases, you may need to do your best to create a useful citation which conforms to the logic of MLA/APA/IEEE, or whatever system is used.

I suspect the APA guide editors don't get invited to many parties. But correct citation will validate your paper as conforming to a scholarly community's standards, and may protect you from potential accusations of plagiarism. Fortunately, citation does become a rote habit, just as a novice typist or musician has to decreasingly often look at the keys or strings. However, I've only focused on citation and not quotation, which is again so important as to require a new chapter. The good news is that quotation allows more scope for personal style and variation, although as a result there are fewer automatic rules to guide writers.

8 QUOTING

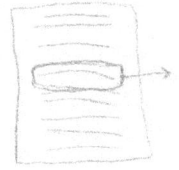

Quoting as an overall activity in academic writing includes citing, but this chapter will focus on the choosing and phrasing of the quoted text. I know that for most readers of this book their paper content is the priority, and writing a paper on it is a means to an end. That's fine—I know most will not be composition theorists. But I think you should take quotation seriously, for handling it with agility and economy really is a power move that will distinguish a professional's writing from a student's. This is hard, even for a L1 speaker of English.

8.1 Seven Ways to Quote

The basic frame for arranging a quotation is some variant on "according to" + quotation + citation, which I call an author-focused form. But that can get repetitive, and there are other and more interesting ways to quote which are also better tailored to different discursive approaches taken during the paper's flow. Perhaps you are by now expecting another set of three—but I can think of seven distinct arrangements to accomplish this.

Author-Focused
Advantage: Easy
Disadvantages: Boring; can waste space

In this sentence construction, the author or speaker is explicitly stated, and is really the focus of the sentence. This phrasing is useful where the name is important or recognizable, and stating it is of interest to the reader or will build ethos credibility. In basic form, begin with a signal phrase which lists the author(s), give the quotation, and then the citation:

MLA

According to Finnish economist Leo Staggers, "Covid-19 will probably show typical financial recovery patterns to earlier pandemics" (8).

APA

Stanford nutritionist Sheila Ford notes that despite the growing numbers of overweight Americans, "many providers still remain in ignorance about the health danger to older or low-income citizens" (1993, p. 5).

In the chapter on editing I will list some alternatives to the tired phrase "according to," so that your reader will not want to jump off a cliff. Again, it gets tedious to see the same structure used over and over. Here you could also invert the order, so that the author's name is given after the quotation:

"Designing a dream city is easy; rebuilding a living one takes imagination" could be urbanist Jane Jacobs's advice to the planners of the Singapore project.

The downside of this form is that if the author of the source is not well-known, stating the name may look frivolous—or worse, like a freshman trying to paper-pad:

According to medical lawyer Walter Hallam, writer of *Court Briefs in Irish Pharmaceuticals*, as well as a banjo player and a loving father of two children and a dog named Badge...

This is deliberately ridiculous, but—with no offense to Walter Hallam (who is fictional anyway), the reader doesn't really care about these details. If the writer feels they are germane, this is what footnotes are for. But it would be better to emphasize the quote and leave the author's name in the citation.

Quote-Focused
Advantage: More compact
Disadvantage: More difficult to write a signal phrase around

Here the quotation is the focus of the sentence, and the source citation is listed but not usually discussed. The quotation might come before or after the signal phrase.

MLA
Invariably in fantasy novels, "elves are troublesome even if they are well-intentioned" (Keller).

APA
"No one wants to make the large and expensive changes to prevent this event from recurring" is the remaining elephant in the room (Hove, 2009, p. 8).

Avoid Orphan Quotes!
If I may interrupt here, please do not write sentences where there is no signal phrase at all—that is, ones that are only a quotation:

The 1980 election was held in an atmosphere of fed-up voters. "The stock market limped along, the auto industry was asthmatic, and the trade deficit was at an all-time high" (Gardner). **x**

These are also known as dropped quotes. The problem is that these sentences feel awkward or jarring, for the quotation is floating by itself, unconnected to any introduction or phrasing from the writer. It would be better with some smoothing words, or at least a colon:

The 1980 campaign featured a president with dismal approval ratings whose policies had given rise to stagflation and an energy crisis: "The stock market limped along, the auto industry was asthmatic, and the trade deficit was at an all-time high" (Gardner).

Split Quote
Advantage: Builds variety
Disadvantage: More difficult to write a grammatical sentence around

From here on, I will use MLA and APA examples without marking them, as you by now recognize the citation patterns. In the split quote form, you break the quotation in the middle somehow and bracket it with your signal phrase and citation:

"No one wants to make the difficult and expensive structural changes required," argues economist Peter Hove, "but in future there may be no choice" (8).

Obar and Wildman (2015, p. 3) mention two further germane characteristics of social media services, namely the creation of "user-specific profiles for a site or app" and the facilitation of "linking profiles with those of other individuals or groups."

You might again use this form for variety, but also if you have an over-long sentence in your source and only the beginning and ending parts are useful for you. You can in this way easily clip out the middle. This also works if you would like to use two separate but topically-connected phrases from the same paragraph or page:

Norris Lacy calls the poem a "roman rose," a conflict-less piece of entertainment rather than drama which conveys "not event but the presentation of event" (22).

Key-Word Quote
Advantages: A power move; looks confident, and very word-efficient; easy to grammatically write a sentence around
Disadvantage: A nearly complete new sentence must be written around it

In the key word form, the writer uses only a short key phrase from the source and builds the sentence around it. This is often favored by advanced writers as it credits the source while using minimal space. It also works well when the phrasing or verb tense of the original does not match your paragraph:

Despite the growing incidence of obesity, many private providers still "remain in ignorance" about the rising health dangers (Ford 5).

Rose of Sharon is so shocked by the loss of her baby that she "struggled and pushed herself up" (469).

I prefer this arrangement myself because it is economical, though I don't want you to think any one of these is 'best.' This would be a boring book if it merely turns out replicas of me—you will have your own favorite writing style, and that may include a favorite quotation style.

As well, with any of these quote forms, there are ethical issues of accuracy, and this is likely an especial danger when writing key-word quotes. Be sure that you do not misrepresent the author's meaning when you select portions of sentences:

Interview Source: No one can say that I like eating mushrooms. Until the end of my life I will hate them.

Larissa Milton writes that "I like eating mushrooms" (217). **x**

Block Quotation
Advantage: Optimal for deeper or extended quotation
Disadvantages: The writer is tempted to overuse them to pad the paper

A block quotation is four or more lines of text, which is approximately 40-50 words or more. When applying one, skip a line before and after the block quotation, and indent on the left side. There are no quotation marks, as the indentation and spaces before and after signal to the reader what you are doing.

MLA

Canadian analyst Peter Hove makes an important point:

> There were really no inventors of the modern stock trade system as now used on Wall Street; it is a system which has developed over centuries based on its European, and mostly British, ancestors. Rapid expansions and crashes are built into the system, but what is lacking is resolve. No one wants to make the difficult and expensive structural changes required. Better software can help, but in future there may be no choice. (8)

For some reason, MLA puts the period before the citation in a block quotation. APA puts it after.

> ... Better software can help, but in future there may be no choice (p. 8).

I am single-spacing throughout this book, whereas in course papers and thesis/dissertations most text is double-spaced. Some paper writers also single-space their block quotations to make them stand out, but generally style manuals advise consistent double-spacing them as well.

Guilty Knowledge

At least once a semester, after discussing block quotations in class, I will receive an undergraduate paper consisting of long and frivolous block quotations shoveled in to pad space. I'm not stupid. I know what the writer is doing.

Guilty knowledge is an ethical concept referring to potentially dangerous information which someone is trusted with knowing for good reasons. Thus, a chemistry class might learn how dirty bombs are made, or a computer science class might learn how hacking is done—not so that students can make bombs or hack mainframes, but so that they can understand and predict what others do. I sometimes feel like teaching block quotations is also tempting students with guilty knowledge.

At a thesis/diss level, or in post-graduate writing, a paper appearing to cynically consist of unnecessary block quotations in order to fill space would destroy any respect the reader has for the paper or its writer. When I was an undergraduate this was called 'shoveling'—and the reference was to manure, not to flowers. But how many block quotes are too many? There's no rule, but I average about one every ten pages, and I would need to see strong reasons for them to appear much more frequently than that in the papers I grade or review. Otherwise, there is little reason for a stranger to read such an essay—why not just read the quoted sources directly if the paper has nothing substantial to add about them?

This is an observation and not a rule, but I nearly always recommend more, shorter quotations in student papers, as opposed to fewer, longer ones. Longer quotations often unnecessarily waste space and can be pruned down, a process I'll return to later. As well, citing a larger number of people is likely to be more persuasive to the reader. This is a metric known as citation density.

Paraphrase Quotation
Advantage: Easy to write: they're your words
Disadvantage: May lack the authority of the original text

You can also rephrase someone's writing in your own words. This is useful if you want to recap or simplify a long quotation, or if the original is strangely phrased or in a foreign language. In science and engineering papers this form is the preferred method, where data results are the important details to convey and not the author's phrasings. Notice there are also no quotation marks in a paraphrase.

MLA
Analyst Peter Hove argues that shortsighted unwillingness to make larger reforms may cause serious problems in future (8).

But notice what happens here.

APA

Despite the growing occurrence of obese Americans, many medical providers still know nothing about the health risk to the elderly or poor (Ford, 1993). x

If you remember the earlier quotation examples, this is pretty much the original phrasing with only a few words replaced by synonyms. That's not very ethical, and borders on gray plagiarism—a topic I'll return to. A paraphrase should be in your own words:

As Ford suggests (1993), despite the growing prevalence of obesity, its risks for senior or low-income citizens are often not seen or taken seriously by providers.

APA 7 (2020) does not require that you list page numbers in a paraphrase, but you might still do so if the information comes from one specific place in the book or source.

IEEE

Compressive strength was measured by using cylindrical concrete specimens (Ø 100 mm × 200 mm) at 3, 7, 28, and 90 days [17].

Without consensus in our society on the scope of data retention and surveillance laws, big data programs risk being negatively impacted or even stopped by public backlash and legal challenges [13].

Third-Party (Indirect) Quotation: x says "quote" (cited elsewhere)
Advantage: Seldom better; but sometimes it's all you have

Occasionally you will find a source where yet another source is quoted, and you want to use it. Ideally, you should hunt down the original, but this may not always be possible, especially when a writer is quoting someone speaking and not something in print. In your citation you need to indicate that you are quoting someone else's words and not the writer of the text it appears in.

MLA
Before taking off, Pope Francis said he would "pray earnestly" for the victims of the terrorist attack (qtd. in *Newsweek*, 34).

APA
U.N. representative Frank Satchel described the water shortage as "impeding our ability to rebuild a severely war-damaged city, but probably only temporarily until their rainy season" (as cited in Christer, 2004, p. 4).

You can paraphrase an indirect citation as well:

MLA
Before taking off, the pontiff promised to pray for the victims of the terrorist attack (qtd. in *Newsweek*, 34).

APA
U.N. representative Frank Satchel noted that the water shortage was serious but would probably only last until rainy season (as cited in Christer, 2004, p. 4).

In your end-text list, include only the text you directly read—the one you took the indirect citation from (Christer or *Newsweek*).

I'd like to add two qualifications before we move on. One is that paraphrases might be shorter (a summary paraphrase) or longer—a paraphrase could expand upon a short and pithy statement, whether direct or indirect.

Dyatlov's remark in *Chernobyl* that the situation is not good but not terrible has become an internet meme for its nuance of a cool, offhand response to danger, but this ignores how rash and fatal the comment originally is.

A second note is that it should normally be unnecessary to cite both the year of the indirect quotation and the year of its appearance, but if you feel this is important you might work the dates into the signal phrase:

Sullivan (1843) foresaw that England would go "railway mad" long before the rapid expansion of lines (as cited in Bergson, 2001, p. 143).

8.2 Quoting Fictional Characters

As with citing works of literature, *quoting* them also presents special problems, because the text might be the characters' words or the narrator's—not the author's. This may need to be distinguished. In the following sentence, who is speaking is clear.

Hagrid tries to make Harry feel better when he says, "Come with me an' see the Great Hall, looks a treat" (PS 212).

But imagine a sentence like this:

Rowling says, "Come with me an' see the Great Hall, looks a treat" (PS 212). **x**

This is confusing, because it gives the impression that Rowling speaks in her own voice here, whereas the speaker is Hagrid, not her.

Rowling writes, "Come with me an' see the Great Hall, looks a treat" (PS 212). **½-x**

This is a little better, but it might still confuse a reader who does not know the book. In novels the characters may also write letters. If we say "Hardy writes...," who is writing? It would be better to have "Tess writes" or even "Hardy's Tess writes." Here there is speaking, not writing, and it would be better to distinguish the activities:

Rowling writes that Hagrid beckons to Harry, saying, "Come with me an' see the Great Hall, looks a treat" (PS 212).

This may seem an esoteric or obvious argument, but it's always important in citation to be clear. A work of literature's author, narrator, and characters are not the same, even if they are created by the same person:

There is no good and evil. There is only power, and those too weak to seek it. – J. K. Rowling

But this is absurd—this is what the villain Voldemort says, not Rowling's viewpoint. Yet I regularly see this error committed on social media, such as when people post witty epigrams by English author Oscar Wilde.

A man can be happy with any woman as long as he does not love her. – Oscar Wilde **x**

Such quotations try to make Wilde, or the person quoting him, sound sophisticated or jaded. But Wilde never said this—his fictional antagonist, Lord Henry, did in *The Picture of Dorian Gray*, and he's the villain. In other interviews and statements Wilde clarified that Henry did not speak for him. As with the Rowling example, it is both incorrect and unethical to portray this sentiment as Wilde's opinion. Again, when you quote characters, distinguish the speaker from the author:

Lord Henry says that "a man can be happy with any woman as long as he does not love her" (*Dorian* 31).

Wilde's Henry dryly says that a man can be content with any woman "as long as he does not love her" (*Dorian* 31).

Or, as another example:

According to Dickens, "I'm very fond of flowers" (Hard Times 11). **x**

Again, Dickens did not say or mean this. You don't need to write *qtd.* / *cited in*, as Sissy is a fictional character, but the fact that she speaks the words needs to be fit into the sentence:

In *Hard Times*, Sissy pleads, "If you please, sir, I'm very fond of flowers" (31).

The same applies to narrators. Usually the narrator in a story is a created voice and not the author speaking:

Jane Austen notes that the Bennets were "proved to be marked out for misfortune" (47). **x**

In a sense this is true, but it's not clear—the narrator of the novel, and not necessarily Jane Austen, believes this conviction:

In Jane Austen's novel the neighbors see the Bennets as "proved to be marked out for misfortune" (47).

Austen's narrator notes that the neighbors view the Bennets as "proved to be marked out for misfortune" (47).

Woolf's Miss Barret is subjugated to a limited life because of her supposed illness, and "she sometimes kept the house for weeks at a time" (*Flush* 41).

In some fiction, the narrator is a named person, such as in Joseph Conrad's *Heart of Darkness* or *Lord Jim*, where the narrator is a specific person, Marlowe. This makes signal phrasing easier, although again, the writer needs to distinguish the narrator from the author. As an extreme example, in Salmon Rushdie's controversial *The Satanic Verses,* the narrator is evidently the devil, and the reader gradually realizes that much of what is reported is lies. Writing "Rushdie says" may dangerously mislead a reader into believing that the narrator's values are Rushdie's. It would be better to use a phrasing like "Rushdie's Satanic narrator says."

Admittedly, such as in some older literature, the narrator-author difference is small, and in a Dickens novel there is often the sense that they are the same. As well, some semi-fiction or essay-type literature may involve the author directly speaking, such as a humor essay by Mark Twain, or Frank McCourt's biographical memoir-novels of his own life:

McCourt remarks bitterly that "Mr. O'Dea hates England and you have to remember to hate England or he'll hit you. If you ever say anything good about Oliver Cromwell they'll all hit you" (97).

Such situations may call for a common-sense judgment; but it should be a considered one.

8.3 Quotation Grammar

In using any of these citation forms, you need to be sure that in writing words around the quotation, that it makes for a correct grammatical sentence. For example, it's easy to get verb tenses confused:

In future it will be important for the French school system "were flexible enough to accommodate rapid inflows of immigrant students" (Surette 25). **x**

That makes no sense. If you aren't sure, remove the quotation marks and read the sentence to see if it feels natural. Use only the parts of the original source that will fit the grammar of the sentence, or change your signal phrasing.

In future it will be important for the French school system to be "flexible enough to accommodate rapid inflows of immigrant students" (Surette 25).

Here is another set of examples. Notice again in the repaired sentences how the signal phrases connect grammatically into the quotations.

One study discusses "then there was the University of Nebraska's 2013 'Unplugged' experiment that asked 200 undergrads to forgo all online technologies for a week" (Dokoupil, 2014). x

One study discusses "the University of Nebraska's 2013 'Unplugged' experiment that asked 200 undergrads to forgo all online technologies for a week" (Dokoupil, 2014).

Jack is degenerating, from "can sing C sharp" (Golding, 22) to "his nose only a few inches from the humid earth," and "his sandy hair, considerably longer than it had been when they dropped in" (62), finally into a murderous savage. x

Jack degenerates from being proud to be able to "sing C sharp" (Golding 22), to being a half-animal with "his nose only a few inches from the humid earth" with hair that is "considerably longer than it had been when they dropped in" (62), finally into being a murderous savage.

My suspicion is that some Asian languages which are less strict about number agreement, articles, and perhaps verb tenses, have an advantage here. In English you can't change the original text (with a few exceptions); you need to shape a sentence which fits the quotation's grammar, or else you need to crop away words from the quote until you have a phrasing that fits:

Heaney's descriptions reveal that he is far removed from his ancestors' lifestyle and he concedes, with some guilt, that "but I've no spade to follow men like them" (line 28). x

Heaney's descriptions reveal that he is far removed from his ancestors' lifestyle and he concedes, with some guilt, that he has "no spade to follow men like them" (line 28).

Here is another example from one of my own papers. Again, the quotation begins where the signal phrase grammatically ends:

The frightening dystopia of *Brave New World* "frequently causes modern readers to overlook the fact that it is a rather witty book much of whose parody is amiably comic rather than morally indignant" (Stableford 254).

Quotes Beginning With Capital Letters

How can you write a grammatically correct quotation sentence if your quotation begins with a capital letter, after your signal phrase? It feels like there is a conflict here between correct grammar and reproducing the exact original source:

Even though Slartibartfast is tired and dejected, he asserts, "What does it matter? Science has achieved some wonderful things, but I'd far rather be happy than right any day" (193).

The practice in MLA is to retain the capital "**W**hat" in order to preserve the original source's form. But as is the culture with MLA, this practice isn't strict, and I would recommend that as long as you are consistent, you can probably get away with lowercasing where it is grammatically correct.

In the APA papers I see, sometimes writers also capitalize, and the world seems to go on, although if one is to follow APA's pronouncements exactly, the uppercase letter is replaced by a lowercase one in brackets to show that there has been an alteration:

On Instagram, it is even possible to use a hashtag emoji like #☺, "[b]y using the # character to mark particular keywords."

Dykas et al. (2007) note, "[t]he dynamic load test result shows that the structural stiffness of the bearing decreases with excitation frequency and amplitude of motion."

Citation Placement

Perhaps this ought to have been covered earlier in the discussion on citation typography, but I didn't want to overload you with minutiae. Do citation references always need to go at the end of the sentence? That is where they usually are placed, but you can also put them next to the words being referenced if you prefer, or if you feel there is a risk of confusing the author's information with that in your signal phrase or other original sentence elements.

Turnaround time is the lead time before take-off after landing. While it averages 45 minutes for full-service carriers (FSCs), low-cost carriers (LCCs) take approximately 20-25 minutes (Yang, 2005); for this reason, some airports have modified…

The term *infodemic* (Naeem & Bhatti, 2020) refers to a social media situation in which…

Critics complained that Shaw's "perfectly ambiguous" (Meisel 177) ending was a precedent justifying later editors…

Changing the Quote

As a rule, you shouldn't change a quote. You should change your signal phrase or other wording to fit the quotation, for writers have an ethical responsibility to retain the original source exactly as it is. But there are limited occasions where a minor alteration to make a quotation fit your sentence is allowed or conventional, but do so sparingly, and indicate that you have made the change. One change is already mentioned—making an initial capital lowercase—and you might also add an [s] or [ing] to make the quote match your sentence's verb tense.

Original source: The company's numerous refusals to release documents obscure the essential problem.

The continuing impasse "obscure[s] the essential problem"

(Witte, 1998, p. 55).

Original source: The prototype EV runs for 43 miles on one US dollar's worth of electricity.

Even by 2009, a "prototype EV [ran] for 43 miles on one US dollar's worth of electricity" (Megat, 2009).

Similarly where necessary, minor emendations of switching *was* to [is] or [are], or adding a [the] could be done. But doing this sort of Franken-quoting is addictive. Normally it is the writer's job to rearrange the signal phrase around the quotation, not the other way around. Readers may feel you are not playing fair with the original text if such emendations are constant.

[sic]

The purpose of *sic*, a short form of Latin *sic erat scriptum*, 'as it was written,' is to show that you are reproducing a source faithfully that has an error, and that it isn't your error.

E. E. Cummings replied, "maybe I just growed" [sic].

The witness testified that "I saw the plaintiff [sic] shred the document."

Cummings (who never himself used lowercase for his first name) is being playful with language. As well, suppose in the second example the witness means the defendant, but has confused the terms—this is a valid situation where noting the unintentional factual error is proper. The problem is that overuse of *sic* can become gratuitous:

Catherine warns her sister that Miss Bailey "disappear'd [sic] from her chaise and was wont to drop the connexion [sic] entirely" (90). **x**

That's extreme and more than a little pretentious, to flag every antiquated spelling in an older text which is no longer correct. It would make a paper on Chaucer or Shakespeare a sea of *sic*s. There is also a fine line crossed where a writer passive-aggressively notes trivial *sic*s to undermine a source he or she doesn't agree with—or at worst, labels a disliked opinion as a transmission error "The president is a very smart person [sic]" **x**. The term has a use, but is probably best applied sparingly, as are most Latin tags such as *etc.* or *viz*.

There may also be different disciplinary cultures at play here. Some of the most technically exact academic writing you will ever see is done by lawyers, and such briefs or papers usually care little about rhetorical beauty or economy—text will be applied or reproduced extremely carefully. For example, some of the legal challenges brought by ex-president Trump after the 2020 U.S. election contained spelling errors, and a lawyer might certainly indicate a brief says "the Untied Stats of America [sic] election" in order to show some claim—that a junior clerk flubbed, that the mistake was intentional sabotage, or it was made to limit a legal team's future exposure (we only claimed the election of the *Untied Stats* was fraudulent).

In such a case these tiny typos may be very significant. I am not suggesting that accuracy in papers outside these disciplines is not important, but over-correcting where the difference is trivial—quoting "I'm not sure either are better [sic]" because *either* really should take singular *is*—may appear pedantic.

Dot, Dot, Dot...

An ellipsis (...) is used if you are leaving out text from the beginning, middle, or end of a quoted sentence, and wish to show that you have removed something.

Zins remarks that "information practitioners in the field were originally subject specialists who worked to improve scientific and scholarly communication... in their respective fields, or in general."

Chi (2014) argues that "[a]uthor name ambiguity greatly distorted the results of co-citation analysis..." However, in a follow-up study, Mainz (2018) qualifies this to say that

Here, sentence portions, or even several sentences, may have been removed, and the ellipsis in both examples shows that this has been done—that the original quotations have been altered. But often the use of an ellipsis is both a grammatical and an ethical matter. If the clipping is trivial, or the quotation is obviously not a complete sentence, it might be skipped.

Original source: "Historically, information science developed out of special librarianship and documentation..."

Do you need to indicate,

Zins remarks that "...information science developed out of

Or would this be adequate?

Zins remarks that "information science developed out of

I would probably do the latter, as that one word (*historically*) is not likely to be seen as a significant change. Similarly, in this next example:

The French school system will need to be "...flexible enough..." to accept more foreign newcomers (Surette 25).

Here again, "flexible enough," without the ellipsis, is fine. The reader can see that you have only used a portion of a sentence. However, there will again be situations where you may need an ellipsis to show that the original sentence does not end where your quoting of it does:

Source: Author name ambiguity greatly distorted the results of co-citation analysis, and it was found that the English indication of

Korean and Chinese names is a primary reason for this distortion (Kim, 2014).

Kim (2014) argues that "[a]uthor name ambiguity greatly distorted the results of co-citation analysis…" However, in a follow-up study, Kim (2018) qualifies this to say that

APA is stricter on this matter, and in such a paper the ellipsis should follow the quoted text. MLA's culture is more to allow the writer's discretion, so long as the reader is not misled.
 Conversely, similar to a key word quote, an ellipsis could be dishonestly used where it should *not* be, in order to distort a source:

Original: "I have not yet begun to fight." – Capt. John Paul Jones

Captain Jones famously said, "I have… begun to fight." **x**

This silly example is similar to the "I like eating mushrooms" one, where twisting the source has been done to create false evidence. The sample here is also an extreme one to illustrate an idea, but it does happen that academic paper writers misrepresent sources without realizing it through this means.

Quoting Text with Quotation Punctuation Inside

Sometimes, the source may have its own quotation marks, particularly in literature when characters are speaking. You will need to include them, as they are in the original source, but you will have the problem of confusing the reader with multiple sets of quotation marks:

Sillitoe adds, "Arthur took off his overcoat and laid it on the ground. "We'll be comfortable here," he said softly. Brenda spoke, the first time since entering the woods, "Won't you be cold?"" (50) **x**

This is a mess. Here as well, an exception to the rule of exact reproduction is allowed. The convention is that you differentiate your punctuation marks from those of the characters by marking their words in single quotes (' ')—or in double quotes (" ") if you use single ones.

Sillitoe adds, "Arthur took off his overcoat and laid it on the ground. 'We'll be comfortable here,' he said softly. Brenda spoke, the first time since entering the woods, 'Won't you be cold?'" (50)

The barman is perplexed to hear a nonsensical answer from his visitor: "'No, no,' said Ford, 'it's just that the world's about to end'" (18).

This also needs to be accounted for in your end-text list, particularly when using MLA format, where many Works Cited titles are set with quotation marks:

Lim, Gary. "'My Horse, a Horse, my Kingdom for a Horse!': Arondel in *Bevis of Hampton*." 44th International Congress on Medieval Studies, Kalamazoo, MI, May 2009.

Verb Tenses in Signal Phrases

You might be wondering why the examples have Sillitoe *says* instead of *said*. A Bangladeshi graduate student once also asked me whether source authors should be indicated as "Dr. x says" (present tense) or "Dr. x said" (past tense) when introducing a quotation. There is no rule on this matter in MLA or APA, although there are typical conventions or commonsense distinctions.

MLA
MLA usually employs what is called the historic present in quotation, particularly in literature where, in a sense, fictional events do not exist or happen until they are present in the reader's experience:

Walter Mitty fantasizes piloting a navy hydroplane, commanding, "Throw on the power lights! Rev her up to 8,500! We're going through!" as he plods along the street in his car with his scolding wife.

In a proverbial statement the present tense might also be used:

Heraclitus advises, "No one steps into the same river twice."

Churchill tells us, "Success is the ability to go from one failure to another with no loss of enthusiasm."

When quoting direct evidence from a source, I tend to use present tense myself.

In his introduction to a 1988 anthology, Harold Bloom patronizingly damns Steinbeck with faint praise, commenting that he retains "fairly constant popularity with an immense number of liberal middlebrows" (4).

But the past tense isn't wrong, and there may be situations where it feels right to use it. The reference may be to a past historical event; the reference may be very old; or the writer may wish to compare between past views and current ones. For an older but still relevant source, I will use present perfect.

Some critics disagree, such as Robertson Davies, who has called *Sunshine Sketches* a "ferocious and mordant" work.

I tend to reserve simple past for an especially old opinion, particularly if it is now less current in scholarship—or for historical reportage.

The view of the poem's geographical setting has not changed since Skeat called it "an absurd local story about Grimsby" in 1902 (liv).

By the 1200's European patience for crusading had faded. The descendants of the crowds that had cheered Urban II in 1095 now answered "Deus non vult!" ("No, God *doesn't* will it").

APA and IEEE

Writers in social science or STEM (science, technology, engineering, and medicine) disciplines also tend to prefer simple present tense for ease and immediacy, although such fields are typically more sensitive to when the source was published or the survey/experiment was conducted, reflecting the faster developments in these topics. Again, I recommend a similar triage:

Study is recent or its findings are still ongoing and relevant: *present tense or –ing*

Rayden & von Hahn (2021) are finding that
The latest UN DESA data [2] show that

Study is older but still shapes the issues: *present perfect (has)*

Alarum (1998) has found
Jordan (2013) has demonstrated

Study is much older and less directly relevant to current scholarship: *past or past perfect (had)*

Evans, Donnelly, and Hume-Loveland (1973) conducted
Clarke (1954) also explored
Ma and Yeh (1980) studied

Or, in sentence example format, note the verb tenses used for the year dates of these studies:

Studies that analyze search behaviors based on user log data are presently being conducted (Choo et al., 2019; Park & Lee, 2020;

Choi et al., 2018).

Weber and Stock (2013) have found that "it is possible to apply only some of the characteristics shown in the model" (p. 15).

Husserl argued in 1968 that the electrical prototypes were only useful in industrial applications (p. 10).

Some supervisors or APA/IEEE writers may also have departmental or disciplinary conventions on verb tense, so that facts or findings which are always true might always take present tense (the data show that), whereas provisional or previous findings might take past or present perfect (the test showed, earlier experiments have shown). Otherwise, I don't think this issue needs to be overthought, and the topic or logic of the sentence may easily suggest what seems more accurate or understandable.

More on Paraphrasing

I am sticking this in here so as not to make the "Seven Ways" section even longer: the skill in paraphrasing is to explain someone else's text in your own words, in such a way that the original information is accurately conveyed but the phrasing or emphasis fit your purposes. This may again involve abbreviating, lengthening, or clarifying the original text.

Original source:

Wikipedia emerged in the bloom of what has been dubbed by some as the Academic Spring. This social movement started among reformist academics who viewed current institutional and cultural norms in academia as obsolete in the digital age. With the advent of near-free, media-rich asynchronous communication, traditional publishing practices have gained the reputation of being too slow and too profit-oriented. It can take years to get a paper published, but only a few hours to get similar information featured on a blog; and published papers are often hidden behind paywalls, making them inaccessible to a majority of the world's population. But blogs and Wikipedia articles have no such limitations (Konieczny 81).

A direct quote-focused sentence might do fine:

New research has shown that traditional publishing models "have gained the reputation of being too slow and too-profit oriented" (Konieczny 81).

Or, you might choose a paraphrase to condense or adapt the text for your own uses. Again, a paraphrase could be shorter or longer than the original, depending on your purposes. Your paper might have little to do with Wikipedia specifically, and so your emphasis might be on a particular subtopic within the source.

Social media posting has evolved into other uses as well. In a 2015 study, Konieczny found that traditional scholarly paper publishing can be too slow a process in comparison with digital forms such as blog posting (81).

A central facet of capitalism is artificial scarcity, such as efforts by academic publishing to enforce access paywalls. New online platforms such as blogs and Wikipedia have threatened some of this scarcity (Konieczny 81).

8.4 Quotation Sandwiches

I am leading you into bigger fish to fry regarding the finer details of quoting, for you have hopefully noticed in my longer examples that they interact somehow with the quotation. Optimally, your discussion has something to say about the quote or cited evidence.

One of the student problems I see regarding quotation is papers that dump one in to 'prove' a claim and then move on to begin a new idea or paragraph. Composition scholars Gerald Graff and Cathy Birkenstein call this a "hit and run" quotation.

In general, I don't end a paragraph or discussion with a quotation unless it is particularly self-explanatory or reads well. The following excerpt reads abruptly, because the quotation ends the paragraph with a jump to a new idea in the next one, with no engagement at all with the quote.

Rowling does not give the children modern technology so that their achievements at using spells to solve problems will be emphasized. Toward the end, Dumbledore tells Ron Weasley, "for the best-played game of chess Hogwarts has seen in many years, I award Gryffindor house fifty points" (Chap. 17).
Another reason that Rowling avoids technology at Hogwarts is to separate...x

Here the quote about Dumbledore and Weasley is used as evidence, but there is no explanation of the quote or discussion of how it supports the paper's claims. Graff and Birkenstein would argue that the "they say" of the paragraph is not connected to the "you say" part—or rather, there is no "you say" part. The reader wants to know how you interpret and respond to the quotation, and a paragraph that moves on can feel lacking. This next example reacts to the quotation.

Rowling does not give the children modern technology so that their achievements at using spells to solve problems will be emphasized. Toward the end, Dumbledore tells Ron Weasley, "for the best-played game of chess Hogwarts has seen in many years, I award Gryffindor house fifty points" (Chap. 17). Here Weasley achieves praise both for utilizing his magic and for understanding an abstract and medieval game.

The additional sentence explains how Dumbledore's statement relates to technology, and in a sense has a conversation with the source, explaining it and linking it back to the writer's argument.
It is now time for another food analogy. A better practice in quoting is to build 'quote sandwiches,' where you introduce the source, state it, and then discuss or contextualize how it relates to or supports your arguments.

8 QUOTING

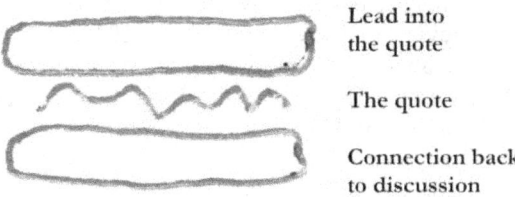

Lead into the quote

The quote

Connection back to discussion

1. Signal phrase / intro to quotation
2. Give and cite the quotation
3. Connect the quote to the discussion

I don't want you to think there is one magic formula for quotation arrangement, and having the same pattern would become boring anyway; but I do find that discussions which have a form of dialogue with their quotations are more interesting, just as in real-life conversation—which is what papers are in a sense modeling.

Here's a student writing sample which handles this concept well, giving a quotation and then relating it back to the dialogue.

Women were not supposed to choose or direct their partner. But Jordan doesn't seem to follow these traditional gender roles. At the first Gatsby party, Jordan says to Nick, "Let's get out, this is much too polite for me" (3), and this shows that Jordan leads the action.

Here's another example which I have written. Notice how the discussion makes the claim, uses a quotation to add support and shading, and then bounces off it to segue back to the paper's arguments.

If Mr. Collins's proposal to Elizabeth consists of affected clichés, at least they are methodically planned ones. I believe we have missed a small but enjoyable joke here, for Collins's pastoral training should draw attention to the preaching situation he creates during the proposal. Shapard posits that Collins probably employs "similar rhetorical device[s] in his sermons" (207), but how Collins speaks to Elizabeth does not seem different from that activity. What helps make the scene funny is that Collins's proposal is not really a proposal at all; it is a sermon.

Clustering Quotations from the Same Source

As a variation on this, if you are quoting repeatedly from two or three sources, it may be better to group them together rather than switching between authors. For example, if x, y, and z are so important to your paper that you discuss each one at length with multiple quotations, you might have one paragraph only discussing x, beginning with "x's ideas are so influential that they might be examined as follows," or similar. The next paragraphs would do the same with y and z.

But this is only a suggestion—you may wish to go concept-by-concept (how x, y, and z feel about idea 1, and then the same for idea 2) instead of source-by-source, if that is clearer or easier to write. As well, some writers clump together overviews of how x, y, and z feel in footnotes/endnotes. I find thickets of lengthy footnotes in tiny text off-putting, but each to their own. If the footnotes are short summaries, the paper could be easier to follow when content is marked off in this way.

8.5 Advanced Quotation 'Waves'

I am gradually moving up in scope, from the sentence package of signal phrase-quotation-citation, to quotation 'sandwiches,' and now to the larger rhetorical patterns which might inform an entire paragraph or section. Here I take some ideas from a good recent book which also discusses research writing at the graduate level: Eric Hayot's *The Elements of Academic Style: Writing for the Humanities* (2014). Hopefully you will read it after this one (and not instead of this one).

Hayot advises building body paragraphs in a rhetorical

hooked shape, which I liken to waves. In this pattern, content difficulty runs from 1 (easy) to 5 (hard). In his model, paragraphs begin with introductory or transition material (1), move up into textual or secondary evidence (2, 3), climax by raising the level of difficulty and abstraction to a peak (4, 5), and then fall back down into summarizing or concluding material (3) that can link into the next paragraph.

As well, as the illustration depicting Hayot's thinking shows, the level 3 which ends one paragraph is now the level 1 of the next one, as the discussion continues to become more complex and informed.

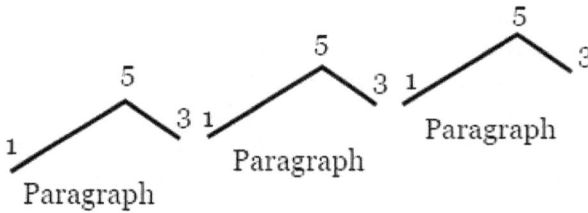

This may feel contrived or forced. It is a suggestion, and not a one-size-fits-all formula. Yet I agree that a paragraph with only ponderous high-level material (5) will probably seem dense and overwhelming, and a paragraph with only low-level quotations and evidence (1, 2) may feel flat and obvious. Putting this together, here is another example from one of my own papers. Note how there is a natural progression in the paragraph arc: A claim and information are given, there is a qualification, and then a discussion follows which analyzes the evidence and summarizes by relating it back to the claims of the paper.

Level 1: Topical material is introduced
Scholars lack agreement on the value of explicit correction of grammar errors (see Ellis, 2002).

Level 2-3: Discussion is developed
Pica (1985) claims that classroom teaching is "of no consequence" in improving usage of *a*, although her sample is

speakers of Spanish, an article language (p. 217).

Level 4-5: More sources and a more complex discussion
Some theorists dichotomize mistakes as *global*, those which cause rejection of the statement as incomprehensible, or as *local*, phrasings which are awkward but understandable (Ferris & Hedgcock, 1998, p. 204). Master claims that article errors "rarely lead to miscomprehension" (1997, p. 216), conceding only that poor usage of articles creates a negative impression in the professor who grades the work.

Level 3: Moving down to summarize and lead into the next subtopic
Nevertheless, one reason article mistakes are prevalent is that articles themselves are so omnipresent: in written English *the* is the most-used word in the language. While lower-level learners have other priorities, advanced writers grasp with issues of credibility in supporting arguments or writing for professional purposes.

Here three more examples from student papers. Notice that the scientific paper samples have fewer direct quotations, but still follows a similar wave pattern in its rhetorical structure and content difficulty.

MLA: *The Tempest*

Level 1
It is true that Miranda loves Ferdinand against Prospero's will and makes a conflict. Her behavior towards her father changes in a way that is "not as meek and submissive as she is often portrayed" (Vaughan 27).
Level 2-5
For example, she disobeys her father by meeting Ferdinand and telling him her name. However, Prospero wants her to love Ferdinand in reality and just pretends to disapprove because he does not want their love to be easy "lest too light winning make the prize light" (I.ii.629-630). For that reason, Prospero forces

Ferdinand to work for him by carrying logs; "Ferdinand's service is short-lived, however, and he is rewarded with Miranda as a bride" (Vaughan 26).
Level 3
Therefore, it is not a real conflict, rather a fake one that is resolved easily later.

APA: CO_2 Storage

Level 1
The rock formations can be largely classified into three main types: igneous, sedimentary, and metamorphic.
Level 2-5
Large sedimentary basins are best suited here, because they have tremendous pore volume and connectivity and they are widely distributed (Bachu, 2003, p. 12). Sedimentary rock can also be further classified into different types of rocks like sandstone, limestone, siltstone, and shale. Šperl has presented the physical properties of different types of rocks in Table 2, after performing laboratory testing (Šperl et al., 2008, p. 4). It shows that the average porosity of sandstone is better than other types of rocks, which means that the porosity is neither too high nor too low for carbon sequestration.
Level 3
Thus CO_2 sequestration occurs better in the sandstone as compared to shale, because the sequestration in sandstone resulted in decreased porosity, whereas increased porosity was observed in shale (Xu, Apps, & Pruess, n.d.).

IEEE: Failure Prevention Software for Autonomous Vehicles

Level 1
To overcome the limitations of the backup systems, we utilize existing techniques [4]. Figure 3 shows the basic structure of a cyber-physical system in which process migration techniques are applicable.
Level 2-5

Through this structural diagram, it is possible to explain the technique of finding alternate nodes proposed in this study. The first CPS node performs the most important function, and if there is a problem with the node, the master node finds the second CPS node, which is the replaceable CPS node. The routing table inside the master node provides a continuous recovery scheme that can detect replaceable nodes by detecting each failure of the lower node.

Level 3

As a result, the routing table maintains information about the running process, process priority, and adjacency between nodes of all the lower nodes connected to the master node and migrates the higher-priority process to a replaceable node whenever a failure occurs.

To Summarize: Entering a Conversation

In 1941, literary theorist Kenneth Burke made this analogy about a writer as a guest at a party of intellectuals:

You come late. When you arrive, others have long preceded you, and they are engaged in a heated discussion, a discussion too heated for them to pause and tell you exactly what it is about... You listen for a while, until you decide that you have caught the tenor of the argument; then you put in your oar. Someone answers; you answer him; another comes to your defense; another aligns himself against you... The hour grows late, you must depart. And you do depart, with the discussion still vigorously in progress.

I have included this quotation here to finish off this section because visualizing yourself as a participant in an ongoing academic dialogue is a good posture to take as a writer. Graff and Birkenstein agree that writers might best situate their paper's contributions among others in the "conversation." Most people have probably sat through class presentation days which were no more than students or groups taking their turn delivering monologues, with no one responding to anyone else's ideas. The information stated may have been sound, but such classes can be boring. What often gives interest to a session of presentations, a conversation, or even a live jazz concert, is the interplay of people reacting to each other's ideas and moving them forward. A paper can't do this in real time, but it can still engage with other writers.

Here my experience is that humanities writers can learn something from writers of science and engineering papers, who often do this naturally, being careful to foreground their research among other studies and conclusions reached by peers and forebears. Earlier I stated that one approach to making a conclusion more memorable is to relate your findings to the reader's interests. In a sense, this tries to make the reader part of the conversation. Placing your paper's argument as an answer or addition to differing opinions might also be a way to make your paper more relevant and connected to ongoing ideas and findings. You might do this overall in your essay, or as a conclusion strategy.

8.6 Plagiarism

This is a gloomy way to end the chapter, but it is necessary. I have spoken about quotation ethics, but there is really be no graver ethical violation in academia than plagiarism. There are few offenses you could commit as a student which would be more damaging to a potential scholarly or professional career.

I generalize out of necessity, but non-western students often do not appreciate how seriously plagiarism is taken in the west, and how inadequate "I didn't know it was wrong" is to the charge. I have seen undergraduates fail courses, graduate students expelled, and professors lose their jobs for it. Plagiarism charges dating back from college nearly ruined the career of U.S. President Joe Biden in 1987, who had planned to run for president in that year. More recently, German defense minister Karl-Theodor zu Guttenberg not only was forced to resign from the Angela Merkel government but had his Ph.D. revoked.

I've had Asian students give me cultural excuses of it's-expected-to-share and everybody-does-it-here, but no Asian university I know actually *allows* plagiarism—all condemn or forbid it at least in theory, and increasingly there is teeth in the regulations. I have seen Korean university departments suspend students or fail their thesis projects for cheating, as well as media scandals where rising young politicians have their careers torpedoed by someone digging up plagiarism in their past.

Something that former undergraduate students do, and perhaps it reflects human nature, is to avoid or act embarrassed around me if I previously gave them poor or failing grades. I generally don't have anything against students who failed, and may even like them; I know what it's like to fail, too. But nearly every professor has contempt for the plagiarist, who not only insults his or her intelligence but mocks the integrity of the subject the professor has spent a career studying. I am even more furious with senior students who lie and say they were "never taught about plagiarism." But I'm unsure that there is anyone who likes plagiarists outside academia, either. Most people would prefer that the surgeons operating on them understand the medical concepts and ideas they wrote about in their classes, as opposed to copying them from someone else's papers.

Having said this, there are two broad types of plagiarists. One doesn't care and believes he or she can get away with it. That type probably isn't bothering to read this book anyway—so I will address you as the second type, which is at least somewhat concerned about avoiding plagiarism, or being accused of it. To do so we ought to define it as best we can.

Plagiarism is likened to theft, but it is not the same as how we conventionally see stealing. If someone burgles your smartphone, that is theft in a simple, tactile zero-sum sense—that person has your phone and you don't. The object is non-shareable. Media companies call file piracy theft, but it isn't quite the same, as nothing has been removed; the file is still there online, and has merely been duplicated elsewhere. What has been stolen is the software file's value.

Plagiarism is different—it is the theft of the author's work and reputation. It isn't monetary theft, because it's perfectly legal to quote or cite small portions of a text in your paper for free.

Most developed nations have fair use laws allowing students and academics to do this, so long as the result is not sold or given a commercial use. (This is an additional reason that plagiarism has such a terrible odor to it, that no one can claim they are merely poor—you don't have to pay anything to use external sources; you only have to say you did so.) But there may be a theft of *labor* if you allow or tacitly encourage readers to believe that you wrote someone else's words or conducted their research.

Where it Gets Hard

Admittedly, plagiarism is complicated. What if it's not stated, but obvious that you are borrowing someone else's work? As noted in an earlier chapter, I sometimes see playful paper titles which riff off familiar phrases:

I Can't Get No Satisfaction: Customer Care Information Collection Using MVP Statistical Packages

Shake It Off: Noninvasive Adolescent Tibia Fracture Diagnosis and Physical Therapy Solutions

Tomorrow is Another Day: Dreams and Dreaming of the Future in Toni Morrison's *Song of Solomon*

I made these up, but you hopefully recognize the references, and that recognition is what makes them humorous. But I don't think any writer would list the Rolling Stones, Taylor Swift, or *Gone With the Wind* in their end-text. The reasonable expectation is that the reader knows the source, and the point is that the writer wants the reader to see the allusion, not hide it. This is a concept I will return to when I discuss the concept of common knowledge.

Second, I once had a frustrated friend sarcastically ask me, why not cite every word in the paper, because surely someone else has written it elsewhere?—Should I cite every "the" I write? Of course not, for everyone knows this to be impossible; but the question exposes a central problem of plagiarism, that it's subjective. Much like the borrowing of a song lyric, the writer's intentions matter.

Unfortunately, there is no cut-and-dried definition of plagiarism. Some style manuals and university boards have attempted to make clinical definitions of plagiarism, such as the rule that plagiarism is three or more words taken from a unique text, but this is still unpersuasive. In the previous paragraph I wrote "of course not," and there are probably thousands or millions of writings in the world using this sequence—but common sense says that isn't plagiarism. Thus we are left with the problem of defining a unique text.

My answer is not going to satisfy everyone, but it's all there is: making a case for plagiarism often involves an instinctual sense that the text has taken credit for someone's original phrasing or specific information, and that it's not coincidental. As Supreme Court justice Potter Stewart said about pornography— "I know it when I see it"—plagiarism typically evokes an intuition of bad-faith usage. For this reason, accidental plagiarism is in my experience rare. Nearly every example I have encountered as an educator has been fairly obviously through malice. I have also occasionally had a student convince me of his or her innocence where the match really was a slight one.

During the writing process it is taken for granted that your contents will reflect a mix of your prior knowledge and what you have learned by reading sources—and listing them in your end-text references sufficiently credits these sources. You also don't need to cite information where there is a reasonable expectation that everyone knows it (World War I ended in 1918, e-mail means electronic mail); nor do you need to cite your analyses or opinions, for the reader knows they are yours.

But you must indicate specific data or verbal/textual sequences which you did not create, and where there isn't a reasonable expectation that the reader knows this. You need to cite, both so that the reader can find the source to obtain more information if wished, and to protect yourself from accusations of plagiarism. Most people would not already know this:

Postwar trading was tumultuous for the Belgians, but there was a noticeable pattern between 1919-29 regarding the differing trade fortunes, depending on whether one was a victor, loser, or neutral nation (Pym 63).

Reproducing this verbatim in your paper would be outright credit theft of Pym's words; but even explaining this specific observation in your own, without citing Pym, might be 'gray' plagiarism. It is possible but improbable that numerous sources all somehow stated this same conclusion independently.

Fortunately, it is easy to cite if you are in doubt, and it's unlikely anyone will complain that you are over-citing. The latter is definitely the lesser of two dangers; your professor or editor can always advise that you remove frivolous citations, but inadequate attribution is a far more dangerous matter.

For another example, consider this original text and the different forms a writer could reuse them in.

Original Text [from pg. 16 of a book by Avery]
Although the official pronouncements of the immigration branch in this period stressed that only farmers, farm laborers, and domestics would be recruited, exceptions were frequently made to accommodate the needs of businessmen in the expanding sectors of the prairie economy.

Good Use of Direct Quotation
Although immigration directors instructed that "only farmers, farm laborers, and domestics would be recruited, exceptions were frequently made to accommodate the needs of businessmen" (Avery 16).

Bad: Plagiarism
Although the official pronouncements of the immigration branch in this period stressed that only farmers would be recruited, exceptions were frequently made to accommodate the needs of businessmen.

The bad example is plagiarism because it's a direct copy from the original, with no source cited.

This is fine because the author has been credited, and the words from the source are indicated by quotation marks.

Bad: 'Gray' Plagiarism
Even though the public statements of the immigration officials stated that only farmers and house maids would be accepted, allowances were often made for business needs.

This is gray plagiarism, or semi-plagiarism if you prefer, because some words have been changed to make the text look different, but the statement still has the same information, phrasing, and sequence as the original source. It would be better to use a paraphrase quotation:

Good Use of Paraphrase
Although immigration managers wished to exclusively accept agricultural and domestic laborers to the new country, they often needed to make exceptions for the growing needs of business (Avery 16).

This is good because the information has been rephrased in the writer's own words but still cited.

Common Questions

Question #1: You think you're so smart! What if I buy a paper from a black-market website that does quote and cite correctly? How will you know?

Answer: I may not know—although if other students buy the same paper (the website is run by criminals—why wouldn't it cheat you as well by reselling it?), it may appear in plagiarism software. As well, you've only hurt yourself—you paid tuition (and paid a website) to learn nothing. Do you normally order pizzas and not eat them, and believe you've won?

Question #2: What if a student was so determined to plagiarize that he or she painstakingly changed the words and phrasing of the source and carefully blended it into the paper?

Answer: That student is a fool. High-quality, bulletproof plagiarism would take far more time than writing the paper would. No intelligent thief would spend $5,000 to steal a car which could be bought for $4,000. It's usually easy for me to recognize plagiarism, as it tends to be badly done. I call this Ken's First Rule of Plagiarism: The people capable of plagiarizing well usually don't need to.

Common Knowledge
Well-meaning Question #3: How do I know if something is common knowledge?

Unfortunately, as with plagiarism, there is no clear boundary on what is considered common knowledge. One current definition is, any piece of information in multiple sources independent of each other. Another criterion used is whether the information can be found in a reference source, such as a dictionary or Wikipedia. A good rule of thumb is to ask whether your peers would commonly know this information. It is specificity and rarity that often are danger signs, where the information is so precise that no one would be expected to know it.

I can only reassure you that, if you honestly have good intentions, common knowledge and plagiarism are going to be less of a problem in your postgraduate writing than you might expect. The punishment distribution of plagiarism is not equal—blatant, defiant plagiarism at a faculty or dissertation level may incinerate your academic career in a day, but a young undergraduate who gets confused and quotes a clause from SparkNotes improperly might only get a scolding. Most professors are not monsters, and try to determine how intentional and serious the plagiarism is.

As well, again, if in doubt: cite; there is little risk of over-citing, and superfluous citations can always be removed. A writer also has the right to optional citation here and there where it isn't necessary, but is a helpful aid for the reader in identifying the source—you might cite a Biblical proverb or popular expression, or a source discussed broadly in your paper with a "for more information see x" footnote/endnote.

Examples of probable common knowledge:
1. Tom is angry when he discovers Daisy is having an affair with Gatsby, hypocritically excusing his own.
2. Shakespeare was born in 1564 and died in 1616.
3. Julie Andrews played the young heroine in *The Sound of Music*. Much of it was filmed in Salzburg.
4. Most people don't want spam e-mail.

Information which is probably not common knowledge, and should be cited:
1. The last names of the visitors to Gatsby's parties subtly reflect the ethnic discrimination of the period, as the Anglo-French names come from East Egg and the minority ones come from West Egg.
2. William Shakespeare's last signatures are shaky, suggesting that he had arthritis or possibly even a sexually transmitted disease, as some speculate.
3. Shaw may have based Henry Higgins in *Pygmalion* on a real-life linguistics professor named Henry Sweet, also known for his explosive temperament.
4. Spam e-mail was named for a 1970 episode of *Monty Python's Flying Circus*, where a sketch features Vikings repetitively singing "spam" without any meaning.

Questionable cases:
1. The European common market did not originally allow free movement of labor.
2. Japan's problems were exacerbated by the earthquake's proximity to nuclear power plants, a large source of electricity for a nation with few natural energy sources.
3. It's proverbially said to be better to live on the edge of a roof

than inside with a nagging wife.
4. Home 8mm movie film was shot by running one side of 16mm film through the camera lens, and then flipping the reel to shoot the other side. In developing, the film was sliced down the middle and joined up.

These last questionable cases are likely matters of personal discernment, depending on how familiar you believe your readers are with the content. I would voluntarily give a citation for the third (Prov. 25.24) to help them find it. Before the 2011 earthquakes in Japan, its power plants weren't commonly known about, but they are now—and in ten years this information may again need citation. As well, an Asian readership and a Scandinavian readership probably have different knowledge levels about Japan. The latter might appreciate the citation.

Popular knowledge varies and evolves, indicating again that such issues can be frustratingly subjective ones. But demonstrably good intentions do mean something, and you are not alone—your professors who write are in the same position as you are regarding this matter.

Is ChatGPT or AI Generators Plagiarism?

Is using an AI platform to write your paper plagiarism? Probably not in a technical sense. The legalities of AI-written text are still being worked out, but AI-text isn't currently considered plagiarism because it isn't a person. But its commonality with plagiarism is that you are taking credit, perhaps in a literal sense, for text you did not create. Your professor's job is to assess whether you learned the writing skills to justify course accreditation toward a degree program or profession.

9 EDITING

Substitute *damn* every time you're inclined to write *very*; your editor will delete it and the writing will be just as it should be. — Mark Twain

Cut out all these exclamation points. An exclamation point is like laughing at your own joke. — F. Scott Fitzgerald

9.1 Rest Before Editing

Let's return to our trinity of the steps of academic writing: planning, writing, and editing—and focus on the last step. It also moves in mysterious ways. But editing is an effective and underappreciated way of improving your writing. Editing is the 'secret sauce' that can make a difference between a workable and an excellent paper.

I will assume in this chapter you are editing yourself. But professional academics, novelists, and journalists typically also interact with external editors. Some seasoned writers have egos and especially need someone to reign in their excesses. As a copy-editor I have encountered senior experts in a field with an "I'm too busy for details; that's for the little people" attitude. No one is too important to edit, however serious your subject and high-level your discourse is; the reader will have the impression that your writing feels disorganized or unfinished, whoever you are.

Mediocre writers approach writing as a one-step process. One concept I teach my students regularly is that of diminishing returns. This refers to the fact that output at a certain point does not always match input due to external factors. For example, if you have a bakery that makes 100 loaves of bread in 6 hours, the bakery might make 200 loaves in 12 hours but not necessary 300 loaves in 18 hours, or 400 in 24. At a certain point output starts to fall because of efficiency limitations such as supply or labor. Similarly, the sixth snack you eat will not be as tasty as the first, even though the snacks are the same.

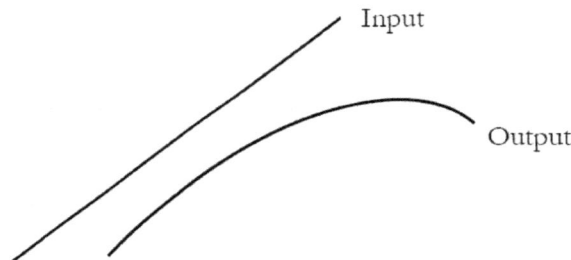

Fig. 1. Law of diminishing returns

I find this law also applies to studying, researching, and writing. If you work on your paper for six hours you might achieve 6x, but working on your paper for 12 hours does not mean you will accomplish 12x. For the last few hours, you will likely have trouble concentrating. You might even only accomplish 5x, muddling together what you earlier learned or planned. This is why I tend not to sympathize with students who protest how they stayed up all night and put in so many hours on their papers. This isn't an efficient practice, and readers and journals don't know and don't care how long you spent writing. What matters is the paper's quality.

Similarly, a skill you should be developing as a writer (as well as for many life tasks) is time efficiency, and my experience is that the steps of writing and editing shouldn't be done on the same day. Unless the writing task is brief, such as a few paragraphs, it would be better to leave it and sleep, or at least do something else for a few hours, before coming back fresh. I find my brain works like a computer's hard drive in that I can't quickly switch between write mode and read mode, or 'edit mode.' Perhaps your brain is an SSD, but mine isn't.

The reason I use this analogy is that in the editing stage we tend to view the paper as a prospective reader, and the task involved is scanning the text to anticipate and troubleshoot potential problems. When you return to your paper after some time away from it you will see things that you did not when you were too close to your text. As well, recall that when writing a paper you know all its contents, but the reader learns it only as it is read. Because the reader doesn't know all of the parts of the paper when beginning it, he or she experiences it differently from the writer. Seeing your paper from that viewpoint is a good conceptual approach to beginning editing.

Writing It: Slow and Steady, or Git 'r Done?

I haven't conveyed much about the actual activity of writing, but here it relates directly to editing. I mention a few times in this tome that should you not be a person who writes introductions well, it's no crime to lay down placer text for that section, write the body and conclusion, and then return to re-write or improve your introduction. What if you were to do this with the entire paper—that is, to quickly type out a rough version, and then go back to fill out and repair the essay? Studio musicians do something similar to this, in that they may lay down a "guide vocal"—a temporary singing track, which allows them to record instruments around it, later erasing and replacing the guide vocal with a better recording.

I have tried both approaches: of rapidly writing a rough form of a paper with minimal quoted evidence or finish, doing heavy editing later; and of carefully going slowly through, with comparatively less editing later. It is one of the benefits of word processors that the first option is easier to do than in the old days of editing pens and correction fluid. I am not sure which workflow is better, and suspect it as usual comes down to individual personality. It feels like a cop-out to write this, and I imagine readers scoffing, there he goes again with the everyone-is-different fluff to avoid giving an answer; but it is true that our writing personalities differ, and our writing topics differ. I also know that I'm not even consistent in how I write on any given day.

I suspect the advantage to writing a loose version of your paper quickly and doing more editing later is that it builds confidence, particularly if the project is difficult or intimidating. Even though I know that 400 words a day of fairly-finished text is better than 1,000 words of slap-dash work, seeing a completed paper structure feels good. The downside is that returning and doing close editing may take longer overall. Conversely, crawling deliberately through the paper may allow closer concentration and focus as you mull over every word and quote; but you may end up spending too much time on small details and lose the larger picture of the essay. I am not criticizing either style if it works, and thinking about how you write is usually a beneficial activity which will make future projects easier.

I do have two caveats. One is the false assumption that slamming down text will overall finish the project faster. It may or may not, for the reasons I've listed—you may spend longer fleshing in and amending text. A second is to again be wary of the romantic notion that working hurriedly in a brilliant passion is somehow more authentic or 'real.' This is perhaps so if you're a beat poet, and I have conceded that all writing has some artistic dimensions, but overall this isn't really a mindset for an academic paper on mitochondrial pairs or consubstantiation.

Overall, as I've alluded to before, my experience with STEM writing is that more advance preparation work is involved, for experiments must be run and analyzed; but the actual write-up is quicker, for such papers are more formulaic in sequence. In comparison, humanities papers usually require few lab days, but arguments must typically be more thoroughly planned and defended in text. There may be less difference in a scientific paper between Slow and Steady or Git 'r Done approaches, or other styles. I know this may annoy some readers or inspire a flurry of exceptions. Nevertheless, if experimentation is valuable in a laboratory, experimentation with writing techniques should also be worthwhile.

9.2 Two Levels of Editing

Now that I have advised when you should edit, let's elaborate on some strategies for how to edit, and divide the task into two broader goals or levels.

The first purpose in editing is obvious. Much of editing is fixing and correcting mistakes. You might get out of bed and go to your computer and read your work and find grammatical errors; you may express wonderment or disgust at carelessly missing a period or misspelling a word, or having a vague pronoun reference, or seeing paragraphs that do not make sense or connect. A claim or discussion point might be duplicated, or missing.

This level of editing is an important and valid activity, and I'm not denigrating it. It is easy to write the following late at night, as most word processor grammar checkers will not recognize the issue:

More case studies on Facebook use in Asian countries are needed to understand the phenomenon in libraries worldwide (Aharony, 2014; Ho, 2019). Therefore, the study tries to fill the research gap by analyzing the use of Facebook as a connecting tool

But what is "the study"—your paper, or that of Aharony or Ho? It is obvious to you, but not necessarily to the reader. It would be better to edit to this:

Therefore, this present study tries to fill the research gap by analyzing the use of Facebook as a connecting tool

In my writing classes I normally make students read their papers out loud in peer-editing groups. This is done partly to build cohesion in the group by having everyone literally on the same page, for there is something primal in how we respond to being read to. But it is also because for many people, their ears notice things their reading eyes don't. Nearly all languages originated as speech, and sometimes things sound wrong that we don't observe in silent reading. Your audience may notice errors where what seemed obvious to you is not to others; or where a term you assumed everyone knew turns out to require explanation or definition. If you have no group or you feel shy you can still try reading your paper out loud to yourself when alone—to notice whether your own ears catch mistakes you didn't previously see.

Again, amending mistakes is important. But ninja-level editing is making the paper *better*. This involves improving your text by moving around text, tightening and bolstering arguments and evidence, and crucially, clearing out dead wood. Editing sometimes means making the text longer, by adding more content. But the more usual mindset of high-level editing is, as the modernists say, "less is more." If you can convey information more clearly and persuasively in the same number of words, or even fewer, that is superior editing.

This doesn't convince everyone, and it is a difficult gestalt for my undergraduates to understand, because they think of writing as getting *up* to a word minimum. If I sometimes use my undergraduates as negative examples, I'm not doing so to make fun of them or condescend, for I was once one too; but if the professor assigned five or ten pages I thought it was a long space to fill. Writers in this frame of thinking are reluctant to take things out because it would make the paper shorter, which is the last thing they want. I can only promise that when you become more experienced and write for post-graduate purposes, you will have a different perspective. You will more typically have an editor who gives you a maximum length. Your thoughts will then be on how you can fit your text within the word limit stated.

This is when editing becomes important in terms of reducing superfluous words, sentences, or paragraphs. When you look at a text segment and realize that it adds nothing or repeats what is said elsewhere, erase it (if the addition or subtraction is significant, you might make a quick note on your outline so that you remember what you did). Editing is sometimes less an intellectual exercise than an emotional one, for you can grow proud or sentimental about what you wrote. But if it is irrelevant or duplicative, or worse, adds needless complexity or potential confusion, it shouldn't be there.

Having said this, brevity is a goal, but not the *ne plus ultra* of writing, and one can overdo it. I mentioned earlier that I dislike the drill-sergeant school of writing instruction, which can give you the false perception that making your writing as joyless and flat as possible is some ethical virtue. At times duplication is good; I stated that sometimes I encapsulate my argument at the start and then expand it at the end of the introduction. I am repeating my thesis by doing so, but I think in that situation there is a reason to. I will waffle a bit here by holding that concision is *usually* optimal, while conceding that accomplished writers may lay in digressions or flourishes and make them work. But these are exceptional situations for calculated effect, not an excuse for sloppy writing. When you are Picasso, you can flout the rules.

9.3 Cutting the Dead Wood

Cutting excess text can happen at the paragraph, sentence, or word level. For example, the following may feel lofty or grand to the reader, but contain redundant information:

I firmly believe that x is y
We can only conclude that x is y
One can assume that generally x is y

Who else believes this but you? Your cat didn't write the paper, and the reader already assumes that the paper's opinions are yours, unless you are citing those of others. I did mention that there are times to hedge or to appear less overconfident. But this statement otherwise might be easily replaced by: x is y.

This is also a good occasion to speak about the dreaded "I" in academic writing.

The Infamous "I"

From the way it is described by some academics and manuals, students may feel that using 'I' or 'we' in professional writing will bring the essay police to their door. I discussed this briefly in the section on evidentiary pathos, but again, using personal pronouns in writing is variously acceptable in different fields and geographies. I find if I submit a paper to an American journal with 'I' references the editors or copy editors will storm and gripe and make me remove them, but this is less so with a UK or European journal. French academic writing commonly has many personal interjections and references, and is less concerned with the Anglo-cultural mania for authorial objectivity.

Disciplines and subjects also vary in frequency of personal pronoun references. They will be rare or nonexistent in a conservative field such as history or law, but occasionally plurals (*we*) appear in science papers, which are often group-written and employ "we applied Bromley's theory" phrasings. Some social science and STEM fields even use 'we' for a single-authored paper, again on the supposition that writing 'I' is a hanging offense. Composition theory scholarship itself is very lenient with personal pronouns, reflecting the aforementioned confessional or emotional style of much 1970's discourse, as well as the fact that writing tends to be a private and reflective activity that meshes with a personal approach. I use 'I' references throughout this book, but would only do so in my papers on literary texts very sparingly, and probably average about once a paper.

Thus, *caveat scriptor*—let the writer beware of the varying cultural or disciplinary tolerances for personal pronouns. But it might also be helpful to discuss this as an editing issue. At a broader content level, overusing *I/we* can tempt the writer into forgetting about the subject and writing about oneself, as noted. I also find it can be pretentious, and in much recent scholarship I see the annoying repetition of the trendy phrase "we argue that x is y." I also find it confusing when multiple aims to the paper are continually stated. Which one of these numerous things "we argue" is the paper's thesis?

As well, to return to my earlier point, personal pronouns often are redundant, and this is why I treat it here as an editing concern. They may commit the further editing sin of wasting space, for it may be perfectly obvious to the reader that it's you who feels x is y.

~~I am curious why~~ Miss Kenton in *Remains of the Day*, who is such an accomplished career woman, is frustrated when her maid Lisa runs away from Darlington Hall. ~~I think that~~ this is because of the emotional personality of Miss Kenton, of course, but ~~I also think~~ there are more factors that make her frustrated. For example, the two women are different in their attitudes about the men they love. ~~So I wanted to write that~~ there are two basic reasons which make Miss Kenton frustrated: her disappointment at Lisa's elopement after she believed in her, and her romantic failures in comparison to Lisa's success in love. ~~I will write about how~~ these three factors need to be discussed by comparing Miss Kenton and Lisa to the footman and Mr. Stevens.

Here is an example of *I-itis*. The constant interjection of the writer into the discussion drags the focus away from the novel and towards the writer. These 'I' phrases add little information and can be deleted, with perhaps a bit of smoothing text. The result will be tighter and stronger.

What about Passives?

Just like the belief that *I/we* in academic writing is bad form, the idea that passive phrasings in English are also pure evil persists. But passive constructions have been used in English for centuries, and have a legitimate use in situations where the agent is unknown or irrelevant. They also are a useful way to avoid personal pronoun references for skittish editors and professors.

60ml of fluid is added to the solution.
220 volts was applied to the device to check its RPM for one minute.

That being said, the passive should not be a default usage in writing; it should be employed where there is a reason. Too many gratuitous passives make the reader tired, as the logic of the sentence needs to be continually reversed in order to interpret it. Passives also can be an editing matter in that they often result in longer text than active ones does: "the cat chases the mouse," is plainer and shorter than "the mouse is chased by the cat," to use a simple illustration.

Unnecessary Dictionary Definitions

I occasionally receive papers beginning with a dictionary definition of the topic or issue at hand. This may be helpful where terms or ideas are obscure ("protein folding, according to science.com, is"), but generally definitions scream "lazy student writer filling in space."

Abortion is, according to Merriam-Webster, "the termination of a pregnancy after, accompanied by, resulting in, or closely followed by the death of the embryo or fetus."

This isn't wrong, but it wastes space. Everyone knows what abortion is, and at worst readers are insulted by feeling the writer is being patronizing. Some students honestly believe that such definitions are an effective way of framing the issue, or of sounding authoritative, and this may be so. But otherwise use dictionary quotations frugally, and chiefly for terms or concepts the reader is unlikely to know about.

Pretentious Introductory Epigrams

Sometimes authors also begin longer papers with a pithy epigram or ironic quotation about their subject, perhaps from a famous novel. This could be done as a standalone sentence before the introduction begins, with or without quotation marks:

But it makes an immigrant laugh to hear the fears of the nationalist, scared of infection, penetration, miscegenation, when

9 EDITING

this is small fry, peanuts, compared to what the immigrant fears - dissolution, disappearance. – Zadie Smith, *White Teeth*

But the quotation could also be embedded within the first sentence of the paper to segue into the discussion, and with fewer words:

In *White Teeth*, author Zadie Smith writes that "it makes an immigrant laugh to hear the fears of the nationalist... compared to what the immigrant fears - dissolution, disappearance." Studies and journalism on mass migration, particularly in light of the recent Syrian conflict, have been

I also really like what one student here with an embedded quote. Instead of a free-standing epigram, the student neatly gets the name of the book and a framing quotation into the first sentence of the paper.

Leah Guenther, in her essay on *Bridget Jones's Diary*, confirms the idea that Bridget cares about her image but also accepts herself as she is, telling us that "while Bridget does censure herself at many points, she is far more likely to absolve herself, to accept herself as flawed and unchanging."

I'm not telling you to avoid standalone epigrams; I've used them in this book. They may sometimes be succinct or poetic leads into the concept about to be discussed, as my quotes at the beginning of this chapter by Twain and Fitzgerald hopefully are. I noted earlier that in my MA thesis on *Beowulf* I had a *Hagar the Horrible* comic starting a chapter, as it described the popular perception of Vikings. I still feel this worked, as it was both relevant and the sudden change in rhetorical seriousness made the chapter more interesting.

But tread carefully, and resist the lure of ladling on aphorisms to give the paper a magisterial look, for instead of adding gravitas the move can backfire and look affected. I once made this mistake in a seminar paper by including:

The past is a foreign country: they do things differently there.
– L. P. Hartley

This looked grand to me; but I have now seen this literary maxim used so many times by every humanities graduate student that it looks tired and clichéd, as though the writer is trying too hard to seem wise. I wonder now if my professor then felt the same, and wince when I occasionally read my thesis. As an editing matter, question whether the epigram frames the paper or looks over-precious, or worse, has the look of padding space.

Rhetorical Question Addiction

Smartphone apps have become popular everywhere. Why are they popular? It is because they allow people to have the benefits of a computer without the size. What are these benefits? The benefit is the ability to receive and send information. Nevertheless, this ability comes with dangers. What dangers? Many young people are addicted to these apps

This can become annoying to the reader as the discursive flow is constantly interrupted. Too many rhetorical questions in your paper can resemble an insistent child who asks 'why' about everything. These sentences also waste space, for the reader is already led by the discussion to anticipate you answering these questions: if you state smartphones apps are popular, of course you will probably analyze why or how. As with my *I/my* references, I probably average one rhetorical question a paper.

How can we edit rhetorical questions out of a paper? Often it's exactly that: we can delete them entirely.

Do you know what MSG is? MSG is an additive which is used to give extra flavor to food.

The text reads just fine without that sentence, and sounds less like an advertisement.

MSG (monosodium glutamate) gives extra flavor to food when used as an additive.

I know in this book I am perhaps showing off with my own papers. Guilty as charged. But I think I employed rhetorical questioning well here in a paper on Huxley's *Brave New World*:

A more recent example is Mel Brooks' *Spaceballs* (1987), where the Darth Vader-like antagonist is introduced by the music and visual cues as powerfully dangerous but struggles to remove his helmet. Similarly, the World State's image as presented by received wisdom is deflated by its incongruities and mundane human foibles.
    Who cares? The reason this is significant for criticism is that it allows interpretation of *Brave New World* and Huxley's technique with a clearer metric, for if the text is judged as darker satire or straightforwardly predictive...

I'm glad I wrote this. The rhetorical question helps signal a shift point in the discussion, it's short, and it gives the discussion "air" by quickly varying the level of seriousness, as did my *Hagar* cartoon.

Verbal as Opposed to 'is' Sentences

I find this next practice difficult to maintain, and may be guilty of breaking it, but you might try replacing static 'is' phrasings with verb-driven sentences that do something. My doctoral advisor disliked 'is' in papers and urged me to reduce them to make my writing leaner. Often this can be done by removing passive constructions, as we did with our mouse sentence, which replaces 'is' with 'chases.' But you can't rephrase "the grass is green" as "the grass hues itself greenly." The result has more words, not fewer, and sounds ridiculous. The goal is to make the sentence more concise while retaining clarity. Sometimes there is no practical alternative to using 'is.'
    But rather than writing "the invention of robot-assisted

surgery is a good thing," we could have "the invention of robot-assisted surgery revolutionizes communication." The second sentence is briefer and has a stronger, more immediate feel. Or, instead of "internet society is changing and this is unsettling for many people," you could have "internet society changes are unsettling for many people." This again is pithier with the same meaning.

Reducing Empty Qualifiers

A related matter is the removing of excess qualifiers.

> orange in color
> the field of medical science
> the game of backgammon

Readers know that orange is a color. Unless these qualifiers have a specific function (or you need to distinguish an orange hue from the fruit), you might discard them: *orange, medical science, backgammon*. The same applies to doubling phrases, which are often banalities.

> each and every
> the last and final
> one and only
> where and when

These phrases can be replaced with *each, the last, the only*, or the second word (*every, final, only*), and will be less likely to bore the writer with verbal clichés.

One technique writer William Zinsser recommends is to scan over your text looking for these filler qualifiers, such as *somewhat, rather*, or *quite*. Sometimes terms need qualification, but these words might add nothing, or even clutter the text or dilute its meaning. Instead of "the sun was somewhat/rather/quite hot," write "the sun was hot."

> Winter is cold.
> The rumor was foolish.
> Prof. Eckert's book is boring.

There will be times to hedge or be tactful, as I will discuss. But these statements all have a direct meaning to which nothing is added with the noncommittal pastel-wash of *somewhat* or *a little*.

Similarly, you might scan, or use your word processor's search and replace function, to find incidences of *very* and then decide whether they are necessary.

> The music was very unpleasant.
> Prof. Eckert's class was very long.
> The argument was very heated.
> The scenery was very pretty.

It's not wrong to write *very*, but there may be places where it adds nothing (you can't be very unique—you are or not), or where a stronger adjective could take its place.

> The music was obnoxious.
> Prof. Eckert's class was interminable.
> The argument was frenzied.
> The scenery was gorgeous.

The overuse of *very* is as annoying as students who feel they are writing for a travel blog and call everything *incredible, fantastic, amazing,* and *the most important*. Not everything requires superlatives. When I assign papers on social issues, I usually receive openings such as "one of the most important issues nowadays is x." If I have 30 papers about different social problems, they can't all be the most important. Some can be merely important and get on with the business at hand.

So far as I know, I have never written an essay with the phrase "as it were." Nor have I ever read a paper in professional life using it where it added anything. It basically means nothing and looks pretentious—exactly what good editing ought to remove. We all have go-to phrases, myself included, that we are fond of. Some of them are apt or powerful, but it is easy to overuse them.

But again I stress, you need not view editing as self-mortification. You can overdo deleting until little remains in your paper but a summary. If you remove all nuances from your diction you might end up with only a shadow left of the original essay with none of its interesting detail or flavor. I tend to like my modifiers and pet phrases. As a private joke, every paper I have ever published has the word "juxtapose" somewhere in it. There are worse infractions.

Latinisms

If I may add or repeat a last quibble, it is with the overuse of *etc.* in formal writing: "We will need such things as eggs, cheese, bread, etc." Here it is redundant. The reader can intuit that the list is not exhaustive, and the "such as" phrase has already indicated this.

There are other Latin abbreviations or acronyms variously used in formal writing:

e.g., *exempli gratia*, for example
i.e., *id est*, that is
etc., *et cetera*, and other things
ibid., *ibidem*, in the same place
viz., *videlicet*, in other words

I have no quibble with these expressions so long as they serve a purpose and are not, as *etc.* often is, overused and littered throughout the text where their meaning is obvious. If the reader can see you are making an example, you may not need *e.g.* as a prefix to it. The last two on the list are likely less familiar—*ibid.* was at one time used in Chicago format to mean "the same source as the last entry in the list." *Viz.* is for some reason popular among East Indian writers, but in North American English is archaic and sounds as though the writer is a Victorian scientist.

Editing Secondary Sources

Your quotations and paraphrases of secondary sources can usually be reduced and made leaner and more efficient by close editing. This may merely involve varying your signal phrasings. Yet often the best results come from paring down the quotation into a key-word citation, removing excess words from the quotation while retaining its essential information. I again need to be careful in admitting that key-word is my favorite style—because it's not always best; but often it is the most efficient.

Weisman has complained about critics who "believe that because I have a certain setting that it necessarily comprises a key to the work" (Jagger 120).

Weisman has complained about critics who assume that the settings of his books are "key to the work" (Jagger 120).

Notice also in my examples I try to avoid using "says" or "according to" *ad nauseum*. Here is a list for which I thank Stephen Brown at UNLV:

writes, argues, contends, states, notes, relates, describes, remarks, asserts, maintains, implies, suggests, holds, mentions, concludes, announces, declares, insists, observes, discusses, relays, finds, surmises, theorizes, ventures

Note that these words are not only variation on "says," but also add nuances. How firmly does the writer of the source endorse the claim? Do you or other experts support or remain skeptical of this writer's viewpoints? It may be helpful to build in this information into the verb used in the signal phrase:

Source text strongly argues	Source text neutrally reports
Finds	Notes

Concludes	Observes
States	Indicates
Asserts	Remarks
Source text only suggests	Source text is controversial or dubious
Posits	Contends
Theorizes	Maintains
Ventures	Insists
Guesses	Holds

All of these convey more than "according to" and signal an attitude to the source. Using such verbs to suggest agreement or doubt in the statement, by you or an academic community, will make your sentences clearer and may allow you to delete a sentence by telegraphing that, for example, most scholars are skeptical of a certain claim.

In editing a quotation, you might reconsider whether it is even necessary to your paper. New writers under-quote out of lack of skill in quoting or researching—but mid-level ones may over-quote because of a lack of confidence in their own ideas, which causes them to cite in support of obvious points. Established senior writers in a field often drift back to fewer but stronger quotations. Quotation is good, and published papers often have more citation density than course essays; but a paper dominated by quotations has little purpose for existing. The reader may as well read the Wikipedia entry.

As a last note, in a more quantitative paper you might also convert plodding lists of data items into a table for word economy—and to be more visually appealing to the reader.

Government statistics show that KTX ridership rose from 37,315,135 in 2007 to 41,348,500 in 2010, while Saemaeul train numbers saw a smaller climb from 10,014,723 to… **x**

Table 1. Number of Railroad Users in Korea

Korea Railroad Statistics (2007-2010)			
	KTX	Saemaeul	Mugunghwa
2007	37,315,135	10,014,723	55,320,438
2008	38,016,405	10,814,239	57,383,295
2009	37,476,940	10,932,361	55,335,056
2010	41,348,500	10,924,731	58,564,906

Source: Ministry of Land, Infrastructure, and Transport

Table 1 indicates healthy increases for KTX and Mugunghwa ridership and a smaller climb for Saemaeul.

Tabular data is frequently seen in social science and STEM papers, and less so in the humanities. But there's nothing wrong with it—and similarly, it might be a more word-concise and attractive way to present brief items. Here I charted the silly faces a character makes in a novel (Kingsley Amis's *Lucky Jim*) to show a progression.

Emotion	Expression	Occasion	Visibility to Others
Suffering	Flushed torment face (8)	Speech by Welch on recorders	Imagined
Suffering	Shot-in-the-back face (27)	Summoned by Mitchie	Hidden
Suffering	Consumptive face (30)	Thinking about contract	Hidden
Disgust	Obscene gestures (56)	Locked out of bathroom	Caught by Margaret
Disgust	Crazy-peasant face (74)	Looking at Welch furniture	Unseen
Disgust	Martian-invader face (91)	Hearing Welch's name called	Hidden
Disgust	Obscene gesture (94)	Christine discussing Bertrand	Hidden
Disgust	Eskimo face (97)	Mitchie and special course	Hidden
Disgust	Edith Sitwell face (102)	Telephoning Bertrand	Hidden
Disgust	Lemon face (141)	Christine discussing Bertrand	Obscured
Contempt	Mandrill face (174)	Watching Welch falling	Open but unseen
Contempt	Obscene gesture (175)	Discussion with Welch	Welch suspicious
Contempt	Angry grimace (179)	Trousers ripped from car	Caught by Welches
Contempt	Lascar face (189)	Telephoning Mrs. Welch	Unseen
Release	Welch, Principal, Nazi trooper (223-6)	Merrie England lecture	Open
Command	Obscene gesture (241)	Bus driver	Open
Playful Joy	Sex Life in Ancient Rome face (250)	Walking with Christine	Open
Playful Joy	Sags as if knifed (251)	Laughing at Welches	Open

9.4 Raising Academic Tone

In the discussion on evaluating sources, I noted that where there is little information about a text's origins, we can make guesses about its value from its vocabulary and sentence complexity. During your editing process it is also possible to cultivate an academic tone by using more scholarly words and phrasings. The goal is not to create marathon strings of unreadably dense clauses, but to cultivate a more authoritative and precise voice. This also applies at an individual word level. I would like to acknowledge Dr. Brown at UNLV again, my own professor in the past, for his advice on this additional editing practice, which he calls "upgrading your diction."

It can be dismaying to see some of the verbal sophistication and complexity of historic political speeches, and to see how far we have fallen. Not everyone will agree with me, but I lament the contemporary obsession with making speeches plain and folksy—and literally so, for I notice U.S. presidents no longer say 'people': it is always 'folks.' Some leaders seem addicted to the word 'good' in their statements: "We had a good meeting with the French. The treaty is a good one." These are informationally weak sentences, and using *good* repetitively is imprecise and monotonous, as it is with *folks*.

One technique in avoiding such tedious words is replacing them with more precise synonyms (people, citizens, individuals). There is nothing wrong with *good*, and I have used it throughout this book. But where possible, try to use more exact, academic, or interesting words. "We had an *effective* meeting. I knew they were *honest* people. The treaty will be *advantageous*." Instead of "Overpopulation is a big problem," describe it as a *serious, critical, dangerous, worsening, treatable, perennial* problem. *Nice* is tepid and vague (unless you mean "a nice distinction," a precise one); instead, x was *considerate, thoughtful*, or *obliging*. As you pass through your paper, look for those words which are flat or dull and change them, using a thesaurus or your word processor's search-and-replace function.

One caveat is that a better word is not necessarily the longest or most obscure or difficult one. The goal is precision and clarity, not pedantry. Imagine Martin Luther King saying "I harbor custody of a personal aspiration." That has nowhere near the same rhetorical impact as "I have a dream." I suppose my point is that your vocabulary should match your audience; a more intellectual-sounding lexicon may sound authoritative, but overdoing it may confuse the reader, or seem pretentious. I remember encountering someone on an internet forum years ago who deliberately used inflated diction ("this lugubrious and sesquipedalian bifurcation has been an inchoate and jocose coruscation") to intimidate people. But this didn't convince others, as they couldn't understand him, and people finally called him out on this ploy and he was discredited.

Second, if you are using an electronic dictionary or app to find replacements, be careful about false or partial synonyms. I remember a Mexican friend asking me, "How much do you win at work?" She had typed in Spanish *ganar*, which translates to both *win* and *earn* in English (cognate with *gain*). Similarly, I had a student write that she was going to meet her *paramour*. The dictionary gave this as a synonym for *boyfriend*. But *paramour* in English has an archaic nuance suggesting a secret lover, or someone you are having an affair with. A good dictionary will tell you these nuances.

9.5 Sexist Writing

Some of the nonsexist terms innovated in the 1980s have not aged well— "waitperson" sounds silly, and "herstory" is largely now used ironically (Old English used *tale*; Greek *historia*, ἱστορία, had nothing to do with *his* or maleness). Conversely, I have almost given up insisting that 'mankind' is historically a unisex term—in Old English if one specifically wanted to denote a male, *wer* or *guma* was used (modern English 'werewolf' and 'groom').

Yet the use of gender pronouns in academic writing deserves consideration. Using 'he' and 'his' exclusively in examples and analogies was once acceptable but is now seen as marginalizing female readers. To be honest, my first response to reading Graff and Birkenstein's *They Say / I Say* was annoyance, as the authors seem to prefer female authors for text samples, and whenever a fictive example of bad writing is presented, it is inevitably by a male. Yet while this sort of political correctness makes me feel disregarded, I can see this is how some women may feel when reading books with endless male references.

Some languages don't normally indicate pronouns, and the issue is avoided. But how can we avoid them in English? Some writers sensitive to this issue use *s/he* or a similar form, or alternate between 'he' and 'she' examples. Singular *they/them* is also becoming more common. Using 'one' ("one must remember to improve oneself") works but its overuse can rapidly feel awkward or affected.

These are controversial waters, and I'm staying out of them. You may encounter professors or editors with firm ideological beliefs or rules on this. But I will approach sexist writing as an editing matter: if you can convey information equally clearly, why grammatically state any gender if you don't have to?

An engineer must see his ethical responsibilities.

You could pluralize:
Engineers must see their ethical responsibilities.

Or, you could rephrase with a passive construction:
Ethical responsibilities must be seen by engineers.

Or, you could rephrase with no pronouns:
Engineering ethics must be recognized.
An engineer must see ethical responsibilities.

Both sentences in this last group are slightly briefer, communicate the same idea, and are less likely to give offense.

9.6 Peer Editing

Peer editing isn't the same as peer review, a term you may have encountered which refers to formal evaluation of a finished paper submitted for publication. Peer editing means exactly that, submitting your working draft to a small group of people at your skill level who will read the work and comment on it.

I often assign peer editing in my classes toward the end of the semester, and there's no reason that students can't meet informally at any time to read each other's work and make constructive criticisms. Why do I do this, when grading papers should be *my* job? The activity is a way of preparing for future career situations where the all-knowing professor isn't there, as well as a means of showing that the professor isn't all-knowing—sometimes students have equally valid opinions, or have subject knowledge the instructor doesn't. This can easily happen in my graduate classes where members belong to outside departments such as sciences and engineering.

Constructive criticism does not mean polite evasion ("everything looks wonderful") any more than it means cruelty ("your paper is stupid and pointless"). It means comments meant in good faith to improve your paper or your writing:

> I like this part.
> I don't understand this argument.
> Maybe this paragraph would be better here.
> I know a website that talks about this.
> Why not use this example here?
> Who is the 'they' here?

If you are shy about critiquing someone else's work your group might consider making the evaluations through e-mail or a blog site (I suppose this could be done anonymously, but I feel that would be asking for trouble). Where possible I let students choose their own groups so that they work with people they trust. I don't know why, but in my experience groups of three or four people work best. Pairs do work, but beyond four or five, members become nervous and feel they have to 'perform'; or the group fragments into sub-groups.

Group peer editing of course doesn't mean that the group co-writes the paper. When I worked in a campus writing center as a doctoral candidate, the most frustrating undergraduate students were those who wanted to drop off their essay and have us 'fix' it for them by the next day when they pick it up. The purpose of the writing center is to improve the writer, not the writing—this act of cheating would defeat the purpose of the assignment, just as doing your friends' mathematics problems doesn't help them to learn. But my experience is that most people are instinctively aware when this line has been crossed; the paper no longer feels like something you made.

My experience is also that peer editing is quite binary, and works either well or badly. When the latter happens, it may be from lack of motivation, but it's more typical that students are so leery of offending anyone that they say nothing of value, or the session deteriorates into a superficial and too-safe grammar-check. For this reason I reiterate that reading papers out loud is more effective, for the shared experience bonds the group together. There really is something ancient and deep in us which loves being read to. I have also noticed that peer editing someone else's paper improves your own writing by making you think about the rules you reflexively but unthinkingly apply to others.

I actually find that paper drafts in the later stages of writing, but not finished, respond best to peer editing—thus the distinction between peer editing and review. While bringing half a paragraph or a fuzzy idea to a peer review will not accomplish much, as counterintuitive as it sounds, I find that completed papers also don't result in much productive help for the writer. My suspicion is that when we see the paper as done, we feel a sense of closure or pride, and become defensive or resistant to suggestions that we alter it.

I once had a graduate student who was so pleased with the help he received during peer editing that he asked if he could cite me and his fellow students in his dissertation. This normally isn't necessary, but academics do thank others for editing help in their acknowledgements in published articles or books, something I have done after particularly thoughtful feedback. We're human, and it can be hard to accept that the critiques others give us are well-meant. Academic writing also involves interpersonal skills—more on this soon. For now, it is time to more formally examine the longer thesis/dissertation project and workflow.

10 SEMINAR PAPER & DISS SECTIONS

We're now at a point in the book where the five-paragraph model is too simple—and remember that I have repeatedly stated it is only an abstraction which we can scale up. I could have gradually introduced formal paper components such as literature reviews and methodology sections, but this may have been confusing by covering too many topics at one time. This chapter now discusses these advanced elements. Writers of an honors thesis or graduate thesis/dissertation will need to be familiar with them, not only because your professor or department may require them, but because planning a long paper may be easier when multiple smaller portions are specified and accomplished.

In short, this chapter discusses the structural parts of a paper in the 20-30 page ballpark, such as for a graduate course, with the understanding that most of these terms and concepts will apply identically to thesis/dissertation chapters and published articles when we discuss them.

MLA

Unless your department or journal specifies otherwise, a typical MLA humanities paper consists of the following section options. MLA is comparatively laissez-faire on these sections, however; some may or may not be included according to the writer's needs, and the use of explicit headings is often a matter of personal preference.

1. Title page (although strict MLA doesn't have one)

2. Table of contents
3. Abstract
4. Introduction (usually with a thesis statement somewhere)
5. Background information or definitions
6. Literature review
7. Main body (for some reason, seldom actually *called* this)
8. Conclusions
9. Acknowledgements
10. Works Cited list
11. Tables and appendices

APA/IEEE

A typical paper in a social sciences or science/engineering discipline will have most of the following sections, although the selection will also vary according to the writer's purposes. Again, I know why the caged bird sings: APA/IEEE paper structuring is in some ways easier because there are fewer decisions to make than with MLA, where you may need to reason out or justify divisions. Reflecting the disciplinary culture of social sciences and STEM, APA/IEEE have a longer and more prescriptive list of sections and explicit headings (e.g. "LITERATURE REVIEW").

1. Title page
2. Table of contents
3. Abstract
4. Introduction (establish a problem, or gap in knowledge; indicate the paper's purposes and how it will accomplish them, possibly via a set of questions)
5. Background information (terminology and basic ideas/history needed to understand the topic)
6. Literature review (leading sources/studies/experts on the topic)
7. Methodology (principles underlying paper's methods), and/or Methods (explanation of how data were collected or analyzed
8. Results and discussion (the main body of the essay)

9. Conclusions (defend the importance of what was done; note limitations and recommendations for future research)
10. Acknowledgements (thank people and funders who helped)
11. References list
12. Tables and appendices

As an example of an introduction section, the following is a fairly difficult-level excerpt from an engineering paper.

1. INTRODUCTION

For construction material, concrete is the cheapest, least time-consuming material. As current structures require higher durability and strength, supplementary cementitious materials (SCMs) have been used for decades. But the supply of conventional SCMs is limited due to transportation fees between production and construction sites, and because of limited sources, prices are rising. For such nations willing to reduce CO_2 emissions and costs, development of new materials which can replace conventional SCMs is vital.

Ferronickel slag is a byproduct from nickel and stainless-steel alloys which are mostly landfilled and cause environmental contamination. Annual worldwide production of ferronickel slag (FNS) is more than 30 million tons [1]. 30 tons of ferronickel slag are obtained from 1 ton of nickel production. Therefore, application of ferronickel powder as cementitious material is an emerging issue to reduce CO_2 emission in concrete manufacture and disposal cost of the ferronickel slag.

In this paper, blast furnace ferronickel slags varying in fineness were used to ensure physical properties and chemical resistance of the concrete, then the hydration process and microstructure of ferronickel slag concrete were analyzed using several microscopes.

Note how this introduction fulfills point four in the list above—it establishes a problem and explains how the paper will show a solution to it.

10.1 Section Headings

The above text is a section heading—ironically, one that says 'section heading.' Do you need to explicitly have section titles (headings) in a longer paper, or can your essay divisions be assumed by the reader? Much of this is up to the writer's discretion, and again, they're more common in APA/IEEE. A paper could have headings like this:

4. BANKING REFORM

Essentially, banking reform needs to be implemented at a multinational level if it is to be effective.

4.1 Case Study

While the modern banking system is in fact centuries old, most literature until the eighteenth century still focused on the practice of usury. It is worthwhile to examine the Croydon affair of 1802

Or a paper might continue to the case study in a new paragraph with no heading, trusting that the reader will follow your lead:

Essentially, banking reform needs to be implemented at a multinational level if it is to be effective.
 While the modern banking system is in fact centuries old, most literature until the eighteenth century still focused on the practice of usury. It is worthwhile to examine the Croydon affair of 1802.

Scientific papers may have an even larger number of nested and hierarchical headings to mark complex sets of tests, tables, and results. I sometimes see divisions in APA papers that would not be made in an MLA one:

2.3 Literature Gap

Even in MLA there are a few standard divisions which are

normally marked—title, abstract, acknowledgement, and works cited sections. But other headings are optional or reflect practices within your field or department (I notice Korean journals, even English-language ones, use more than western ones do). You may feel it is important to signpost a discursive switch in the paper's direction, or you may decide that the transition is clear and a heading will waste space.

I try to be sensitive to these disciplinary cultures, but I have graded papers where I felt the meta-commentary was overdone, where there was such a tangle of headings on every page that it crowded out the text. Reading papers like this is tiring, because the reader needs to continually stop and process another frivolous title, fragmenting the text into endless trivial sub-sub-sections. This also may give the impression that the writer is filling space with superfluous divisions. I cannot specify a rule, but to me more than two or three headings per page seems excessive.

MLA Headings

If you wish to use explicit MLA headings, their typography is not strict but is conventionally as follows. As with citation practices, remember that this typography may change in later updates of MLA style.

If numbered, there's no special formatting:

1. The Early Crusades
1.1 Theology and Practice
1.1.1 Saladin and Negotiations

If not numbered:

Level 1: bold, flush left
Level 2: italics, flush left
Level 3: centered, bold

The crusades

Theology and practice
Saladin and negotiations

APA Headings

APA *always* marks titles, abstracts, and references with explicit headings, and usually does so with literature reviews, discussion, and conclusion sections. Other sections can be marked as you wish, such as "Case Study 1: Malaysia"—or, as ever, there may be (annoying) departmental or in-house journal variations on such rules.

Introduction sections should not be marked with a heading, as of APA 6, as they are obvious, but writers seem to insist on using them anyway—it will be interesting to see if APA style in future gives up and permits or specifies them. You can still list an introduction in your table of contents if you wish.

If you use them, APA's headings are as follows:

Title or Level 1: Centered Boldface
Level 2 Heading is Left-Justified Boldface
Level 3 Heading is Boldface Italics

Proposed Method
Language Models for Category Selection
Problems With Acquisition Measurement

Some writers ALL-CAPS the first-level heading (PROPOSED METHOD), although this is non-standard APA. APA also directs that writers not put numbers before section headings:

3. PROPOSED METHOD
3.1. Language Models for Category Selection
3.1.1. *Problems with Acquisition Measurement*

—although writers often do it anyway, particularly when there is an extensive nest of multiple-level headings that may confuse readers.

The first paragraph after a new section heading isn't indented, as you can see in this book. Often new paragraphs after a table or figure are also not indented. This of course is redundant if you skip-a-line instead between paragraphs.

"Compressed" Grammar in Headings

As with newspaper headlines, academic paper headings often employ a "compressed" or minimal grammar, with articles and some prepositions removed:

3.1. The Features of the Demographics of the Respondents **x**

It would be better to shorten this:

3.1. Respondents' Demographic Features

10.2 Abstracts

An abstract is a brief summary of your paper's content, arguments, and findings. Abstracts are *not* a part of your paper; they go before the paper, usually on a separate page—although sometimes I see them in printed journals on the same page, or even after the paper. Usually the abstract is a single paragraph in block form without indentation. The length depends on the editor or department, but abstracts are typically 100-200 words in the humanities, and perhaps twice as long in social sciences or hard sciences, where there might be multiple paragraphs.

In academic writing the abstract is important because many readers view the abstract to decide if the paper is worth reading. As well, on some websites or online article databases the *abstract* may be freely available to view, but the paper isn't. The abstract is thus an important tool not only because words from it may be indexed in search engines, but because viewers might be inspecting it to judge whether or not to seek out the paywalled full-text. This is one reason citations are almost never in an abstract—the reader may not have access to their references.

In business or political or economic policy papers the abstract may be called an executive summary. An executive summary often has bullet points or other non-sentence elements, and is longer—as much as 10% of the length of the paper. Naturally, in different disciplines practices vary, and a science or engineering abstract might emphasize the experiment process or the applicability of the results obtained in a more regimented form. Typically, a STEM abstract is also a bit longer and may have marked-out divisions for research questions (R1, R2), a statement of research gap or problem, an overview of methodology applied, and findings.

Again, a common error in abstract writing is to assume it replaces the introduction, and that the information in the abstract need not be repeated in the paper. I have seen theses where this happened—where the introduction lacked key information, because the writer assumed that these details were already covered. Once again remember that the abstract is not technically a section of your paper, but more like a synopsis preceding it—and in some journals it is placed at the *end* of the paper.

I discussed earlier how introductions and conclusions differ in their temporal perspectives, by looking forward or back. It might be helpful to visualize an abstract as looking out at the entire paper.

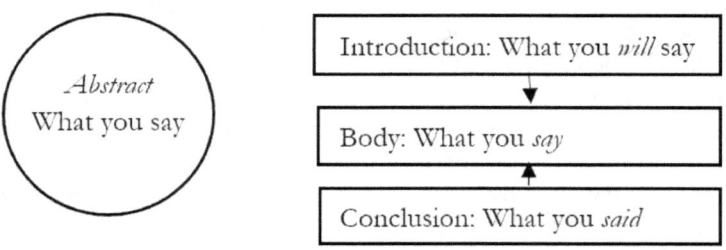

To use an imperfect analogy, before movies start at the theater you will see trailers for upcoming films. These trailers highlight the movie's attractions in order to entice people to view them, but they aren't part of the actual movie—they don't replace portions of the film itself, and no movie would begin assuming its introduction is unnecessary because people have already seen the trailer and know the setup.

This analogy is only useful up to a point, as a movie trailer would not tell you the ending of the story, whereas a good abstract states a paper's key conclusions, or at least provides a useful summary. Some weak abstracts report the paper's outward structure in list form but do not speak substantively to the paper's information: "The article has an introduction, literature review, discussion, and relevant conclusion section, along with recommendations." Thanks for that.

Here is a short abstract based on a paper I wrote as an undergraduate about Japanese civilian internments in Canada during World War II:

Bitterness over atrocities committed by enemy nations during World War II led to resentment of immigrants from those countries, explaining the hostility toward Japanese citizens in Canada during the war. Yet were the Japanese interned for reasons of national security or merely to gratify a desire for revenge? The same question applies to the German inhabitants of Canada at that time. This paper seeks to examine why the German internments happened, and provides a historical overview and analysis.

This abstract is doable but not optimal, because it merely lists the paper's sections and does not even answer the main question posed. There are few specific terms likely to be indexed by a search engine. Similar to my advice on thesis statements, don't try to build suspense in an abstract—recap its arguments and basic findings. Note what I have appended here in a revision and expansion.

…This paper seeks to examine why the German internments happened, and provides a historical overview and analysis. In brief, the period evidence suggests that whereas the Japanese internments were driven by racism and xenophobia, the restraints placed on German Canadians stemmed from a perceived Nazi threat rather than prejudice.

This addition isn't better merely because the abstract is now longer, but because it's now better—it summarizes the findings and reasons regarding the questions asked. A reader is more likely to become curious about the paper's discussion and read it, even if he or she disagrees with the position taken.

I have had students ask if it is acceptable to copy and paste sentences from their papers into their abstracts—whether doing so is repetitive, or is in fact a form of plagiarism. I don't see any professional or ethical problem with re-using sentences, although I always end up altering them anyway to suit the needs and length boundaries of the abstract. 100-200 words may seem like a decent-sized space, but here your editing skills might need to work the hardest to fit your abstract into a word limit.

Key Words

Many writers append a line immediately after the abstract called "Key Words," where they list 5-7 important terms or topics in their paper for search engines or other indexes. Italicize *keywords* on the line below your abstract and separate terms with commas.

Keywords: European Union, euro, Germany, bailout crisis, economic reform

Examples

The following abstract is for an article I published using the "challenging conventional wisdom" frame, where I disagreed with the majority interpretation of a novel. Notice how the abstract begins by 1) stating the majority critical view; 2) declaring a thesis opposing that view and giving reasons; and 3) stating how the result of this thesis helps to understand the novel. Again, whereas an introduction would clarify what the rest of the paper will be about, this is a précis of what the whole paper is about.

Juan Rulfo's *Pedro Páramo* has been read as archetype, capitalist critique, or modernist surrealism. Its religious interpretations have generally seen the novel as pessimistic and its characters damned. However, the text gains clarity and religious meaning once Comala is understood as a Christian purgatory with an indeterminate geography, physicality, and time, and we realize that Juan arrives already physically dead. Some of the novel's characters spiritually stagnate or decline, as does Pedro Páramo and Rentería, but others are purified and attain self-understanding, as do Dorotea and Juan. Climactically, Susana's death and salvation affirms the purgatorial aspect of Comala as Páramo's defeat results in his dissolution and regeneration for the town's inhabitants.

Keywords: Rulfo, Pedro Páramo, Christian purgatory, modernist literature, death literature

Here is a graduate student's abstract for a paper on second language acquisition.

In the second language environment, how to acquire a second language has been a main issue for many scholars, and several language acquisition theories exist. This research is based on the Interaction Hypothesis which describes interaction as a major role in SLA. The aim of this research is to demonstrate the effectiveness of interactive education for pre-school children by analyzing IE experiments in classroom environments which contain interactions between child and child, and child and teacher. On the basis of these experiments, IE can be considered as an effective method for SLA for children.

Keywords: interaction, interactive education, language acquisition, L2 acquisition

A final abstract is from an IEEE paper, referenced earlier, on preventing software failure in autonomous vehicles. The IEEE website advises minimizing unusual typography such as mathematical notation, as it may not reproduce correctly on an article database website.

A Cyber-Physical System (CPS) is a system which consists of multiple cyber and physical environments interconnected via a network. System recovery is possible by repositioning the critical mission to another node. In a vehicle system where the safety of passengers is the top priority, safety functions must be uninterrupted, and a fault-tolerant system is needed to guarantee that the safety of passengers is not threatened by sudden unintended acceleration or stop shorts. Although a conventional fault-tolerant system uses a highly reliable backup system, it is expensive to configure a backup system and can only be recovered once. In this paper, we implemented a process migration platform on the EV3 robotic vehicle, implementing a resilient system to find alternative nodes in order to recover the main process autonomously in the failure of a primary node. The platform successfully dodged accidents caused by stop shorts, unlike backup systems, to reduce costs in configuring the system, and to take advantage of a continuous resilient platform.

 **Tip**

When should you write your abstract? I don't think this matters. If it helps you to build confidence or ideas, you can begin your writing process with it. But I always write my abstract last, as I would otherwise need to revise or rewrite it anyway. I have never written a paper which didn't turn out slightly different at the end from how I intended it.

10.3 Tables of Contents

Tables of Contents (TOCs) are commonly mandated by universities for a thesis or dissertation project, but they are not otherwise compulsory in APA or MLA, and may be frivolous in a five-page paper. My experience is that somewhere around 15 pages they become useful for helping the reader to find paper divisions. If you have one, place the TOC on a separate page. For some reason abstracts and references tend not to be counted in TOCs. Here is an example—but note the error:

TABLE OF CONTENTS

Abstract 3
1. Introduction 4
2. Literature Review 5
3. Methodology 6
4. General Analysis 6
5. Case Studies 7
   5.1 FAO case in Thailand................................ 9
   5.2 IFAD case in Nepal................................. 10
  6. Conclusions 11
  References 12

This is a correct table in terms of format, and I don't mean that having a page number for the abstract or conclusion sections is the error. Rather, the student made it manually, which means typing *dot dot dot* incessantly and still getting a ragged right edge. This is a path to insanity—the numbers will *never* be straight. It is worth learning how to automate TOCs in Microsoft Word or whatever word processor you use. This also allows you to move around portions of your paper and not have to continually repair your page numbers—all you will need to do is click to update the table. You can of course see another TOC at the beginning of this book, and a further benefit to using Word's auto-table function is that the e-book version is automatically tabled as well.

10.4 Literature Reviews

A literature review answers the question, what sources do I need to read to gain a basic knowledge of this subject or the major opinions on it? It is less typical as a formal section in humanities papers, and so my discussion will prioritize APA/IEEE ones for the social and hard sciences. 'Literature' here refers to scholarship in general, not the narrower meaning of works of fiction.

A literature review is a short overview of sources that others have written on the subject, within which you intend to frame and defend your own arguments and findings. Its function is again also to indicate to your reader where they can learn more to understand your paper and its subject. It typically comes near the beginning of the essay before the general discussion. A lit review will likely list many, but not every source in your reference list—there may be minor statistical sources or other texts in your reference list which aren't essential to the review or to understanding the subject.

A lit review *can* be a free-standing paper on its own, but it ordinarily forms a section within a research paper or thesis/diss. To me a good yardstick is that your lit review should be about 10-15% of the length of your paper. In a brief essay a paragraph might be enough; in a seminar course paper you might need a page; in a full thesis/diss you might require 4-5 pages. To me anything much beyond that length starts to distract from the proportionality and flow of your paper—or like an over-long introduction, it begins to discuss what the body section should. I have sometimes seen such lit reviews spin out of control, so that after it ends there is little left for subsequent sections to do.

A brief lit review can be a simple summary of the key sources, but a longer or more helpful one has some sort of organizational pattern or logic. Your review might be broken down into different major schools of thought if the subject is controversial, or you might have a direct chronological progression from old to new sources. For example, in a paper on an issue spanning a good length of time or a long developmental trend, you might point out chief works written on the subject in representative periods. Another common breakdown is to move from general works to more narrow sources focused on your paper's specific topics. The following are examples.

1. Topic is highly controversial with marked camps: divide by the major viewpoints (political/scientific/ethical views on stem cell therapy; liberal/conservative views on cancel culture)

2. Topic has a long history with different period views: divide by period (what did critics say about novel x when it was published in 1878?; what did critics say in the twentieth century?; what do critics say now?)
3. Topic is broad, but your paper covers a small area: divide from general to specific (e.g. net-zero homes in Newfoundland: discuss solar energy; discuss solar panels in retrofitted homes; discuss solar panels in retrofitted homes in cool marine climates)

The review may refer to conclusions or viewpoints you don't agree with; it is still important to include them so that the reader can later contextualize your claims against those you oppose or intend to qualify. It's true that you are tailoring your review to your paper by examining past and current research and ideas regarding its subject, looking for gaps or problems. Yet lit reviews are usually more objective or neutral than the rest of your paper. They mainly list sources and might briefly note their influence or major arguments. You might indicate that certain works are more important, controversial, or relevant to your subject, but a lit review generally doesn't pursue your paper's thesis argument—that's the work of successive sections. Again, if you get too thick into debating with your sources, your lit review might take over the paper, and so part of a good one is knowing where to end and move on to the next division.

Here is a literature review for a paper about surrogacy markets, that is, paid arrangements where an outside mother is contracted to carry the pregnancy of another couple's child. The writer has chosen to discuss only three key sources at length, and that's fine.

The paper strongly relies on literature which examines general contents of surrogacy contracts.

Spar (2006) says that there are flourishing surrogacy markets and we need to understand how they structure their trade. Spar examines the historical context of the trade and suggests that governments need to play an active role to regulate surrogacy markets. Four models of regulation are discussed: the luxury model, the cocaine model, the kidney model, and the hip replacement model.

Seo (2009) also analyzes current surrogacy contracts with a focus on Asia. Most countries in the region have no surrogacy laws, so Seo insists that surrogacy regulation is needed and suggests a theory of legislation through social reaction to surrogacy and legal examination, in regard to the permission range of surrogacy contracts, parental rights, and adoption systems.

Further, Ramkie et al. (2017) point out a growing trend of surrogacy in several countries, presenting their views on surrogacy. The article notes a controversial case example from Australia to show the problems of current surrogacy. Moreover, it presents specific statistics on surrogacy market prices and the number of babies that are born through surrogacy in the countries.

This next example is a shorter and 'tighter' single paragraph review of research on gender differences in writing acquisition:

There are only a few studies on gender differences and language learning in the activities of writing, listening, and reading, as well as speaking, directed toward Korean students. If we look at studies conducted on English literature, Choi and Park (2009) found that writing performance differs depending on gender, and they argue that writing should be educational. Ga (2011) also explored writing and writing-effect development for 6th graders and 10th graders in Korea, and urged students to provide meaningful writing and success experiences to form positive writing attitudes and enhance writing efficacy. Lee (2023) more recently asserts that the gender of teachers is an important factor in modeling writing.

In my paper on Amis's *Lucky Jim*, I didn't write a formal lit review, but I wanted to give a historical overview of critical opinions of the novel. This paragraph was situated between the introduction and body as is usual, but was not marked with a heading title, as again, MLA tends to use fewer of them.

Period criticism of *Lucky Jim* did focus on Jim Dixon but was absorbed in situating the novel as an example of the Movement's "Angry Young Men" of the mid-1950s, suggested by its plebeian concerns and cynicism for postwar austerity. This categorization led to deliberations on the morality of the protagonist, with many seeing Dixon as another fashionable Teddy-Boy dandy, with a representative anti-authoritarian peevishness that would metastasize into violence in Burgess's *A Clockwork Orange*. Somerset Maugham bitterly denounced new literary models like Dixon as boorish "scum" who "have no manners" (qtd. in Green 135-36). Yet the romantic or scandalous aura of the 'Angries' has perhaps mercifully faded from discourse, leaving it open to more skepticism; as Bradbury observes, many of its supposed members were neither angry, young, nor men (318) (Iris Murdoch was none). Yet Dixon is still read as what Christina Larkin Galiñanes calls "an uncouth menace" (146) or what Frederic Carpenter sees as displaying "amoral opportunism" (446) and a duplicity hardly better than that of his colleagues.

10.5 Methodology & Results/Discussion

The methodology section is another optional division normally included in APA or IEEE science/social science papers and less often in humanities. In a paper on interpreting a literary text the evidentiary process is usually self-evident: examination of the text and sources discussing it. Not as many literature papers include surveys or experiments, or have concerns with replicability.

But where needed or relevant, a methodology section indicates what sort of process or type of evidence the paper focuses on, so that other researchers can either better understand your findings or reproduce obtaining them. Typical methodologies are qualitative methodologies, ones which accentuate reasoning and examples, and quantitative ones, which emphasize data and statistics, such as survey or experiment results. A social sciences paper might also identify itself as having a single or comparative case study format, as we discussed earlier on argument modes or frames.

Quantitative and qualitative data were collected for examining the improvement of students' overall quality of writing. Quantitative data sources are pre- and post-tests, and qualitative data sources are grader interviews.

Or:

A survey was conducted on 25 teachers, who had experience studying abroad (3-5 years) or majored in English literature. The survey questions are shown in Table 1.

Longer papers may have a methods section, which overlaps or may include a methodology section, but the two are slightly different—a methodology section briefly explains or justifies why the paper takes the approach it does, and why using calculations, surveys, experts, or other emphases are best, at a more theoretical level. A methods section instead may give more concrete or practical information on how the paper's information was assembled, or what steps were taken.

Cylindrical molds and 12 concrete specimens were prepared for each exposure condition. After 28 days, the specimens were immersed in two parts, distilled or deicing solutions. Then for F-T cycling, samples were stored in a chamber keeping temperature between -20°C and 20°C for 12h. The using equipment and specimens used are shown in Fig. 1. After F-T cycles, the specimens were taken to a tap water for removing loose samples. The fragments were gathered in paper, and then the samples were spaced outside for air-drying condition. Finally, both compressive strength measurement and weight loss were measured according to KS F 2403 [6].

Even longer methods sections may also have their own subsections with headings. A paper I received on surveying learning styles had within its methods section the following subdivisions:

1. The participants involved
2. The physical setting of the tests
3. The tasks assigned
4. Post-test questionnaires

Or, in a paper in information science:

1. Research design (documentary and qualitative: 20 studies)
2. Research instruments (data collection form and structured interview form)
3. Data collection (information gathering from online databases)

Results/Discussion

While the background information, lit review, and/or methodology or methods sections of a paper are important, you can't spend forever in the tomatoes and cheese of your paper—eventually the reader will become impatient for you to get to the meat of your essay, the main body. Again, I don't want to seem over-prescriptive when papers vary in style and purposes so greatly, but my experience is that by one-third into your paper, or at least by the halfway point, the paper needs to address its main task: proving its thesis argument and claims, and discussing how or why it is true, or why it matters.

Usually, MLA doesn't bother having a heading title at this point, although if you want one it can be there—so long as it has a useful name such as "Case Study" or "Discussion." Please don't call a section "Section 2." Thanks for that. In a paper I wrote on Fielding's *Bridget Jones's Diary* I had the rubrics

III. Bridget's Fantasy of Poise
IV. Bridget's Fantasy of Control
V. Bridget's Austen Fantasy

as a way of marking and dividing the body section. This is very much the writer's choice, although I recommend you don't call your body section "Body Section," which wouldn't tell the reader much, and would look pretty amateurish. Here is an example.

Discussion

A key argument why CO_2 emitted by human activity is not the sole cause of global warming is because temperature change is a natural phenomenon. This is proved by the existence of a medieval warm period and little ice age (Bolinas & Soon, 2001). The medieval warm period was from the ninth to thirteenth centuries in the medieval era, and in this period, the average temperature was much higher than now (Singer & Avery, 2007). Many famous European works of architecture and churches were built during this medieval warm period, which indicates that they had enough food and labor force to conduct such projects (Lamb, 1995). Throughout this period, despite the warmer climate, there were no drastic changes in ecosystem, or the extinction of species as recent scholars have argued. After this period, there was the 'little ice age.' From the thirteenth to eighteenth centuries, there was a period of cooling starting from Europe to all over the world, and it demonstrates unpredictable climate change (Fagan, 2000).

APA/IEEE are as ever more prescriptive here, and while title names may vary, typically there will be results and discussion sections. Note that a 'discussion' section normally has a different and more specific meaning in these papers.

Results: What was discovered or found by obtaining the information or evidence?

Discussion: What do the results mean?

These are formal ways of dividing up or sequencing a body section, and some writers merge them into a single title anyway (Results & Discussion). But these two heading titles are common in such disciplines. I suspect one skill necessary in writing a discussion section is to avoid having it steal the fire of your conclusion section, and my observation is that science and social science papers usually keep the discussion section short—or they might alternatively merge it with the conclusion instead (Discussion & Conclusion), thus avoiding having a paper ask "what does this mean?" twice.

Conclusions

As with introductions, we've already discussed conclusion sections. In MLA they are optionally marked. In APA/IEEE, again, this heading could be combined with your "Discussion" one. Or, you can call it "Conclusion" without a plural; I've also seen "Conclusion and Recommendations" or similar variants.

10.6 End Materials

Acknowledgements

Acknowledgement notes typically thank those who gave help or support, or acknowledge a funding source. They look a bit obsequious in a short course paper—it looks pretty obvious what you're trying to do if you compliment your professor—but they are often found in longer works. In a thesis/diss or book there might be a separate page or short section for this purpose. In journal or conference articles the acknowledgement is marked with a heading title and usually comes near or at the end.

There are few rules regarding acknowledgement sections, as not even the unsmiling, ruler-snapping APA mavens are petty enough to dictate the correct way to thank someone you love. Within common sense, you may write what you like. The phrasing is usually third person ("The authors would like to thank x for the many kindnesses shown"), but not always. In some disciplines and journal cultures some humor or wit is allowed to pass. The only advice I urge is to keep acknowledgments short. In a book or diss you can offer a prayer or thank your spouse, mother, dog, or hairdresser at length; but in a published article where printed space is precious, it will annoy others to go over three lines or so. Thank your readers, editors, professors, or the institution which funded you, and be done.

Appendices

An appendix section might list extended survey, experiment, statistical, or other data that is too lengthy to place in-text without distracting the reader from the main discussion. It also normally takes some identifying heading title.

I suspect few people bother to read appendices, and my practical advice is that you probably shouldn't put anything too critical in one, or anything that seriously impacts how the paper should be received; it might be safer to assume it won't be read. Some writers provide a summary or shortened version; others just list a hyperlink to some online repository where full data reports can be downloaded.

Bios

I won't reprint mine here as an example, because it is on the last page of this book. Occasionally a journal or other platform will want a biographical note about the author to accompany the article. It might go on the first page in a footnote, but often appears at the very end. Korean journals often place both abstracts and bios on last pages.

Again, it's your bio. Write what you want. If you're a student or young academic and haven't published much, focus on your interests. But be brief—a typical note is about 80 words. Like acknowledgements, third-person is usual, and if possible, you might look at bios by others to see how serious, playful, or personal they are.

11 THE THESIS/DISS PROJECT

I have discussed the common sections of longer papers, and now turn to more concrete matters of organizing, writing, and possibly defending one. If I've used terms that are unfamiliar, perhaps this is a good time to distinguish them. Understand that these words aren't used in the same way everywhere, and that lengths are guesstimates.

A paper/essay: Generically, any academic writing project.

Honors thesis: A final research paper of 20-40 pages completed as a capstone project by undergraduate seniors.

Seminar paper: A class paper of 20-ish pages written at the end of a graduate course for credit.

Thesis/dissertation ("diss"): A paper of anywhere from 50-500 pages written to complete a graduate degree program (not to be confused with a *thesis statement*, a paper's central argument).

In North America, a thesis is for a master's degree and a diss is for a doctorate degree, but some countries reverse this, or use the words interchangeably, as I do. In a medieval European university a lecturer would state a position (thesis), followed by a disputation with students (dissertation), thus the conflicting terms for the same or similar thing.

Articles, publications, monographs, book chapters, conference papers: Scholarly work done by professors or academics that is usually not for course credit or a degree.

ABD: 'All But Dissertation.' A candidate who has completed all courses and exams, but has not yet finished the thesis/diss. This may still allow the candidate to seek work or other opportunities on the understanding that the diss is in progress.

To repeat what I discussed in Chapter 1, academic writing will improve and solidify your subject knowledge, but will also cultivate your ability to think critically, to communicate your ideas clearly, and to work independently. These are immensely valuable skills for a scholar or professor, and thus the written dissertation has remained the basic capstone requirement for university graduate degrees for centuries.

Academic scholarship and the expansion of knowledge runs on written communications—but writing is also vital for many careers, especially ones which require individual work habits, problem solving, and written communication. At a practical level, a thesis/diss could make a solid writing sample when seeking a job or applying to further studies or scholarship programs. What organization would not appreciate, for example, a thesis on itself discussing how it could improve its practices or efficiency?

In some cases, where the thesis/diss is especially strong or relevant to a current need, you may even have an advisor who is willing to work with you toward revising parts of it toward publication as a journal article or book. Journals usually publish articles by established scholars, but some try to encourage newcomers in their discipline with the foresight that otherwise there will be no seasoned academics. Because it is less common for a student to be published, it's a respected accomplishment to include this in a faculty or university application. I'll return to this topic later.

This may feel like a strange chapter, because it will somewhat be about the nuts and bolts of the thesis/diss workflow, but also about writers as human beings, who have feelings. Your emotional intelligence and capacity to diagnose good and bad habits in yourself are going to be important factors in such an extended project—not so significant a factor as your intellectual abilities, granted, but critical enough to affect your probability of successfully completing it. There are plenty of jealous or resentful people online who will say that "it's just work, and anyone can do a doctorate." No, they can't; most graduate degrees take raw intelligence *and* motivation *and* personal skills.

I emphasize all this because writing a thesis/diss is difficult, but also a project where you will likely have to rely on yourself more than previously as a student. Perhaps you have already noticed a progression. Whereas you were told what to do in high school and had fewer choices, as an undergraduate you had increasing freedom to pursue subjects that interest you, and this has continued in graduate work, where your professors have become more like mentors, guiding you as you take growing responsibility for your own work—give or take the occasional tyrants. One explanation for the term 'commencement,' referring to the graduation ceremony, is that it doesn't refer to beginning something, but rather to a Latin word for 'eat,' where medieval professors and graduates ate a meal together to symbolize that you are now a (semi-) equal. True or not, this is the direction you are headed in, where your teachers will always be (probably) older than you, but they are becoming near-peers.

11.1 Advisors and Committees

As I always qualify, programs have differing rules, but the usual practice is for diss candidates (you) to choose or be assigned an advisor to guide you in negotiating or choosing a topic. You will then write the diss with guidance/abuse/neglect/revision directions from your advisor, and then defend your project. My own degree programs, and those I teach in, have a common procedure where candidates face a committee of your advisor and three or so other members, who advise and vote on the diss. Some programs have you simply submit your paper, but usually there is a live defense presentation. Some departments have comprehensive exams in addition, which are typically written before the thesis/diss is begun, as mine were.

By far the most important person to you in this project is your advisor—who is also sometimes called a director or supervisor, or called many other things, nice or not. This is normally a professor or faculty member in your department, who again is meant to help you define your topic and hand-hold you through whatever difficulties or questions you have on the topic or researching it. The usual sequence is that you meet with your advisor when necessary and cycle through submitting chapters or drafts, receiving corrections, and then submitting an improved draft, until the advisor feels you are ready to submit a final draft to your committee.

The committee's work is optimally to read your diss and make suggestions as you write it, but realistically they are usually uninvolved until you submit your paper to them for evaluation and your defense, if there is one. They are also usually from your department, although some programs stipulate that one should be an outside member (not in your department) who can bring a different and often more impartial perspective. This was again the case for both of my own programs at the masters and doctoral levels.

If your department chooses your advisor or committee members for you, this may be unfortunate if you aren't satisfied with who you are given, but it does simplify your decisions. If you do have these choices, I am going to give you some realistic realpolitik as advice:

1. For committee members, choose the best, but if you can, run the choices by your advisor first—don't select members who don't like each other, or who have bad blood with your advisor. The last thing you need is people who won't support each other, or you.

2. If you can, choose an advisor you like and have a friendly rapport with rather than the technically best or most prestigious professor—or even the one most closely aligned with your topic. It might be wise to wait until your second year or so, when you know your professors better.

3. Be nice to secretaries and staff, who can help/hinder more than you expect.

I am fortunately not writing this from being burnt personally, and I am grateful that my department was kind enough to leave me out of their faculty politics. But regarding my first point, I've seen squabbling faculty pull candidates into their disputes, and you don't want to be drawn into taking sides or caught in the crossfire.

As well with advisors, while mine were both kindly people (and I have seen and worked in departments where everyone gets along), I also know of horror stories. Happy is the candidate who has someone who strikes a balance between the extremes of not-giving-a-damn and task-master-from-hell. There are lazy or incompetent advisors who agree to supervise a student and then fail to read drafts or offer constructive help, or really do anything—and there are abusive professors who disrespect candidates, treating them as free labor and forcing them to do endless unrelated chores or lab duties, giving them conflicting directions, demanding constant results and meetings, or arbitrarily imposing decisions on them.

You need not agree with me, and perhaps you feel it's better to have Dr. Very Famous as an advisor on your CV, whatever his or her personality. And that's fine—I can only warn that you are going to spend a great deal of time interacting with your advisor, and the thesis/diss project is stressful enough without making things worse by having someone you don't like or trust. And as far as having an advisor precisely within your field, at a certain point you will know more about your exact topic than your advisor does, anyway—you're becoming the expert on it.

I admit I once had to scold my doctoral committee when I felt they were slack. They took it well—they understood that their responsibility is to provide help, and that people need reminders of their duties. As an extreme example, a friend of mine 'fired' an advisor and entire committee in exasperation and chose different people. As a grad candidate you are getting dangerously close to departmental politics and problems. But it must be said that some bad candidates blame their committees for their own problems.

11.2 The Diss Proposal

Even at undergraduate levels of coursework, you may be asked by a professor to submit a short proposal tendering your course paper's subject, such as the following ones I received.

Hermione is a perfectionist and always seems stressed, but she breaks down and cries at one point. I am going to analyze her character, and I think that she is similar to Prof. McGonagall. For example, McGonagall is also a perfectionist and she tries to keep the rules. So, I am going to compare these two ladies.

Here is a more detailed proposal.

I would like to write my essay on *Macbeth*. What I want to focus on is why Banquo's son did not become the king at the end, even though the witches said so in their prophecy. Since Malcolm, not Fleance, became the king, I would like to write about some different theories on what happened and what Shakespeare had in mind. There are some historical influences so I also would like to do research on this.

I require these proposals to prepare my students for a future when they will be asked to write a longer or more formal one, for an employer, editor, or advisor. But why do they want one? Partly proposals are sought for the needs of others—so that people can anticipate and organize your project, or allocate funding or resources, or avoid over-duplication of topics.

But a paper proposal is mostly to help *you*, to allow your professor or advisor to use his or her experience to refine or steer your topic, or warn you away from a poor or un-writeable one. I alluded to this in the planning chapter, but the most typical feedback I give, or which I heard myself as a candidate, is that the topic is too big. This advice was for my own good.

Thus graduate programs typically require a proposal to be submitted and signed off on, for no one wants you wasting months or years on an impossible project no one warned you about; funding might also be involved. In regard to formats, some universities or departments will have standard forms with boxes and checkmarks for thesis/diss proposals, and others don't. Both my masters and doctoral proposals were coincidentally roughly 1,700 words, and this seemed about right. At any rate, both were accepted, and I'm sure the details of both were forgotten about minutes later. I've never heard of a committee which asked at a defense why the diss doesn't match Line 6 on the proposal; your committee had to write these projects as well, and most members will understand that your topics and ideas will shift.

I have reprinted my actual 1999 MA thesis proposal here, with some slight modifications (I've trimmed most of the reference list). I didn't use MLA formatting at the time, but my committee members evidently accepted this informality in my proposal.

Department of Graduate Studies
Department of English Literature

M.A. Thesis Proposal
Ken Eckert

Area of concentration: Medieval literature: Old English
Paper title: It's About Time: Kingship and the Character in a Contemporary *Beowulf*

Thesis chapters:
1. Introduction
2. *Beowulf* and a government in transition
3. Beowulf as a realistic character
4. Time and contemporality in *Beowulf*

5. Conclusions

My position in this paper will be to argue that *Beowulf* presents no lost, idealized past as Bakhtin would and Tolkien does argue, but rather that the narrator depicts an accessible past which is relevant to its time period, whether this be the eighth or tenth century.

I propose to examine the poem from three aspects relating to the idea of contemporality. I would first like to look at the changing concept of kingship in the poem. Kings in *Beowulf* are not fixed in their roles, but rather demonstrate a progression from being warriors elected among peers to having the Roman trappings of primogeniture and divine right of rule. Through this I would like to establish how the civilization of *Beowulf* is one in transition.

I would second like to look at Beowulf as a realistic character. Much criticism treats Beowulf as a combination of legendary and idealistic traits. My argument is that Beowulf is not a fantastic creation but rather a realistic role model whose actions are practically justified.

Last, I would like to tie all of these issues together in a chapter which examines Bakhtin's thesis that the epic must out of necessity pose a fixed hero in a closed past. I will argue that Beowulf is a fluidly developing hero in an accessible and changing world, and this section will examine the representation of time in the poem.

Introduction

Summary: In this section I will introduce general ideas by pointing out that much of the poem is concerned with establishing a continuum between past and present. I would also like to demonstrate that aspects of courtly behavior exist in Beowulf, in an effort to establish a literary continuum rather than an abrupt change in style.

- Opening thoughts
- How did kingship and chivalry change in the middle ages?

- Is Beowulf a 'courtly' character?

Latin and Germanic Kingship in Beowulf
Summary: According to Michael Swanton, a chief tension in *Beowulf* is the progression from primitive society to civilized. The role of king, with its transition from a society based on kin to one based on primogeniture, is relevant to *Beowulf,* for this change is expressly seen in the poem.

- Differences between Roman and Saxon concepts
- Is Beowulf the new type of king?
- Faith to one's lord is a virtue in both concepts

Beowulf as a Realistic Model
Summary: The poet expresses Beowulf's altruism, kindness, and prudence. These are not unrealistic ideals but rather the traits of a role model for the audience; Beowulf is not a superman but rather a character to be emulated.

- Is Beowulf a real character?
- Is Beowulf a good king or reckless in facing the dragon?
- Heaven swallows the smoke: is Beowulf to be judged favorably by God?

The Past and Present in Beowulf
Summary: Bakhtin describes the epic form as one in which a fixed, knowable hero operates in a closed past. *Beowulf,* by these criteria, is not purely epic in that it has concrete links to the present and features a character which changes and has private thoughts. The poem is not a story of bygone events but one with a fluid link into the world of the poet.

- Time in *Beowulf* and its link to the present
- Moral development in Beowulf?
- Change and the future in Beowulf's world

Conclusion
Beowulf is ultimately a transitional work between a primitive world and a civilized Romano-European one in that its endorsement of the heroic code is qualified. The poet synthesizes the two viewpoints by placing Beowulf in a time which is relevant to and flows into the issues of his own world, indicating a poem concerned with the present.

Working Bibliography
Abraham, Lenore. "The Decorum of *Beowulf*." *Philological Quarterly*, vol. 72, no. 3, 1993, pp. 267-87.
Chickering, Howell D. Jr., trans. *Beowulf*. Anchor Books, 1977.
Mitchell, Bruce, and Fred Robinson. *A Guide to Old English*. Blackwell, 1964.
Skeat, Walter W. *The Canterbury Tales*. Modern Library, 1929.

Structurally, the proposal has this form, minus the last element.

1. Proposed name of thesis
2. Proposed area of concentration
3. Proposed thesis chapters and summaries of each chapter
4. Working reference list
5. Proposed timetable or schedule

The *last* thing I wished to do was to commit to a deadline without being obligated to—because even in 1999 I could see potential risks to getting the project done.

11.3 Emotional Skills: Common Dangers

a. Greedy candidates
b. Passive candidates
c. Ghost candidates
d. Scared candidates

Social media is jammed with jokes, memes, and grumblings about how terrible and stressful grad school is, so much that an outsider must wonder why anyone goes. I had bad days, but also enjoyable ones where I was learning new things, chatting with interesting people, and doing something I felt was fulfilling and important. But I was older than most graduate students, and life experience helps. The same applied to the workflow and writing of my thesis and diss.

Again, part of the reason you are given the thesis/dissertation assignment is for the end product itself, but also for the professional skillset you are developing as an independent scholar and researcher via writing. I want to emphasize that some of these skills are intellectual and others are personal or interpersonal ones. I have seen people drop out of diss projects and quit or fade away. Some leave for not-great but rational reasons, such as an employment offer, or they simply realize they're not up to it academically. Some sadly have health, money, or even relationship problems. The saddest are those who burn out, and I can diagnose four reasons why it might happen, and they are all emotional in nature.

Greedy Candidates

I don't mean candidates who are selfish, but those who choose far too large or ambitious a topic, and find they can't finish it. This may be because an advisor did not properly warn them, or because they set such an impossible standard of perfection for themselves that they can't meet it.

I've never seen a peer or candidate who is actually intellectually dull finish a graduate degree. Again, those who stand outside these programs and snipe that 'anyone can do it if they do the work,' don't know what they're talking about. But I will say that I've observed competent but not stellar people finish their thesis by diligence and persistence, and very gifted candidates who bit off more than they could chew, and became frustrated.

My advice for the potentially greedy or the purist is to see the project realistically as it is: one paper that few will read afterward, and not a magnum opus or a judgment of your life.

Ideally, your thesis/diss is an introduction to your professional career and not its summation. Its purpose is to demonstrate that you can do scholarly work, and is not solely itself the scholarly work. If you are in this danger zone, it is the time to ask for help from your advisor or committee members—that is what they are for. They may assist you to reduce the size of your project.

Passive Candidates

Candidate z, who I did supervise myself, was bright but lazy, and flitted from topic to topic without ever working to develop it past a superficial depth. The candidate eventually lost interest and quit the program after repeatedly missing deadlines and meetings. That's an extreme example, but I do see students who make me wonder, why are you here if you don't want to? If I have to natter you to do things and you sulk like a child being told to clean your room, why are you doing this?

Perhaps this sounds harsh. We all have good and bad days, and responsibilities or temptations. Sometimes I was excited about my master's thesis, but I was also working in a campus bar and playing in a band, and some mornings I didn't feel like writing. And that's fine—people need fun and rest. But these days were the exception, and I compensated on days where I was working. Overall, graduate school, let alone academia, is no place for passive people who need to be told what to do, or for martyrs who see the diss as an unmerited burden. The project is meant to foster your ability to self-regulate and to develop independent work habits. Advisors will vary, and some are more directive, and others will wait for you to contact them. What they have in common is that they will still get paid if you don't finish your diss. You should not be starting one unless you want it done more than your advisor and committee do, and can attain the self-discipline to persist at it.

Ghost Candidates

You must keep the lines of communication open. Nothing makes your advisor or committee members so anxious as when they write e-mails or messages to you that aren't answered or acknowledged. Some candidates disappear or hide from the advisor because they haven't done anything, or have done insufficient work, and they worry about being scolded or reprimanded. Admittedly there are mean advisors, but most will rather hear that you are still out there trying, even if you have spent most of your time playing video games, as opposed to not knowing what happened to you. Again, your advisor's job is to help you; if you are having trouble or are stuck, ask.

Scared Candidates

Candidates who are in trouble may also become paralyzed by fear or stress, and begin to avoid their work. Again, we all face human temptations. I was a bartender for graduate students during my MA, and there were more than a few barflies who probably typed two words a week, and mostly spent their time chatting and playing pool over beer and cigarettes, positive that they would get serious about their diss "any day now." I suspect they were afraid of failure, but could not admit it to others or themselves.

I suppose this isn't so bad a scenario among the four types I've listed if you're having a good time. But candidates who procrastinate may need to pay continuance tuition fees every semester. They may also ultimately face an exasperated department chair who drops them—or advisers who quit their posts or retire.

One way of making this enterprise less frightening, and of minimizing avoidance impulses, is to break the diss project down into smaller pieces. This is again part of the reason I stress planning so much (and now you hopefully see that the simple concepts I discussed in early chapters now scale into larger activities); but during the writing phase as well, you may want to parcel out tasks so that bite-sized pieces can be done with smaller time commitments. As well, it sounds childish to say that you may need to reward yourself with something fun at the end in order to motivate yourself to commit to some hours of work, but you wouldn't be the first to do so—and if it gets you through a bad patch here and there, there are worse stratagems.

A more benign, though equally dishonest means of avoiding the diss project is righteous procrastination—meaning that you avoid distasteful work by substituting it with something you dislike slightly less, rationalizing what you've done by it still being an unpleasant task. Perhaps you need to complete your tax return, but you busy yourself by washing the dishes or vacuuming, praising yourself that you are working hard.

Candidates sometimes do this with their thesis/diss projects by endlessly putting off writing with the scholarly-sounding excuse of needing more research and reading. These are essential activities, but you can read your life away. I was guilty of this myself during my masters, and had to be told by a department head, "just write the damn thing!" You may need to set a date on your calendar or some fixed limit where you stop reading and researching and start writing. You may need to occasionally return to the former activity, but for some people, making a scheduled commitment to themselves that they will mostly switch to writing mode—and perhaps even concretizing it by establishing a habit of regularly going to a physical place that is allocated for writing—helps give their work structure and focus.

I don't want to turn this writing book into a self-help manual, and I am not a counselor. But I will say that the work habits, or lack thereof, that you develop now may stay with you for a lifetime. Labor also needs limits, for having a terrible work-play-rest balance is no healthier, but the goal should be to work more efficiently, as I discussed in the editing chapter. Avoiding your writing may result in you either never finishing it, or else putting in more time later on to meet an emergency deadline or other stressful situation. It would be better to diagnose, or at least be aware of, the emotional ways in which you may be sabotaging yourself during the project.

11.4 The Diss Defense

Although doctoral degrees date back some nine centuries, the live oral defense goes back only to early nineteenth-century Germany. Some universities and programs don't have an oral defense at all—you submit your paper for evaluation and are done—and others have varying levels of formality to them. Early disputations were public and often lively, sometimes attracting large audiences. European defenses still may have a great deal of pomp, with ceremonial swords and robes. U.S. ones might be just a meeting in a classroom. Others, especially in and after the age of Covid-19, are done online.

What is common to nearly all defenses is that a) candidates are terrified, and b) afterwards they say, "it really wasn't so bad."

If you have written a solid thesis/diss and your advisor is pleased and recommends you go to the defense stage, it's unlikely that your committee will offer any serious challenge; they're on your side, and they want you to finish as well. Some critics even gripe that the modern defense is little more than a rubber-stamp.

But people do fail, or are directed to do revisions, which I'll return to later. The worst thesis defense I ever sat in as a committee member was for an honors undergrad student who seemingly did everything possible to antagonize everyone, by:

a. Distributing copies of her thesis to the committee members the day before the defense, giving none of us adequate time to read it. Don't do this.
b. Ignoring her advisor's advice that she wasn't ready, as she didn't want to wait until after the semester break. Really don't do this.
c. Plagiarizing. Really, *really* don't do this.

The result was a train wreck ending in tears, as she was failed, and half of her committee resigned on the spot upon recognizing her plagiarized sections.

But on a happy note, an amusing story I was told by one of my own professors in graduate school concerned the professor's friend, who needed to fly to another city for his diss defense. His committee met him at the airport and took him to a pub, and likely he didn't wish to annoy them—they ended up drinking all evening and chatting about his project. The next morning he arrived at the defense, hung over and expecting to be dead on arrival. His committee shook his hand, explaining that they had really had his defense the night before when everyone was relaxed. I am not advising you to drink alcohol with your committee, but I suppose, as ever, when in Rome.

These two incidences demonstrate extreme situations at both poles. Yet the majority of defenses, as I say, end in the candidate feeling relief that much of the worrying was for nothing. Your primary concern is your thesis/diss, and again, if it's a strong one, the defense is more a formality. Nevertheless, defenses make a difference, and I should discuss how to strengthen yours, if only so that you are better prepared for future presentations someday where your audience doesn't know you, or may not be sympathetic or good-natured.

11.5 Optimizing Your Defense

The golden rule of diss defenses is simple: brevity. Samuel Johnson said of Milton's *Paradise Lost*, "none ever wished it longer." I suspect every diss committee feels the same way about defenses. They have mostly already made up their minds on whether you will be passed or not. Departmental protocols vary, but generally I see half-hour presentations and then a half-hour for questions. I would be surprised to see committees willing to sit for much more than an hour.

I am sure there are defenses where the thesis/diss really is on the bubble in terms of grading, but generally the purpose of the defense is to demonstrate that you can explain and defend your diss like a professional. In other words, the defense is a rhetorical act as much as it is an examination of the diss contents. You obviously can't read your entire diss in real time, and optimally your committee has already read it. Your presentation should highlight its central arguments and findings, and the real meat of your defense, if any, will probably be in the Q&A.

It's true that some departments dress casually, but I would dress well, or at least as well as your committee members. In some ways your defense is like a job interview to be a fellow faculty member. I say this because acting like a professor is what you want to display during a defense—and it could very well result in you being hired as a professor in the department someday.

PowerPoint Slides

PowerPoint and other slide software technologies weren't common when I defended, but they are omnipresent in defenses now. I am certain that could they do so, some of my Korean students would marry a PowerPoint. But unless they are prescribed, you don't actually need to have slides. You could distribute a handout summarizing the main arguments and topics of your thesis, and sit next to your committee and explain your findings to them in a conversation, taking questions at the end. Many professors prefer this intimacy and immediacy. Yet I understand this advice will likely fall on deaf ears, and so for those who insist on slides, let's discuss how to make yours potentially more effective.

Tip

Give the trees a break and don't make photocopy handouts of your slides. No one will read them, and 100% of them are thrown away. If you must, make a summary handout of your points, with at most a few graphs.

Keep It Simple. If you display a PowerPoint extravaganza of text-stuffed slides and animated effects, the committee or audience may be so absorbed in viewing or reading your slides that they forget you are there—or they may wonder why you are there if your only function is to narrate and advance slides. Moreover, you probably know from experience that there is little more boring than a presentation where someone just reads out their slides. A diss defense is not *supposed* to be fun, but there's no reason to make it drearier.

I'm uncomfortable with the term 'PowerPoint presentation' entirely because it suggests that the slides *are* the presentation; they aren't, or shouldn't be—you are. The slides should be a supporting visual aid to structure your work and help the audience picture your ideas. I will return to this when I discuss conference presentations, but if you have, say, a half-hour space, you might have 30 slides and average a minute for each one.

One feature I noticed in the late Apple CEO Steve Jobs' presentations was that most of his slides had no text on them;

11 THE THESIS/DISS PROJECT

they were visuals, with a mix of photographs and data graphs. When he did use a slide with text, there were only a few words. Simple slides allow the eyes of the committee to stay where they should be, on you. I know graduate students will protest, "but my subject is very complex," and there may be slides where you need more textual detail; but overall the complexity of the topic should be explained by you and not the PowerPoint.

Tell People the Structure. As with the paper, avoid surprising the audience with your thesis arguments, or assuming they can pick it up as they go along. Include a table of contents at the beginning of your slides, or convey one verbally, so that the audience is prepared for the main ideas and subtopics you will cover. As well, periodically remind the audience of where you are within your sequence. Make your table of contents short with three or four main topics so that the audience doesn't forget them. If this sounds like my earlier discussion on thesis statements, it should—the concepts are nearly the same; and if you have planned well, your outline basically is already a table of contents, and you can probably just lift text from it or your thesis statement to form your TOC.

Use Big Fonts in High-Contrast Colors. Slides don't look the same when projected as they do on your monitor when designing them. Projectors can't yet reproduce the same sharpness and brightness, and you can't always make the room entirely dark. Nor do you want to, for the committee should be able to see you—again, you are the presentation, not the PowerPoint.

For this reason, I recommend large fonts in opposite colors from the background. If in doubt, have white text on a black slide, or the opposite. At present, I typically don't use less than a 24-point font, and usually have about 28, with titles in the 40's. I do this partly to prevent myself from having too much text, but also because your committee members aren't student colleagues, and are likely older and have weaker vision. You will frustrate them if you see that they are squinting, or asking you to repeat what the slide text says.

Don't Overuse Video Clips. It's tempting to place YouTube or self-generated video clips in a defense presentation to add authority or flavor, but it will probably be perceived as space-filling, undermining the committee's confidence in your work. Unless they are key sources of evidence, I would not risk any more than a brief clip or so.

Don't Put All Your References on the Last Slide. It might feel odd that I tell you this, for surely your presentation should mirror your thesis/diss. But your audience can't turn pages in one, and doesn't have time to pair each slide to the references. Further, if you have many reference entries, how will you display them without crowding them onto a slide in small print? You may again frustrate your committee, or waste time when someone asks you to back up to an earlier slide to match it with a reference entry.

Instead, I recommend that you place the reference for the secondary source or graphic at the bottom of the same slide on which it appears, as you would a footnote. I suppose there could be stickler committees who demand that your slides also conform to MLA/APA/IEEE standards, but if not, it would be visually easier to do simplified footnotes on the slides. I find that at academic conferences, the audience prefers this, and some people take photos of the slides for later reference.

Handling the Q&A

To repeat, the defense is a test that you can explain and defend your paper's arguments, just as much as it is an evaluation of those arguments. The committee wants to see that you can do this with self-control and professionalism. You need to do this verbally, but also visually through controlling your body language. A presentation where no one can hear you because you are hiding behind a podium or mumbling into a paper script, or you appear unprepared or unsure of yourself, will be judged less favorably even though the content may be strong—recall Aristotle's guidance on projecting visual ethos and authority.

11 THE THESIS/DISS PROJECT

Cultures have different attitudes towards eye contact, but if possible, try to interact with your committee and address them without fidgeting or looking at the clock.

The Q&A is the acid test for this. In my student presentations or in actual defenses, nothing looks more amateurish than presenters who mutter "any questions" at the end and then clench up as though avoiding a chair thrown at them—this body language says that you lack confidence in your understanding of the subject. You must at least appear to welcome questions; and if you enter professional or academic life you will indeed welcome questions, for they show that the audience is interested in and curious about your ideas. In my first professional conference presentation it was far more disheartening to encounter an audience which didn't have questions and was merely waiting for my session to be over. I would much rather hear "you're wrong" than "we don't care and weren't really paying attention."

The common fear is that a question will be asked that you can't answer, and you will look foolish or even fail the defense. That is admittedly a risk, but it's a relatively lesser risk—for you will also look foolish if you evade the question, or lie by saying "I'll find out and get back to you." How will you do this? Everyone in the room knows you won't, even if you can. I have even seen presenters lose their tempers and sarcastically attack the question, believing a good offence is a good defense. This is more than dangerous—it's a downright stupid move which is guaranteed to antagonize an audience or committee.

A strategy I have learned in conferences is to say you don't know and ask if someone in the audience does—often someone will save you and offer an opinion, and all you need to do is agree with it. This might not work during a defense. Rather, during my own one when I was asked a question I couldn't answer, I asked for clarification, and the explanation of the question gave me enough clues to partly respond to it. But if you genuinely don't know an answer, admit it. You are unlikely to fail a defense or lose face over one admission, and in fact the gesture that you don't know all the answers may look better for you.

Easy and Hard Questions

You are the expert on this topic; be prepared for both high level and low level questions. I won't gossip, but on my own diss committee, to put it tactfully, some members put more effort in than others. Your advisor probably knows your subject and thesis well, but likely at least one of your committee members is less motivated and hasn't done more than a cursory read of your paper. You may get very difficult questions about "why did you use source x for argument y on page 213?" (you should of course have a copy of your diss with you). You may also get, "so, what's your diss about?"

You can't get angry with your committee or audience, even if you feel the question is unreasonable. You are again partly being tested to see whether you can act coolly under stress as an academic—there will perhaps be times in your career at conferences or meetings where others ask foolish, mean-spirited, or self-serving questions. I also had an ex-lawyer colleague who liked to ask aggressive, slightly hostile questions, purely as a pose to test the candidate's mettle under fire. You must show self-control as you vary your answers in difficulty or tone to meet the questioner, just as you would explain your thesis differently to your family than you would to a room of scholars.

Stressing Out

To sum up, it's natural that you are going to be stressed about your diss defense whatever I tell you. And some amount of stress is good if it gives you adrenaline and energy. But too much can incapacitate you. Perhaps the silliest advice others give is, "don't be nervous; everyone does this." That usually doesn't help, for nervousness is not usually a conscious choice, or controlled by a switch we can flip.

I repeat that, just as the thesis/diss is a demonstration that you can do serious work in the future, so is the defense. This is a time to learn your own body's preferences regarding presentations. You may find that some light exercise before makes you feel better and calmer (I usually go for a walk). Coffee or other caffeinated beverages may help you—or they may make you jittery, or cause you to need a bathroom break during your defense. Some people really do have a single shot of alcohol to steady them—although probably numerous ones, as Jim Dixon has in *Lucky Jim*, will not help. A heavy meal may either fortify you or upset your stomach. I find a single coffee or water is optimal for me, and I avoid any dairy, as it clogs my throat.

11.6 Grading Metrics

You can anticipate what I will write—that evaluation practices will vary; and that's correct. I will only indicate what is a typical workflow after your diss submission and defense. The two might be graded separately, or combined into one assessment. It will probably be something like this hierarchy of grades:

Best: Full pass. Your diss is finished, and you can graduate. Hurray! (But: this seldom happens.)

Second Best: Pass with minor corrections. Small fixes and additions/changes have been ordered by the committee, but normally no further defense is needed—your advisor can sign off on the corrections. (This usually happens.)

Not Good: Conditional pass. Major improvements and changes have been directed, and another defense must be held to re-evaluate the text or your explanation of it. (This sometimes happens.)

Bad: Fail. The diss has been rejected by the committee, and you may need to start over, either with a new topic, or at best salvaging some of your completed work. (This seldom happens. A good advisor would have warned you long before this stage.)

Depending on this outcome, there may be small bureaucratic

details. For both my masters and doctoral papers I had to prepare a specific print copy using special (and expensive) acid-free paper for the department to submit my thesis to a registry. There may be further back-and-forth between you and your advisor where minor corrections are ordered.

At any point in the thesis/diss project there is a hazard that people will give up; but a real danger zone is entered when candidates are given conditional passes or fails, for they can feel both inadequate and humiliated by their professors. To her credit, the honors student I mentioned who failed her defense did return and pass. Many do not, and some candidates remain forever as ABD, still technically working on their diss long after they have entered careers and their advisors have retired. I have known colleagues 'still finishing' for decades who are likely lying to themselves, particularly if they are in rapidly changing fields where their research from thirty years ago is now near-worthless.

Writing a diss is often compared to childbirth among candidates or on social media. French feminist theorist Hélène Cixous in fact likened writing to a sort of substitute for childbirth for male authors. There are indeed similarities. Childbirth comes with some fun (making the child) and some pain (delivering the child). Similarly, whatever the popular idea is that diss writing is some sort of grisly torture, there will be both rewarding and discouraging days.

But writing a diss is not like childbirth in one important respect, I think. After you have a baby, people want to see the baby and will think it's cute. Few will want to read your diss after it is passed, and you will have a limited window of time to explain it to curious friends or relatives before they lose interest. I am not saying this to discourage you, but to help you keep your expectations in writing it realistic. As the expression goes, the best diss is a done diss.

12 BEYOND THE DISS

The end of the last chapter may have sounded harsh, that almost no one cares about your diss after it's passed. But it's unfortunately true. Not even your mother will want to read it—unless perhaps she works for NASA. Even then she may only skim the abstract. Your friends and family will say what 95% of people do: "You spent all that time working on *that*?"

The good news is that your work can be republished as something that *is* valued and read. I have sat on committees where I felt the work was particularly interesting or relevant, thought it a shame that it will gather dust on a shelf, and advised ambitious candidates to re-use or cannibalize their diss into journal articles or some other publication format. It is not self-plagiarism to revise and publish parts of your diss, and in fact it's an excellent way to jump-start an academic career. I did it too with several diss chapters.

Some graduate students or scholarly readers of this book may already be writing or looking toward post-graduate writing, such as published journal articles, book chapters, monographs, or conference papers—or related writing such as technical, business, online, or creative forms which will leverage some of the skills you have built. I agree with Eric Hayot that graduate programs too seldom offer instruction on how to write the seminar papers and dissertations discussing the content they teach; but instruction on post-graduate writing is even rarer. You may not need or want to publish after you graduate, but if you do, this chapter is meant to help assist you in this task.

12.1 Revising Your Diss

Why publish sections of a diss, when there is no longer a course or degree incentive? As a student or new graduate, you might want to make yourself more attractive when applying to a job, to a further degree program, or as a junior professor yourself. And—because it's there. The work is done and is fresh, and it's easier to turn material from a diss into published work than it is to start at nothing with a different topic. If you are a professor, you likely already know that retention and promotion decisions will be influenced by your publication record, and that in some departments it is a central part of your job responsibilities. Last, in some limited formats, such as monographs, there may be *some* money earned.

If you are starting out, you must see that the training wheels are off now, and the scholarly world is going to be rougher than student life was. Perhaps your committee members were nice as pie, as mine were—and I'm not only saying this because they might read this book—but maybe they weren't. Yet at least they knew you, and had some personal investment in seeing you succeed. Most of the people involved in publishing your work don't know you, and while they may be well-intentioned, they don't necessarily have an interest in your success.

The largest obstacle you will need to cross is that for publishers and conference organizers, your work is a risk to their budgets and reputations, and you are likely competing with other scholars and submissions. Print publishing costs money. It is on you to demonstrate that your work should be published, whereas your committee had a lesser risk. A course paper or diss, or diss chapter will likely need extensive revision to raise its discourse level, as it is being written for professionals who will expect original arguments; it will probably need to be reformatted to the publisher's in-house typographic standards; and it may go through several stages from editors and readers.

After you graduate, you will probably receive spam mail

from publishers telling you that you don't need to do all these things—that your wonderful diss on pickle therapy is perfect as is, and all you need to do is make five easy payments for it to be printed in attractive leather and saleable to university libraries worldwide. These are almost guaranteed to be predatory publishers selling vanity books. There are almost no circumstances where you should pay to publish a book, and these fly-by-night firms will do nothing to promote or distribute your book. Virtually your only sales will be books *you* buy after being nagged or pressured by the publisher, as stores and libraries won't buy from vanity imprints.

I will deal with book publishing in more depth later. For now, I will discuss publishing single chapters or sections of your diss a la carte—which I argue has the *relatively* lowest barriers to entry for a new academic. You might do this as a journal article or as a chapter in an edited book. Assuming either type—and some of this applies as well to books—there are three typical problems at play.

1. Justifying a rationale
2. Raising the originality level and citation density
3. Dealing with rejection

Regarding the first point, publishers usually care about readerships and budgets in a way diss committees don't. My doctoral thesis regarded how medieval romances, a perennially undervalued genre in English literature, influenced Chaucer's tales. My committee liked this; but when I tried to publish my work, book editors asked: why should we risk printing a study of texts that you admit are *undervalued*, which readers probably won't buy?

This is less the case with journal articles, where the financial risk is less or minimal. But editors still want essays that readers will be interested in. Another useful point from Eric Hayot is that sometimes the context for a seminar paper or diss chapter doesn't translate into an outside publication. Maybe it was fun to consider how *Hard Times* and *The Grapes of Wrath* critique economic systems, because you read both in a course. Perhaps your department found it vital to work on a local social or engineering problem. But if you submit such a paper, even an excellent one, to a journal they may ask you how these issues matter to them or their readers. What seemed obvious or important within your campus bubble may have little resonance to people far outside it.

Worse, every field has its done-to-death topics. This doesn't really matter in a university department, where if you've written a diss on Shakespeare, fine. When you try to publish, you discover that thousands of new books and articles a *year* are published on the bard, and you are competing with them for acceptance. I've already alluded to the idea of originality in choosing a topic, and noted that it isn't so much a necessity in undergrad or even grad work. Often my undergraduates *do* write something interesting and new in their papers, but at their level I can't reasonably expect critically innovative research; they are learning the basics. But in post-academic work originality becomes critical. STEM people already know about filling a research gap as a research issue, but journals will not take your word for it—the gap must be proven, and the need for it to be addressed must be defended more vigorously.

I discussed the "who cares" question as a conclusion strategy earlier, but it is now an overall problem for your paper to overcome, and is considerably more pressing when money and journal reputation is involved. You might now address the "who cares" question in your introduction, or even an explicitly marked section within it, and as a result, introductions in published articles are often longer than they are for course papers—rather than 25% or so, your introduction might comprise 33% or even 40% or more of the article length. Literature reviews might also lengthen. Your paper does not have to use the "challenging conventional wisdom" frame, but it does need to be more aware of how it interacts and responds to other research and views.

Again, technical or scientific papers often do this formally or naturally, as the practical application of the paper is typically more an issue. I wrote this, but note that the end of the introduction pays special attention to justifying itself as a paper.

A tiny network of websites exists where home users have patched together their own movie film digitization systems. These typically involve some process of photographing either the projected image or the film frame itself onto a digital camera, with some sophisticated users engineering systems to auto-advance the film and trigger the camera for unsupervised scanning. While such processes may be optimal, they require a high order of equipment, technical expertise, and budget. The general consensus is that this is the only effective way to transfer film, and that flatbed scanners are unsatisfactory in quality. The purpose of this paper is to demonstrate a workflow solution which does make this feasible, by using a Canon 9000F Mark II flatbed scanner with a transparency adapter along with Adobe Photoshop scripting to successfully scan and render usable and high-quality digitized 8mm/Super 8 silent film.

I have also hopefully done this in two humanities papers, where the first two paragraphs also try to signal that "something important is missing that needs a paper to address it—this one." I of course can't be hostile, but I did need to assert that another article in a crowded field is justified, without making it read like cheap clickbait.

Does George Bernard Shaw's *Pygmalion* (1912) telegraph that Higgins and Eliza will marry? In light of more recent concerns in Shaw scholarship of language, class, and gender, the question seems déclassé, if not a stock theme for first-year essays. Yet the question is still not satisfactorily resolved either in criticism or the story's popular reception, despite the voluminous readings dedicated to this quintessential Shavian controversy.

The amount of scholarship on Chaucer's Wife of Bath has been more than *litel*. Yet something small but curious happens in the loathly lady's bedroom lecture in *The Wife of Bath's Tale* which seems as yet unremarked upon.

The third point, which I'll explain and then return to later, is that publishers, reviewers, and conference organizers likely don't know you, and may reject your work with much less tact or helpfulness than your university professors hopefully did. Publishing is career gold, especially in academia, but in brief, it is not for the impatient or easily discouraged. You will need to learn how to deal with 'no.'

12.2 Academic Journal Articles

When academics talk about 'articles' or 'pubs,' they mean short papers of anywhere from 3-4 page reviews to 30 page studies on a subject in their field published in a scholarly periodical journal. Such journals are often housed or subsidized by universities or other institutions, and might print anywhere from 6-8 times a year to once annually. Articles may be single or multiple-authored, and might be print-only or some print/online hybrid. I have already discussed evaluating journal articles as sources and the WoS/Scopus etc. hierarchy, and so this should already be familiar.

If you were on the ball when writing your diss, you hopefully looked into typical article lengths in your field so that you could write diss chapters in that zone. About 15-25 pages or 5,000-7,000 words is typical in my field of English literature; my friends who write in law might go to 10,000 words. These articles are normally at the highest and most specialized level of subject knowledge possible, as they are intended for other disciplinary specialists, and often have the highest citation density. I have hit 110 citations in an 8,200 word paper, about eleven per page, and again, a field such as history or law might go much denser, where every piece of information must be documented for the writer's or firm's protection.

As I'll expand on, Asian universities often apply a point system in evaluating professors, and journal articles are often the most highly-rated forms of research output, much more than are books or conference presentations. But this differs between cultures and fields. The Europeans value books more, and some fast-moving fields such as computing prefer the immediacy of conferences.

Why Not Send It to the Best Journal?

Be my guest. If you can pull off placing an article in a top journal, you will raise your own reputational score, such as an "h-index" or ORCID profile, and might certainly astonish your committee members. But it's a long shot. Once when I was a doctoral candidate, I overconfidently sent a revised seminar paper I thought was particularly strong to the best journal in my subfield. It was promptly rejected and returned to me with a rather "who do you think you are, kid" tartness to it. This just discouraged me from submitting the paper to anyone for several years.

When I discussed judging secondary sources and the "food chain" or informal reputational hierarchy of journals and publishers, I advised that it's common sense to begin with journals or sources indexed in the best academic databases, and work your way down. This is not necessarily the best way to submit your articles. Rather, I advise you learn to target your article to where you realistically see optimal prospects for its acceptance. Choosing the best journal in the field which only publishes the top work and most established authorities may only hurt your feelings, as mine were, when its editors bite your head off. In your mid or later career you may need to consider impact factor or other metrics of how highly your journal is ranked. But early on, it might be more prudent to sometimes settle for quantity over quality.

Having said this, you should not be sending your papers to journals which are not listed on any article indexes or which somehow seem dubious. Comedian Groucho Marx's dictum that he wouldn't join any country club bad enough to invite him to be a member applies here: be wary of any journal which solicits you by spam e-mail. Though this may appeal to a writer's vanity, the journal may be bogus or near-bogus, or may demand large fees for publication—indicating that everything submitted is accepted whether it is groundbreaking or garbage, and may not be reviewed by anyone. In 2005, two scholars infamously submitted a science paper to predatory journal consisting of nothing more than the repeated sentence "get me off your f— mailing list"— and it was actually published after the fees were paid.

The general reputational tree for journal submissions is not much different from my one for judging sources.

Gold Standard
Web of Science indexes for arts and humanities (A&HCI), social sciences (SSCI), or sciences (SCI); top university presses

Silver; Very Good
SCI(E), Scopus, IEEE or other field-specific indexes; well-known and established university or institutional presses

Might be Fine, but Google it
Journal is in no major indexes; journal is online only; journal originates in a non-English speaking nation; for-profit commercial publisher

Stay Away
Journal solicits via spam e-mails filled with inflated compliments and spelling errors; journal is on Beall's list of predatory publishers; journal requires enormous fees

Again, lest I make these providers or organizations angry with me, I am dealing with overall perceived reputations, and there will be exceptions. Some specialized academic disciplines may have their own high-prestige journals which don't necessarily show up on the mainstream indexes. As well, my point on 'non-English nation' may appear prejudiced. There are notable outliers; in such a field as English linguistics, there are prestigious Japanese journals, and probably few engineers or computer scientists would decline an offer from the best Indian journals. But generally, I maintain that periodicals in English but originating in non-English speaking nations should receive more scrutiny.

Should I Pay Fees?

It's not *always* a danger sign if journals demand subsidy fees or Article Processing Charges (APCs), although it's of course up to you whether you can or are willing to pay them. You may have other choices and fish in the sea, just as the journals do. I have a few times paid fees of $50 or so to join a journal's 'society,' which allowed me submission rights, but also all the copies of the journal for the year. It's also fairly common for Korean journals to ask for article processing fees of $200-400, although I've had larger amounts requested which I refused. I once encountered additional nominal fees for paying external reviewers as well. There is scammy profiteering, but sometimes people need to eat, like you do.

This may again come down to a judgment call of whether you can or will pay these fees. I don't mind so much paying the Korean journals because the articles are open-access on their websites and other repositories. Other journals may give you a similar "green" fee option to make your article open-access. As noted, for ethical reasons you may wish to support journals affiliated with open access movements. It's when fees jump into stratospheric amounts, and become mostly what the journal or editor wants to discuss, that you ought to be suspicious that the 'journal' is a predatory scam.

One of my early published journal articles regarded animal symbolism in a medieval romance written around 1300. For years I had predatory animal sciences journals solicit me for articles because their spiders found my article. You will inevitably receive e-mails like this:

Dear *HTTP 404 Error*,
We are so indulged to be privelged to have the enormous honnor of requesting your extremely valuabul article based on your magisteriul work "Bad Animals and Faithful Beasts in Bevis of Hampton" and cordeally welcome you to contribute another expart article to the *International Global World Journal of Absolutely Everything Scholarly Academic Just Send It Now*.

If you are as equally cynical as this e-mail, you might decide that any publication is better than none on your CV. But even if you are willing to pay the fees for these pseudo-scam journals, you are legitimizing what they do; you are guaranteeing a future blizzard of more e-mail invitations; and any hiring committee worth its salt will notice that the journal is suspicious and that you are passing it off as a legitimate scholarly source.

Again, you need to tread into the publishing world with your eyes open. To many people outside academia, the system is lunacy even with legit journals—writers pay a journal to accept their article, which is reviewed by volunteer peers for free, and then the journal makes a profit on its product—which in turn university libraries must pay for access to. It's little wonder that there are predatory journals when this model seems dubiously lopsided in profitability for even the most reputable players. As well, one of the structural problems of the system is finding external reviewers, who being anonymous, usually receive nothing except the feeling of collegial philanthropy.

Unless they are open access, you normally can't even post your *own* published papers online or on social media to make them freely available to friends or colleagues, as they are the property of the journal or press. Uploading them to ResearchGate or ArXiv or other repositories may result in nasty takedown orders. However, many journals will allow you to post your originally submitted manuscript (the Author's Original Manuscript, AOM), or ones at various stages of finish, and I know of none that forbid you to post abstracts. It might benefit you to have profiles on some of these sites, although some are profit-oriented and not necessarily in your best interests. Google Scholar and the ORCID identification systems for publishing scholars are both reputable sites to create a research profile.

This whole system isn't really for the benefit of academics and may eventually crack apart, and is already threatened by online alternatives (more on this later) and pirate repositories. For now, be wise as a serpent, while remembering that some journals and publishers are relatively well-intentioned, and some toiling within them are doing their best. Oddly, higher-tier journals are less likely to ask for fees than low-tier ones, the opposite of what you might expect; the more prestigious ones are probably better-funded by their university or institutional sponsors.

12.3 No: Rejections and Revisions

Normally you will submit a .doc or some similar file format to the journal by e-mail, or by a submission portal, most of which seem to have been coded around 1999. A few still live in the age of dinosaurs and require actual printed and posted paper submissions, as did a medieval studies journal I knew which perhaps took medievalism too much to heart. Obviously, it's wise to read directions on length or formatting—journals may use a standard citation style or some in-house Franken-version. Some submissions are *blind*, meaning you remove your name and those of any co-authors, so that reviewers will not be prejudiced by recognizing the writers.

After you submit a journal article, the article may receive a quick 'desk reject' from the editor if it is immediately seen as unsuitable—either because of its quality or because the paper's topic is outside the journal's subject ambit. A very nice journal will recommend other journals to try. If it stays, it is normally sent out for review to two or three reviewers, who will make recommendations. You won't know who the reviewers are for their protection, and they may not know who you are if it is a blind submission.

Article review can involve a frustrating wait for writers, for the process can take anywhere from weeks to a year, during which time the submission is exclusive, meaning you can't submit it anywhere else. The longest wait I've ever had was 13 months, but that's extreme—and I'll never submit to that journal again. I would say 2-4 months is more common, and one months about the fastest I've ever experienced.

The usual recommendation terms used for journals, at least in my field, are listed here (from best to worst). Note that they are similar in logic to that of a diss committee's grading report.

Accept: the paper is accepted as is, and no changes are required (this almost never happens)

Accept with minor revisions: the paper is accepted, and only small edits are directed which the editor can accept; no re-review is needed (this sometimes happens)

Conditional acceptance / revise and resubmit (R&R): major changes are directed, and afterward the paper goes back to reviewers for a second chance (this sometimes happens)

Reject: the paper is unacceptable and must be sent elsewhere (this often happens). At best, the journal might recommend another journal they feel your paper is suited for.

Article submission requires patience and a thick skin, and some grin-and-bear-it tolerance for what can be random. I have had articles accepted on the first try; other articles underwent submissions to numerous journals over years before they were accepted: my record is a dozen journals over seven years; some simply could not get a break anywhere. It is discouraging to have an article which you have labored on be rejected, and difficult to reach the disappointing but prudent decision that it's time to give up and move on.

Authors are sometimes like tomcats: they distrust all other toms, but they are kind to kittens. – Malcolm Cowley

Malcolm Cowley's dictum, alas, applies more to your professors and you, but not to journal editors and reviewers, who don't know if you are a cat or kitten. Reviewers vary on how much tact or advice they provide. Reports can range from detailed, friendly advice on how to improve the paper for another journal, to a terse "the paper is unpersuasive"; reviewers can radiate collegial warmth or cold condescension. Some reviewers have their own agendas and prejudices, and there is a humorous social media meme and Facebook group about the infamous "Reviewer #2" who hates everything and makes impossible or unreasonable demands. In 2018 such an "R#2" failed my submission and told me that I needed the help of a native English speaker!

What happens if the reviewers disagree? This varies, but the editor might re-send the paper to other reviewers, or break the tie by adding a third vote. I have also had journals which gave conditional acceptances if any one reviewer approved the paper. I'm not proud. A backdoor acceptance is still an acceptance, and the reader will of course never know.

When the Paper is Rejected

I sometimes see contentious threads on the "R#2" forum which asks whether a writer should challenge a rejection report. I suspect this is nearly always a waste of time, and worse, might antagonize editors against future submissions. Worst, the same reviewer might again read your paper for a *different* journal you subsequently submit to.

I have two red lines in article submission. I won't tolerate a review process of over one year, and I'll retract my submission if a journal can't get its act together by then; and I won't accept abusive language. I once received a review which was personally insulting, and I requested the editor to either assign me a new reviewer or else release my submission. The editor complied, but the paper was ultimately rejected. I am glad that I didn't accept such behavior (and it was eventually accepted elsewhere), but my suspicion is that I annoyed the editor, who privately sided with the reviewer; the reply e-mail to my request was carefully couched to avoid in any way seeming to apologize. Such are the seedier politics of academic publishing!

Again, for some reason little is written to guide journal article writers in these issues of realpolitik. I can only give you my own experience here as a template. If my article is rejected and there is little or no feedback, I will usually do a quick read-through and then send it off elsewhere right away before I can forget about it or become discouraged. If there is a reject with helpful advice (occasionally I've had a journal reject my paper but kindly recommend a sister or related journal), then there is more to work with, and I can go into an editing and revision mode. If the review honestly feels the paper is very bad, I may give up—but the article will be stored in case I can use parts of it for something else in future.

When Revisions are Ordered

You may either be receiving directions for minor or major revisions without another review, which is optimal, or at least a second chance (revise and resubmit). Either way, your foot is in the door. It is almost always better to stay with the submission.

The first impulse writers have is frustration or anger, that the feedback is nitpicking, unreasonable, mean-spirited, or biased. It may well be. Either way, it's a human response to vent, and my own practice, and one I recommend, is that you step away from the paper for a day or two to cool down. You may become impatient if you revise when irritable, or worse, you may somehow transmit hostility into the text. This might be the best time to do any suggested additional research, such as locating and reading new sources. You may honestly realize that there were ideas or issues you missed.

The larger problem is that if I've received the reviewer reports months after submission, the paper is no longer fresh in my mind, and I have difficulty stepping inside the paper and keeping all of its sections and chains of arguments straight. What I do is first carry out the low-level fixes ordered by the reports—the grammar or citation errors, the low-level factual mistakes, or other small issues. This will bring me back inside the paper, and will build my confidence that something is getting done. As well, if the reader report says something like "missing citation on p. 8 line 17," it is best to tick off these tasks before you rearrange text to different locations.

If larger structural problems are identified as needing repairing, I number the paragraphs and reverse-engineer an outline so that I can see the overall flow and sequence of ideas at a graphical level. This allows me to move around logical blocks as needed, paragraph by paragraph—or, paragraphs might be deleted or markers inserted to show where new ones are to go. Here is the reverse-engineered list of paragraphs from my *Pygmalion* paper, which allowed me to see the paper structurally at a glance.

1. Quick take: Higgins is a replacement father for Doolittle.
2. Shaw very prescriptive in his plays
3. Shaw did not want them to marry
4. Shaw doesn't have many positive marriages.
4a. Biographical and psychoanalytic readings of Shaw-->his mom
6. Critics still insist that they are meant to marry
  5. No one asks whether Eliza wants to marry Higgins --> move to 7
7. Eliza shows no interest in Higgins
8. The interesting complication is Doolittle
9. Doolittle is a cohort of Higgins in age
10. Doolittle's arrival allows play to show agreement is not sexual
11. Doolittle an absentee father [Lack of dad in Shaw's life?](but wouldn't this show Eliza needs love?)
12. Eliza long separate from her father?
13. Higgins easily takes on parental role (does this explain Eliza's anger with him, transferred from her father?)
14. Eliza's return forms a family, not a romance
15. Act V demonstrates that Eliza sees Higgins as father
16. None of this requires radically revisioning the play
17. Conclusion: lack of dad mirrors Shaw's lack of dad?

Sometimes you can't obey the reviewer directions, either because they contradict each other, or you have some justification to disagree and stand your ground on a particular issue. I have usually gotten away with this by re-submitting the paper with a polite explanation that the reports were helpful, but on notes x and y I differ, and why. Editors will sometimes agree with you over directions and take your side over the reviewer's, or they may simply let you have your own way, accepting that to an extent it's your paper.

Handling Multiple Authors

Revisions can multiply in complexity and headaches when multiple authors are involved. A bit of typical terminology:

- First/Lead/Main Author: The author who did most of the work
- Co-Author: Another author at the same level, who did as much work
- Contributing Author: A sub-author below the main one(s)
- Corresponding Author: A (sub-) author who handles messaging; normally a senior manager who supervises

I have only occasionally worked with other authors, as it is for some reason infrequent in the humanities. The social sciences sometimes has double authors, and STEM is infamous for having multiple authors, sometimes to the point of absurdly long lists. This might reflect the reality that a scientific article project is more likely to require funding and assistants to carry out physical experiments, whereas a paper on a literary text normally doesn't need laboratories. There also seems to be more politics in STEM departments in my experience. My advisors and colleagues would never have dreamed of such a thing—English departments tend to be made up of lone wolves. But sometimes graduate students in science departments find that *everyone* and their dog wants a piece of the pie when it comes to being listed in a published article, especially department chairs with power, whether or not they've written a single line.

Hence to my knowledge, a common problem in science papers is squabbles over author order; optimally, writers want to be listed first, so that they will be (Johns et al.). If the authors are friends and collaborate regularly, they might either alphabetize or rotate the author list. If not, or there are difficult people who wish to monopolize credit and minimize contribution—it would be highly recommendable to clearly lay out and agree on author sequence and task divisions before the project begins.

As a copy-editor outside these issues, I would recommend someone take explicit responsibility for final editing. A common issue I see in group-written papers is that sections are pasted together without much oversight, so that the level of discourse or rhetorical style jarringly changes as contributors switch. Or, a term that isn't defined earlier in the paper is explained in a *later* section. It would be better for a final editor to smooth out these differences.

Being Asked to Review

At some point, you may be fortunate (or unfortunate) enough to be considered competent or authoritative enough on your topic to be asked to review someone else's paper for a journal, and make a recommendation on publishing it. This may happen after a journal has published yours and you are in the loop of contacts.

You can be as cynical as you wish regarding accepting reviews; It's up to you whether you accept the request or not, as you probably won't receive anything and it will be anonymous. But serving as a reviewer could supply a line on your CV or resume, and I suspect that being nice to the journal may cause them to be nicer to you someday if you submit there again. I also think that reading other people's papers may help you to write your own, when you observe things to try, or things *not* to do.

As for the review itself, I have no special advice, for it's your business. I usually do a fast read-through and then a slow one, and then write a report. You aren't helping by accepting everything, believing you are being kind. Equally, I can only appeal to your better instincts that you not repay nastiness with the same, and that you make an effort to give some constructive advice and encouragement if you recommend revisions or a rejection. Raining down snark might be shrugged off by an emeritus professor, but it might also move a first-time writer to give up permanently.

There are usually three things which will fairly quickly cause me to vote for rejection of a paper:

a. Unclear or missing thesis statements
b. Unproven arguments
c. Vague, confusing content

If you have read the book up to now, a and b are predictable—if I don't understand what the paper is trying to demonstrate, I will recommend a reject. I just don't think it's fair to make me work that hard to piece together your point.

An argument paper with insufficient evidence is also understandably a failure; it doesn't persuade. I write this delicately, but I sometimes find papers predicated on social justice issues to assume too much:

What are the implications of Marlowe, Joseph Conrad's racist and sexist narrator?

How can we forward diversity in human resources departments?

We know most people are afraid of robot healthcare workers. How can we solve this?

I am neither endorsing nor opposing these particular premises, but a paper probably should not take it for granted the reader implicitly accepts them without bothering to prove them. Rushing on to build further claims on top of these assertions may be unwise.

As to the third point, I sometimes find papers are so unrelentingly theoretical and abstract that they have no concrete examples or facts to ground them, and I don't understand what the discussion is topically or even grammatically about. I once read a paper on water purification devices in Africa which only treated U.N. initiatives and policy strategies—but never once discussed an example of the actual device operating in a physical location, with interviews with villagers or results. The paper felt unpersuasive to me, as though whether a purification device actually *works* is unimportant in comparison to arcane policy debates a continent away. A photograph of clouds is more meaningful if you can contextualize them against the land, and I suppose a paper also needs to have both sky and ground to anchor each other.

Recall also in the chapter on editing where I advocated lexical precision, not pedantic terms for their own sake. Sadly, it is likely going to be younger academics who are insecure about their abilities who will try to show off by stuffing their papers with obscure or inflated language.

12.4 Conference Papers

Scholars or experts in a common field may meet regularly or annually to discuss new findings and to present papers to each other at academic conferences. Some people attend them out of obligation and view them as pleasurable as a dentist visit, but others enjoy them. You might participate only as an audience member, or you might be a panelist or presenter. Some find conferences supportive and collegial, though I tend to leave them feeling lonely, and prefer going to one with a partner or group. The established ones can feel cliquey to me, as though everyone only wants to interact with the people they have known for three decades.

Often scholars will read an early draft of an article they are working on, hoping that people will give helpful advice or point them to sources. The conference paper may end up in a conference proceedings or, after revision, eventually later in a conventional journal. In some disciplines which are faster-moving, conferences are where the action is, and reading at them may count more towards faculty retention and promotion decisions than journals. I've had computer science colleagues explain to me that because journals have such a slow publication cycle, the technologies they discuss may be out of date by the time the journal goes to print.

Some disciplines have some metrics for which conferences are better or more prestigious, but generally, as there are fewer conferences than journals, your professors or colleagues will likely be familiar with the major established ones in your field that "everyone important" goes to, or at least those in your country or region. Some are a single day, but I have seen some upwards of four days. At some, actual faculty interviews are held on the sidelines, as the MLA is known to do.

Conferences can also be expensive, and might involve flights and hotel stays. University departments may have support funds for these activities, but sooner or later every academic or even grad student will get spam e-mails for semi-bogus conferences. As with predatory journal invitations, you will need to trust your instincts, but there are similar danger signs that a conference is dubious:

1. None of your colleagues or peers has heard of it. New conferences do emerge, but one held by the same university for decades, and which your advisor knows twenty people, ten drinking stories, and two marriages from, is more likely to be reputable.
2. You've been already pre-approved for a major speaking role at it, with over-the-top flattering language, typically filled with spelling errors or wooden phrasings.
3. The conference has a flashy but vague name: "International Conference of Global Scholarship," and seems to fit any academic field. I once was invited as a keynote speaker at a medical or veterinary conference because an internet spider found my paper discussing medieval animal imagery, as I mentioned. Obviously no one cared whether my subject had any relation.
4. It's suspiciously pricey. At least in my field, I don't think I've seen conference fees go much over $100. You may also have red lines on how much you're willing to spend on such an endeavor. As with journals, at a certain point, why are you paying to provide something for free?
5. It's held in an obscure location or obvious vacation resort. This doesn't mean conferences must be held in London or New York, or that those held there are always legit, but as with journals, an unknown city which has no obvious connection to your subject, especially at a private venue and not a university campus, is a red flag. Bali is very nice, but it suggests an excuse for a holiday.

Some universities—and this is often the case with Korean ones—minimally value conference reading because they have been burned in the past by professors taking a subsidized golf break. I've had friends as well who read papers to empty rooms, wasting their money and time in shell conferences that were profit ventures for the organizers. But I don't want to discourage you from going to conferences entirely—some are very reputable and good places to network or make employment contacts. Some are fun; one I attended in Medieval Studies in Michigan had jousting demonstrations, mead-tasting parties, and even a dance.

12.5 Preparing a Conference Paper

Again, I don't want to dishearten you. There may be very good career reasons to attend conferences, and some are enjoyable; there's nothing wrong with traveling to a new or exciting location. As noted, it may also be easier to transition a course paper or diss chapter into a journal article via a conference session, assuming the participants have a welcoming attitude for students or new graduates. Sometimes sessions have an enjoyable informality or humor that wouldn't happen in journal articles, and often session titles are provocative or funny. I just generally haven't enjoyed conference culture.

When you arrive at a conference hall, inevitably you are welcomed by grad students at a table, and given an ugly lanyard with your name on it and a book listing the scheduled sessions and events. Your first order of business is to locate: coffee. You then want to get an idea of where the rooms are, and what sessions will occur. Conferences may begin with one giant session with a keynote speaker or speakers, important authorities in the field who are invited to welcome and set the tone or theme for the conference. There may also be round-table or panel sessions where groups of scholars have a conversation.

But the meat of the conference will be individual (or perhaps pair) presentation sessions. Typically, you will be given a one-hour slot, with about 45 minutes for presenting and 15 for questions—or sometimes a half-slot of 20 minutes presenting and 10 minutes for questions. What all conferences have in common is that time is always short, and everything always runs late, and something always goes wrong that eats up more time. For this reason, at the planning stage you should be thinking in terms of time and not words or pages.

It's possible to simply read your paper old-school style, as conferences mostly did in the past and as elderly professors still do, and this has the advantage of being simpler to plan for or practice—all you really need to do is time yourself reading. You also have a ready-made paper should the conference publish its proceedings. The downside is that this can be boring, and so many academics have a more speech-like approach where they address the audience supported by PowerPoints or other slides. This is more difficult to plan and time, but is usually more interesting.

If you are doing the latter and presenting with slides, much of what I discussed about your diss defense applies as well here. If you are reading your paper, there is less to do—although if you are reading at a steady average of about half a page of double spaced text a minute, you really can't do more than 15-20 pages, and you may need to be clearer about verbally signaling where you are in your paper's timeframe. One good place to edit is to minimize quotations. That sounds odd, that I am telling you to reduce citation density, but your audience can't easily distinguish between your words and quoted words, and it looks silly to be making rabbit-ear "air quotes" all the time.

You should also have a plan for what you will do if you are running out of time, and an organizer announces "five minutes!" when you have more to say or show. What I do during the planning stage is mark cues for "must do" and "nice to have" sections or slides, so that if absolutely necessary, you have some indicators you can glance at on the fly that will remind you what you need to cover and what you can skip. You will hardly impress the audience by panicking or trying to go twice as fast, confusing everyone.

At conferences you are running with the big dogs in a way you were not as a student. There will be the cool kids in the field who receive the best session times; there will be angry people with agendas. In the Q&A there will be people asking belligerent or rigged questions, or using the microphone as a way to talk about themselves and their research for ten minutes without asking an honest query—and there is little you can do other than very politely cutting off a rambling pseudo-question, pleading that time is short. People will get up and noisily walk out of poor-quality sessions. I've seen keynote speakers scold the audience over the beeping of smartphone cameras as they photograph slides (I use a digital camera set to silent mode to avoid this distraction). I admit I've also walked out of sessions where I felt my time was wasted, where the session was more an advertisement for the people involved than any content. Sometimes book publishers or software companies pay to give sessions which *are* literally commercials.

But on the plus side, I've enjoyed the adrenaline of a rousing session, and obtained both good advice from a kindly questioner, and a professional-looking video of my session to show friends or use as a work sample. For some reason conference coffee is seldom good, but I do find people often eat well at them, and some conferences will have lunch or banquet events.

After the conference, some fields publish printed proceedings of the papers read. In such cases, you will be invited to submit a printed version of your paper on short notice. This is uncommon in the humanities, but many STEM fields publish them. My guess is that, all things being equal, proceedings carry less authority when cited in other papers than a journal article would—proceedings are shorter and have undergone little peer review. But they have the value of immediacy in quicker-moving disciplines, as I've noted.

12.6 Edited Collections and Monographs

One of the nicer pieces of candy you will receive as an academic or researcher is an invitation to contribute an article to an edited book. For some reason I never see opportunities to apply for these chapter placements; they always seem to be extended by someone you know, a department chair or some colleague who is in the position of editing such a volume. Unfortunately, this might require 'knowing people,' which as a student you are less in a position for.

I say chapter publishing is nice because such a contribution is likely to be medium-benefit but low-stress; university departments and other institutions probably will not value a book chapter highly, but if you are pre-approved by an editor and have a diss chapter or set of materials ready to write new content, your workload should be fairly minimal. Your contribution has been accepted; you don't need to work so hard to defend or justify your study at the beginning.

The remaining problem will be revising your work to fit the book's subject and space allotment given to you—although in my experience these book themes are usually pretty loose, and might be nothing more than a *festschrift*, a collection of studies on a broad topic dedicated to a beloved senior scholar in that field. This is again a good reason to design a diss as a series of chapters on an integrated idea, which allows you to fairly easily repurpose single chapters for something else—assuming a single chapter makes sense on its own without too much editing or explanation.

Monographs

A monograph is just a fancy word for 'book,' but not all books are monographs. Some may be textbooks or manuals for students or others, or edited volumes as above. A monograph, as suggested by the *mono-* prefix, is a more theoretical work of new information written by one scholar or professor for others in the field.

Professors often write monographs for, again, promotion or career purposes, and it is a common activity during a sabbatical break. It's also common in Europe for young professors to first obtain a doctorate and then a *habilitation*, where they write a book, either of new material or compiled from previously-published journal or conference articles. Many countries take this second qualification seriously, and may require it for full professorships, or endow habilitated professors with higher titles, such as Dr. habil. or Docent. Other cultures, such as Asia, tend to prize monographs less, as many universities are wary of the many vanity publishers which print any book for money.

Monograph publishing may appear like the wild west in comparison to journal article or conference publishing, with different and looser rules. It may seem arbitrary, but it's generally not considered plagiarism to reuse your published articles in your own book. As well, journals as a rule firmly forbid simultaneous submissions to other journals, but this is less the case with book publishers, who may not mind you sending dozens of query letters at the same time to other presses—although I advise it's good manners to tell them.

Another distinction in monograph publishing is that it is the only form of academic publishing I know in which authors are commonly actually *paid*, typically either as a flat rate or per copy sold; some 'rock star' academic celebrities may even receive an advance sum on their contract. Nevertheless, I should warn anyone feeling this is a lucrative opportunity that the chances of having a monograph proposal accepted by a decent press are even worse than for prestige journals, and the payments involved are not large. A typical academic monograph might reach a printing of only a few hundred copies.

During the negotiations for my first monograph, my editor told me that I would probably make enough money to go out to dinner once a year, and he has proven to be correct. There is admittedly better money to be made in writing a textbook, as it will potentially annually be bought by classes of students. But I assure you I have no sports car and swimming pool outside my office—you are still writing for small disciplinary demographics, and a hundred dollars a year in royalties is doing well for a publishing academic.

I will repeat two points I made at the beginning of this chapter on revising a diss into a book.

1. Establishing a rationale for the book
2. Dealing with rejection

There was once a time when it was customary for publishers to print unrevised dissertations as books, but it is no longer 1885. There are far too many dissertations now for most to have such prestige. Much more than journals, publishers are concerned with the practical matter of profits and sales. Whether a diss, revised papers, or new material, a monograph manuscript will need to be tailored to appeal to a wider audience of potential buyers rather than the local interests of your department or committee. As the set-up for a printer is usually a few hundred copies at minimum, the publisher needs to justify the risk—although, as I'll discuss in the next chapter, some publishers now outsource printing to fulfillers that can print single copies on demand.

Another difficulty with monograph publishing is that the submission process tends to be more convoluted than it is for journal article publishing, where at most one might create a profile on the journal's website and complete a form. Some academic or private presses will accept a simple query e-mail to the editor listed for your subject area, and others will want a more complex proposal addressing several questions. In particular, you will likely be asked what the book's potential market is. A typical form asks for:

a. Proposed title and brief description
b. Table of contents
c. Chapter summaries and word counts
d. Date of completion
e. Explanation of the book's potential market
f. Competing or similar books
g. Assurance of legal clearances and permissions
h. References, or a resume/CV
i. Samples from finished work

As many presses ask for similar information, you can often copy-and-paste these details, but creating the initial proposal can be burdensome, even without the later back-and-forth details of contracts and proofs.

It's my experience that dubious or scammy book publishers are less common than they are in journal publishing. But they do exist, as I noted earlier, and I would be careful of working with any publisher that seems too eager—or which cold-calls you with spam e-mails. I have red lines with journals, and I also do with book publishers: never deal with one that requires you to pay money, or which mandates you buy a minimum order of books yourself. You may receive the unpleasant surprise that your book is priced very expensively, and that *you* are the marketing team.

Yet I don't want to discourage you from writing a monograph any more than I wanted to discourage conference attendance. It still looks impressive to people to have your own book, as opposed to a sliver within a journal. The major disadvantage is that unless you are a celebrity or ex-president, publishing a book is glacially slow. I began sending proposals for my first book in 2011 and only saw it printed in 2015, after many rejections and months of drafts, permissions, and discussions on art and typography.

This is partly why monographs are even rarer in many STEM fields than are journal articles. By the time the book comes out your important discussion of Windows XP may be obsolete. This is one reason why alternative digital formats for publishing are gaining popularity and influence—which I will discuss in the next chapter.

13 OTHER PROFESSIONAL WRITING

In this chapter I am going to discuss alternative forms of academic, or at least semi-academic writing, which might be done for professional purposes by a student or as a postgraduate or career activity. This also at least hopefully serves the purpose of distinguishing academic argument papers or diss/thesis projects from these genres.

13.1 Digital and Self-Published Books

Perhaps I might have discussed this in the previous chapter, for self-published books *could* be academic monographs or collections of published articles with the same scholarly register as a conventionally published one. But I include this topic here partly because such books could also include other forms of professional writing, or even creative or personal writing, such as a memoir or family genealogy. As well, the remainder of this chapter concerns online publishing, emphasizing its distinctions from the traditional publishing models that have dominated printing for centuries.

POD (Print On Demand) Publishers

A POD publisher is a standard scholarly or commercial publishing house which does everything except printing. That is, it may do reviewing, production, and marketing, but outsources physical book printing to fulfillers which can make books one at a time. Single POD books are slightly more expensive, but this allows such publishers to accept riskier books with smaller markets, as they don't need to set up books in 250-500 minimum print runs to be profitable.

Should you submit to POD publishers? There is nothing intrinsically disreputable about them—they *may* have the same peer review standards and authority of a conventional publishing house. In practice, I find they are slightly less prestigious, as little obligates such a publisher from having lower acceptance standards when their financial risk is significantly reduced. But after you have gone through the established presses and been rejected, it is much better than nothing, and a good POD one will advise you on book graphics and will assist in marketing and promoting your book. As well, a 'real' publisher is more likely to succeed in getting your book into bookstores.

Self-Publishing

If a POD publisher is sending your book fulfiller, why can't you do the same? This is what self-publishing is: it involves being your own virtual publishing house or imprint, and arranging your own editing, layout, production, and marketing of your book, and contracting with fulfillers such as Amazon or IngramSpark. These companies then sell your book on their websites or provide it to other bookselling sites and physical 'bricks-and-mortar' stores, and then pay you arranged royalties. With e-books this process is even more streamlined, as no book is printed. Normally writers contract with the same fulfillers, but you *could* sell the files yourself.

The disadvantages of self-publishing are considerable ones. One, as noted, you lack the sales and promotion tools traditional houses have. The second is that self-published books are still better than predatory journals or vanity press books, but receive minimal regard from scholars or university departments, and that is why I listed them as 'gray' sources for assessing reliability or prestige. I do have my self-pub books on my CV, but I list them under a separate heading indicating so. The reason should be evident: *anyone* can publish one. There is no peer review or gatekeeping, and excepting an extreme situation of hate speech or copyright infringement, there is no substantial oversight stopping people with no credentials or competence from publishing trash. Book chains such as B&N will automatically list your e-book or print book from the fulfiller's index on their store websites, as they receive a profit from selling any copies and incur no real cost—it's just pixels. But few will stock an unknown self-pub book in print on precious shelf space (apparently the hardest outlet to get onto is airport bookstores).

Then why do it? The first reason is a depressing but realistic one—again, it is extremely difficult for a new writer to place a book manuscript with a well-known or reputable traditional publisher, particularly on an esoteric topic or one with limited sales prospects. Self-publishing may be better than nothing if you can't interest publishers in your work. After I've had an article rejected ten times, I begin to consider whether it's worth persisting with; with a book manuscript, you may need to submit to a hundred presses. I hope I am not damning this present book out of my own mouth, as it is self-published, but its potential readership is small. Publishers are not necessarily cynical people, and they may appreciate that a manuscript is high in quality or important, but their concern is sales numbers.

A second benefit is that self-publishing offers total control over your book's materials and appearance, and if you are a George Bernard Shaw who has absolute and exact opinions on how a comma, indent, or spacing should look, or you have firm feelings on your text's content and cover graphics, you make *all* decisions. You can price it high or low, or at-cost, or perhaps free for an e-book version. The fulfiller incurs no real cost or risk; normally, if you're happy, they're happy.

Further, self-publishing is lightning fast, a huge plus for quickly evolving topics or events. Traditional publishing operates in months and quarters, or at best weeks. Self-publishing operates in hours and days. You may be able to submit, proof, and make your book available and propagated onto major bookselling sites within a weekend. Moreover, self-pub books permit rolling revisions and improvements, so that you might have regular or annual releases, as this book has in the past. For now, self-pub books languish in a sea of bad ones, but occasionally one is taken seriously or sells well, or is picked up by a traditional press. They may in future be a serious and credible publishing route, and they already are undermining the concept of book 'editions' when they may be updated at will.

Preparing E-Book and Print Versions

E-books come in a variety of file types for different vendors, but basically are customized html files. As they record letters rather than images of letters, the files are usually small. E-books can be fiddly to format, and the software for making headings and TOCs and so on is still improving. As well, probably Shaw wouldn't like e-books, as they will look different on every reader depending on the fonts chosen.

I don't recommend you only make an e-book version of your book. I stress that *anyone* can make one, and it will probably mean as much to a department head or supervisor as having made a watercolor painting. I also think academics deserve more dignity than to give their e-books away, but that's my opinion. Whether it's fair or not, there is still some cache in a physical artifact, and there are also people who prefer to read print books.

Print versions tend to involve more decisions and setup. Fulfillers like Amazon's Kindle Direct Program (KDP) will often have ready-made templates based on the book size you prefer. This is your decision, and you may find the book looks more scholarly or less depending on its size, although it's often more cost-efficient to have larger but fewer pages—if you've bothered to measure this book, it is 5-1/4" by 8", a good compromise. I advise you take the cover design and graphics seriously, and optimally seek a friend's or professional's help on it. This is the first and perhaps only impression people will have of your book. It should look attractive both in full-size and as a small icon on a book seller's website.

13 OTHER PROFESSIONAL WRITING

Contracting and Selling Your Book

If all you want is a few beautifully-bound print book copies of your diss to give to family or colleagues, no problem. You are happy, your aunt is happy, and Amazon is happy to make a profit on five copies.

If you hope to sell your book to others, this can get complicated. You are the publisher, remember—and if you like, you can even make up your own imprint name. Books are catalogued by ISBN numbers, and you can receive a free one from a fulfiller, but for maximum freedom your own ISBN is best so that you are not tied to one outlet. They can be slightly expensive (although Canadians can have one for free through Library & Archives Canada).

Amazon KDP will print and sell your e-book and print book on its website. This is nice, and Amazon's sales power is so extensive that for many authors this will be the majority of their sales anyway. But you are not exclusively tied to KDP (unless you agree to be; they have some tiers offering benefits for exclusivity). I find it is better to market my books through a combination of Amazon and other fulfillers, as *in my opinion* Amazon is not presently optimal for international or library sales. You can sign up with dozens of individual bookstore or distribution companies that offer self-pub e-book/print book options if you like—B&N, IngramSpark, Google, Apple, Kobo, and others. I find it is easier to contract with a single agglomerator such as Draft2Digital or Smashwords, which will take a small cut but automates distribution and pay for most of these outlets for you.

The most common mistakes I see self-publishing authors commit are:

1. Wildly optimistic prices. I was only half-joking at the start of this book saying that my royalty is a few cents. I've seen writers feel that strangers will pay ten dollars for their twenty-page e-book. This present book is also for my students, and it's wrong to profiteer from it. As I've said, you deserve to be

paid for your work; but I recommend profit points of roughly a dollar at most.
2. Too-short books. With an e-book, anything goes, I suppose—but I would not sell a print book less than 100 pages. At this point, it looks amateurish, and binding the book and having a printed spine gets very iffy.
3. Lazy, crappy cover graphics made with clip art and juvenile font choices. Again, the book's cover is something that should be taken seriously.

Promoting Your Book

Social media posts are good but will mostly only reach your friends and contacts. Some self-pub authors take out small paid advertisements on social media and book sites, such as Facebook, Amazon, Goodreads, or indie book promotion sites. I have done so, and such websites can be very good at helping you target your desired demographic for even ten-dollar budgets, if you prefer. They are unlikely to pay for themselves, but they can certainly help to sell or kick-start interest in your book.

There are websites that promote costly self-pub packages with outlandish sales promises, which are mostly scams. Statistically, selling 100 copies of a self-pub novel is doing well, let alone for scholarly works. 98% of self-publishing success seems to be writing pulp romances about shirtless cowboys. But not everything in life must make you money, and if you feel satisfaction or validation in publishing your diss or creative work, this also has value.

13.2 Technical Writing

Technical writing is typically writing which describes or directs, such as a document explaining a mechanical process, or instructions for using a device or program. Common forms are instruction manuals, technical briefs, datasheets, compliance reports, proposals, and engineering summaries. This sounds like some of the STEM (science, technology, engineering, and medicine) situations I have discussed in connection to IEEE format, and there is some overlap.

Such writing is typically minimally argumentative and highly formatted. Technical writing may have no thesis argument or viewpoint whatsoever; it is more likely to be expository writing, reporting only exact information and facts objectively. In style it usually favors short, precise, direct sentences with minimum ambiguity over rhetorical persuasiveness or elegance.

I couldn't imagine more boring writing. But that is me, and good technical writing is valued and well-paying in workplaces for those with a talent for it. The danger is that this sort of formulaic writing may be increasingly done by AI software. At best, it may very soon simply be a part of other job tasks.

13.3 Business Writing

Despite the academic politics and wrangling in scholarly writing, there is at some level an innocence to it: you are ideally writing to help people and give them knowledge. Business writing is not always on the reader's side, and is not always altruistically interested in knowledge for its own sake.

Sometimes, like technical writing, business writing conveys information with maximal brevity and clarity. But sometimes it is crafted to be deliberately unclear and ambiguous. When a corporate release announces that it is "initiating a campaign of repositioning opportunities to streamline operations and leverage its footprint," this is a buzzword-filled evasion of saying that the company is losing money and will fire some staff. The realpolitik of business writing often reflects legal or public relations niceties, or navigating client or corporate relationships, rather than beauty or, unfortunately, strict truth.

Many people find such writing dull or unfulfilling if not ethically challenging, but others see it as a necessary activity. In its defense, it has to be done; and firms prize skilled business writing and pay it well. Typical forms include cover letters, résumés/CVs, corporate communications, press releases, inter-office memos, and grant proposals.

These genres of writing tend to be highly formulaic or impersonally polite, making use of standardized structures. Typically, a business letter begins by identifying the purpose of the letter, explaining some request or information, and then ending with some form of gesture or direction to the reader. This might be done for business tasks or promotional purposes, to build a relationship with the addressee, or to promote oneself.

Dear Mr. Van Duson,

In regard to your letter of August 12, I am writing to inform you that the contract information you requested has been arranged to be sent to your office. I enjoyed having lunch with you last week, and would like to say again that if I may be helpful in any way or may provide further assistance in your continuing negotiations with the company, please let me know. I thank you for your attention to this matter and look forward to meeting you at the IQS Conference in Munich on October 8.

Best regards,
Lynette Barker

Business Writing and AI

As with technical writing, up to 2022 I still recommended business writing as a not terribly exciting but well-paying career skill. It is now probable, for good or bad, that it is the *most likely* writing genre to be automated by AI text generators. I have already begun to receive e-mails from people whom I know have weak English skills that are suspiciously flawless—the e-mails were fairly obviously written, or at least edited and corrected, by ChatGPT or the like.

And admittedly, I have less professional or moral ground here objecting to AI generators, for unlike academic scholarship or fiction, business writing doesn't really have an expectation of originality or personality anyway, and again, its formulaic and dry writing style and content breadth lends itself to being auto-generated. It is the sort of low or mid-level drudge work that AI will likely be very good at fulfilling.

Perhaps my earlier advice on seeing AI generators as a tool remains apt. I would not myself trust a bot or app to entirely write a letter, for the subtle gradations of tone and legalese could be spectacularly bungled by a non-human writer; I would certainly want to proofread anything an AI produces. As the expression goes, *garbage in, garbage out*: a competent or careful business writer will still need to develop a skillset for choosing effective prompts to tell the AI what to create.

But AI might be very good at producing an initial draft or outline which a human writer can use as a basis or scaffolding; or, it might be good at suggesting additions or edits or corrections to a nearly-finished text. There are now AI plug-ins that can recommend textual or graphical improvements to PowerPoint slides, and no doubt AI will be used to advise on strengthening cover letters and resumes, as follows.

13.4 Cover Letters and Resumes/CVs

You will normally need a cover letter and resume when applying to graduate school, a job, or an internship—or a more specific type of resume used within academia called a CV, Curriculum Vitae. It's probable that you will only ever write one for yourself, but I'm going to discuss these documents because they do have academic relevance: your likely purpose in attending university was to prepare you for a career, and effective cover letters and CVs may make a difference in obtaining one. As I note, you might use AI utilities to suggest ideas or improvements for your cover letter or resume/CV, but you can't just ask the generator to write you one; it doesn't know you.

This is one situation where it might be nice for the APA style fussbudgets to pronounce a correct standard for cover letters and CVs, for there isn't one. Practices and formats vary, and I can only advise you from personal experience or my students' writings what might be effective. While cover letters and CVs don't have thesis statement arguments, they are in a sense persuasive writing—they seek to convince someone to select or approve you, and give evidence shoring up this recommended action. They also attempt to leverage a certain type of visual ethos in that a strong cover letter and CV look credible.

Keeping in mind the audience of an application letter, which is someone you want to persuade to choose you, is absolutely key. I say this because you are writing for your needs (you want the position or internship), but the text needs to address the *reader*'s needs (to be informed to select the optimal candidate). This may sound cold, but I so often see student cover letters, or actual ones where I am involved in a hiring decision, where the letter is all-about-me: I want this job because I want to do this. Or, there is a begging tone: please choose me and I promise to do x. Why should I? There are other applicants who aren't charity cases.

Thus the first mistake I see in applications is approaching the recruiter from the position of a supplicant or beggar. Recruiters aren't necessarily callous, but their task isn't to make your dreams come true, but to choose an applicant who will be the most problem-free and straightforward fit to the opening. In your cover letter it is better to radiate assurance that you are the candidate who can glide easily into the vacancy—that you're already qualified to begin, or with a minimum of difficulties. Your goal is to convince recruiters not of a zero-sum benefit (I get what I want), but a positive-sum benefit (we win; our needs are mutually served by choosing me).

Make the Little Details Easy to Find

Your name and contact information should be easy to find on the cover letter, and perhaps can be placed in a header on top of the page as well. Do be clear at the beginning of your cover letter what it is you want.

I am applying for the position advertised. **x** *Which one?*

I am applying for the position advertised for Full-Time Intern (LED-#406) in the department of physics.

13 OTHER PROFESSIONAL WRITING

Accentuate the Positives

A cover letter isn't a confession to Father Finley. You most certainly should not lie, or seek to deceive a recruiter (it's often a dismissible offence if caught later), but you are selling yourself; focus on the good attributes.

Though my grades were not stellar, I feel I can compensate by x

There's no need to admit this. If your grades weren't your strongest point in university, discuss other attributes that were, and accentuate those strengths. Many of us are culturally taught to value humility and avoid boasting, and it feels unnatural to advocate ourselves in cover letters. This balance isn't easy to finesse. You can overdo things and seem arrogant, especially if you overuse inflated buzzwords, but you optimally want to project competence, and the readers of the cover letter want to identify your best skills and attributes.

What I'm going to say next may sound moralizing or fusty. But one way candidates sabotage themselves when entering the post-student professional world is by having juvenile e-mail addresses, or by being careless about what they post on social media. It's your life, and you have the right to post what you like, within limits. But if I receive a cover letter with partynaked413@abc.com, or I Google your name and everything is profanity-laden posts about you holding alcoholic drinks in a nightclub, I will make conclusions about your appropriateness for a serious position. The same warning applies about being in the habit of posting strong or controversial political rants. Now, you may feel strongly that censoring yourself online is unjust to you or inauthentic. But you should at least know that committees may search your profile and judge accordingly.

Show, Don't Tell

No one cares about your passion. I have read so many saccharine applications rhapsodizing about the candidate's 'passion' that the word has become offensive to me. The word means nothing, and can be claimed by anyone. This doesn't mean that your ethics or emotions aren't valuable, but that I would prefer you convey a concrete example of your supposed ardor. If you want to be a nurse, discuss the nursing trade magazines you read; the volunteering you've done; or your aunt who is a nurse and has mentored you since you were small. If you want to be an engineer, discuss your past experiences or interests concretely related to the pursuit. What you have actually done, whether formally in placements or courses, or informally by picking up a skill through life events, is more convincing.

Similarly, attention to tangible details show that you are serious. Years ago I was on a faculty hearing to award a winter-break scholarship to New Zealand. Many students spoke vaguely about their 'strong desire.' One student discussed the program's attributes, particular opportunities within it she was interested in, and how it fit into a larger career narrative. She accurately noted some of the sights and amenities in Auckland which I recognized. She had cared enough to investigate the scholarship, and she received it. Similarly, your application or interview should reveal that you've researched and thought about the position—what specifically you want to do in it; what special interests or skills you can bring to it; particular people in it you want to work with; or how it connects to a longer-term plan.

Resumes

Resumes are brief summaries of your qualifications and skills, normally in some abbreviated or point-form format. They typically take three layouts.

1. Chronological, listing from the present backwards.
2. Functional, listing by category of skill; for example, divided into a. Sales b. I.T. c. Management. This is better for people with a variety of careers.
3. Combination, a mix of chronological and functional.

Resumes commonly have headings indicating categories of qualifications or experiences, such as

Education
Work Experience
Volunteer Experience
Other Skills
Awards and Accomplishments
References

This is a typical order, and the one I used in my resume days. But there isn't a rule, and you should probably put your strongest category first. A resume is secondarily a documentation of your past, but primarily the recruiter is interested in how the skills and experiences you had can be used in future. If your degree is not exactly in line with the position—accentuate work experience first. If you have little work experience, place volunteer experience first, or collapse the headings into "Experience."

Similarly, your resume headings should document where and when you did something, but in describing that entry, skills are what is important. "Took a course," "Helped the teacher," or "Worked in the office" is obvious, but any relevant expertise learned, especially managing people or money, is more valuable to a recruiter. Active verbs such as served, supervised, organized, trained, managed, counted, prepared, or taught tell the reader that these skills can be re-applied to the present position, whether you learned them in a job, a volunteer placement, or in a classroom.

Tip

Don't include a photo of you in your resume unless requested, or it's the normal culture. In some jurisdictions, organizations are afraid of being accused of sexism/lookism, and may as policy automatically reject any application with a photo.

Because resumes are typically scanned quickly by impatient eyes, word thrift and tight editing are critical. A common question is how long resumes should be. My rule of thumb is to have as many pages as you have decades of living. When you are twenty, two pages is likely enough. A forty-year-old might need four pages. It would be better to delete less-important content from your resume than to have a lengthy one that people will stop reading, or one with text jammed into tiny fonts and margins that an elderly recruiter can't read. Some people remove anything more than ten years old. Usually I advise that students remove non-special skills—everyone knows how to use Microsoft Office.

An interesting development with resumes, if such a thing can be said, is that they are gradually resembling websites—perhaps because many applications are now completed online. This means that you need to think about design and layout esthetics more than you would for a seminar paper. This will probably vary by what you are applying for; if you are in a conservative field such as law or civil service, a cutesy resume with icons and colors will be disregarded, but in the fine arts or design a visually intelligent resume might be persuasive.

CVs

Some of this guidance carries over into CV writing, although only some. CVs tend to be longer, and may be double the length of a resume. I see some upwards of ten pages, as they tend to be more documental in nature, listing specifics of the degree program and every publication or conference attended. This is mine in structure.

Dr. Kenneth (Ken) Eckert
Professor of English
My university name and address
E-mail, ORCID
(A digital identification number at orcid.org)

SUMMARY
Present Employment: Professor, my university
Degree: Ph.D. in English Literature: Subjects a, b, and c
Publications: x articles published with y in submission; z books
Teaching Experience: x years

EDUCATION
Ph.D. English Literature, specialization
University (year of graduation)
Dissertation title
Advisor and e-mail address

ACADEMIC APPOINTMENTS
Associate Professor of English
My university, location (year begun - now)
Doing x things. Y research grants and z students supervised.

PUBLICATIONS
Research Interests
Single-Authored Articles
Published Books and Other Research (self-published)

CONFERENCE PAPERS
Newest to oldest

COURSES TAUGHT
Name of Course (Numbers and acronyms may not mean anything to recruiters), number of times taught

ACCOMPLISHMENTS & AWARDS
Fluent in these software packages, these LMS
Reading/speaking proficiency in languages x and y
Academic awards received
Member of professional organization x

REFERENCES
Dr. x, Position, Location, e-mail

CVs tend to be more conservative in format, although their readers are probably equally impatient; an easily-recognized typographic logic to your divisions and headings will be appreciated. I find CVs which follow "References" with "Available on request" almost as annoying as letters which extol 'passion.' It would be better to either list the names and contact details of your references, or omit the heading entirely.

13.5 Online Writing

Online writing could involve writing for a sort of modified online journal where graphics and hyperlinks can be included; or an essay for a social media journalism site; or in a personal blog site; or as a webmaster for a department of program in your workplace. It is again unlikely to be of much scholarly value on a CV, but it is engagement with peers and the public in the form of community service. It also has the benefit again of being far more fast-paced than traditional publishing mediums. Instead of schedules being in days, they may be in hours, particularly after important news events.

It may sound clichéd to state so, but the changes wrought by the internet to how we read and digest text are enormous and ongoing, even leaving alone the tidal wave of AI-facilitated text. Scholarship, or at least its indexing, is gradually migrating online, as are some conferences, as I noted earlier. But there are two more subtle changes that are developing because of digital scholarship. One is that online writing is a more visual medium than print is, and so digital writers need to be increasingly adept at weaving pictures, graphics, and audio or video clips into their text, and may perhaps need to make more rhetorical or content decisions on fonts, sizes, colors, and layout arrangements.

How internet and AI writing will conversely change paper writing in return has not yet been determined. By the standards of scholarship, the internet is a recent innovation. But there is already some influence on typography and formatting in online journals—for example, as I mentioned before, less indentation of

13 OTHER PROFESSIONAL WRITING

paragraphs and more skip-a-line—and some experimental moves toward citation systems based on code hyperlinks, with DOI codes a beginning towards this. As well, many textbooks and magazines now use more pop-out blocks inserted into page columns to simulate the busy multi-sectioned design of web visuals. In some ways this returns to medieval manuscripts, which often had side-column commentaries as opposed to a single line of text.

The second change is subtler but even broader: the linearity of traditional print text is being challenged by digital text. By that I mean that books and journals, and the articles within them, have beginnings and ends and are read in a start-to-finish direction. Websites don't—they have pages which may not form any sequence, and which may be freestanding, read only as the user needs or wants to.

This has immediate implications when we consider that a website's 'table of contents' is not usually like that of a printed book. In a journal it may not make a difference what articles are read or in what order, but in most books the TOC has some sequential rationale. Because most people are now used to websites, we probably don't realize how we shift our cognitive gears in using them. As most western writing systems involve left-to-right reading, horizontal site menus tend to be designed to be scanned left-to-right and vertical ones up-to-down, but that doesn't mean we are to click in that order. On a site menu there may be options such as Home, About, Contact, and also other branches and sub-branches conforming to the site's organizational logic, if there is one, but they may not form a sequence.

When I now see early forgotten or archived websites from the mid-1990s, they often feel stiff or lacking user-friendliness. This is understandable considering that early html had fewer design options, monitor screens were smaller, and page writers were applying the logic and conventions of print to the web. Early pages tended to resemble papyrus scrolls, and it's no coincidence that we "scrolled" through long chapter-length pages; like ancient scrolls, they were often freestanding and episodic, much like ancient story cycles or modern sitcoms or animated cartoons are.

Around 2000, sites began to imitate television screens, as though each page is a channel, with its own pop-up or inline components and less scrolling. This trend has continued over the last twenty years with dynamic as opposed to static page design, meaning that pages are created or adjusted in real time to match the user's needs or location. As patience for endless scrolling has shrunk, the nature of the internet as a 'web' has intensified—pages are shorter but have more hyperlinks and cross-references, allowing users to digest brief chunks of text or media and then jump like grasshoppers between other pages on the site or other websites. I suspect the term 'page' itself is now grandfathered as a web term, and may or may not be used in future decades.

These developments may seem exciting, or threatening, or bewildering—in the same way mechanized printing might have seemed to the late medievals, who also saw both new possibilities and dangers. At a career level, it is easy to feel like a dinosaur when technologies are moving so quickly. My belief is that online text will form an everyday means of conveying information, just as radio and television are, but that there will still be a role for legacy text: for conventional books and papers. Some text will remain sequential rather than forming matrices, for human brains don't change much. A paper describing a series of steps in an experiment would be arduous reading if it were divided into small and random links. The conventional formats of scholarly papers and dissertations may change in this century, but I doubt the rhetorical practices underlying them will.

The internet will probably continue introducing interesting changes into how text is reproduced and disseminated. Future computer monitors may incorporate three-dimensional layers of text and graphics, with a whole new methodology of seeing visual hierarchies and relationships of information. Asian web design has generally been very bad in the past, and I suspect this is so because it is seen as an IT and not a humanities practice. This may change, and in any culture there may be valuable career if not scholarly applications in future for those who understand the rhetorical language of digital writing, particularly as much of the coding drudgery may be handled by automated applications.

13.6 Wikipedia Writing

I have periodically mentioned Wikipedia throughout this book, and mostly in relation to it being used as a source. To reiterate, unless your paper's discussion is somehow about Wikipedia, quoting it as a secondary source should be minimal, partly because its reputability and reliability are controversial, but mostly because that's not what it's for—it is meant to be an encyclopedia, a tertiary source which may indicate useful other sources.

But here I would like to recommend Wikipedia as a writing activity; that is, joining the site as a volunteer and creating or improving entries that you feel qualified in. It may seem strange that I do so, as Wikipedia is not argument or even necessarily academic writing; it's an encyclopedia, and many entries are about popular culture or unserious topics. You can't state or pursue a thesis statement on the site, and if you do it will be deleted. There is also less scope for 'new' entries, as the usual practice is to expand existing ones or innovate sub-branches on related subtopics.

As well, as with most of the writing genres in this chapter, Wikipedia writing and editing is not well-regarded as a formal scholarly pursuit within academia. Although the site is raising its standards and improving its tools for identifying casually or maliciously false information, entries are anonymous and crowd-edited, making it problematic to credit scholars with a tangible research accomplishment.

Yet I think there are two solid reasons to contribute to Wikipedia. One is that it is good writing practice, does involve research and referencing skills, and the exercise of working within the different heading and division practices on the site is beneficial, as is negotiating or working with other editors. The rhetorical activity of turning off the need to prove an argument and addressing a different audience with different needs is also valuable. Further, the digital literacy skills I previously mentioned of negotiating code and graphics are also acquired via entry-editing. Wikipedia has its own lexicon of terms (stubs, branches), and conventional article headings that do not always resemble those of scholarly papers.

Last, in a way this discussion circles back to that in the first chapter: why write? For many, a paper or diss is a means to an end, for course or degree credit, and that's fine. But hopefully you also write to help others to understand a subject. I am by no means denigrating conventional scholarly writing, for why else would I write this book—but the readers of such publications might potentially number in the hundreds or thousands. The Wikipedia site averages 18 billion views a month, and to me there are solid philanthropic reasons to pay forward your expertise on such a platform, one which freely provides information to millions of people who either would not understand, or have access to conventional scholarship.

14 GRAMMAR CLINIC

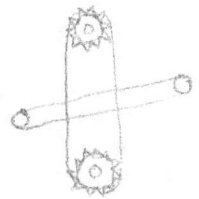

I'm not a second-language acquisitionist, but I do have experience teaching English and grading writing by non-native (L2) learners. I find that it's easy for bare-beginners to learn the basics of English, but extremely difficult to become indistinguishable from a native (L1) speaker. If you are able to read this book, it's unlikely that your grammar levels are 'local' ones that prevent understanding. More probably, your errors are ones that identify you as L2. Whether it is fair or not, that will stigmatize your writing. And in fairness, unfamiliar or unclear phrasings combined with already difficult content is a heavy cognitive burden to place on any reader.

English is a challenging and inconsistent language and I feel sympathy for its learners. Even someone with an L1 proficiency can be confused by someone speaking in one of its many dialects. The elderly can find the slang expressions and emoticons of a teenager's text messages indecipherable. English was not designed by anyone, but has evolved chaotically over centuries, and nearly all attempts at 'improving' it have failed. But it is a human language, with conventions, or a fuzzy logic, that can be internalized.

14.1 The History of English

A good way of better understanding the logic of English is by looking at its history. As you can see from the chart, English began as a dialect of medieval German. Note that English doesn't come from Latin, something I have to repeatedly explain even to native speakers. Other branches include Celtic, Greek, Slavic, Persian, and Sanskrit languages or descendants. Indo-European thus accounts for nearly all the languages of Europe and some of western Asia. One exception is mysterious Basque, which is spoken in northern Spain.

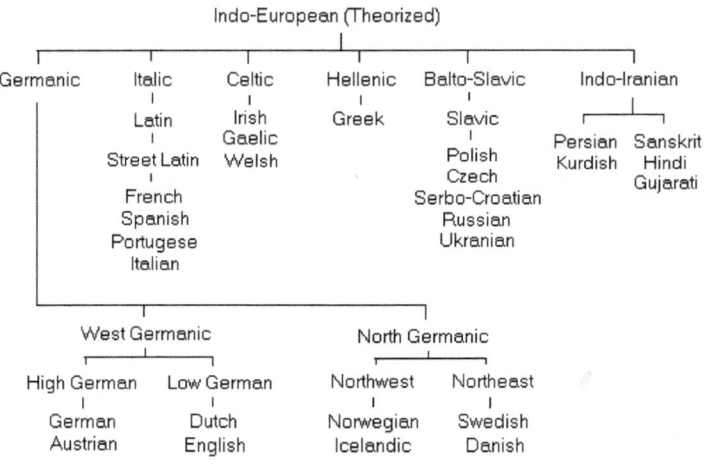

Source: C.M. Millward, *A Biography of the English Language*, 1988.

What the chart doesn't show is the constant borrowing of new and duplicate words from other languages. English was heavily influenced by Latin-speaking missionaries, Norse Vikings, French conquerors, and Greek academics fleeing the fall of Constantinople in 1453. English absorbed words from all these people and their languages partly by force, but partly because it has a grammar and sound system which can easily adopt and naturalize loanwords.

Some languages either have political or cultural resistance to loanwords, such as French with its *Académie française*, or as an extreme example, the stagnant Korean spoken in North Korea; or they are grammatically poor at integrating them, such as Latin—rather than use English 'miniskirt,' the Vatican renders the word as "brevissimae bracae femineae," perhaps semi-humorously. English's voracity for foreign words gives the language power and precision, but is less helpful for learners who are faced with inconsistent sounds and forms, such as the various plurals *churches, children, cacti,* and *deer.*

The influence of other languages, particularly during English's linguistic chaos of foreign invaders and speakers around 900-1100, has greatly impacted English grammar, making it powerful but also maddeningly inconsistent. For example, Old English had fewer verb tenses, and haphazardly imitated Latin and French ones. Thus English adds endings (I learn, learned), changes roots (I run, ran), or changes nothing (it will burst, it burst) or using *have/had.* Some grammarians argue that English doesn't have a future tense, merely implying futurity with auxiliaries like *will* or *going to.* My professors used to joke that "there's no future in English."

14.2 Language Interference

More advanced learners of any foreign language need to deal with the problem of language interference—which refers to the tendency to misapply the natural default phrasings and emphases of one's native language to an acquired one. This can happen at the word level, where a word that sounds familiar has a very different meaning (Spanish *embarazada* does not mean embarrassed, but 'pregnant'), or at the grammatical level, or at the wider discursive level.

This is not only the case with Korean. Many European languages have no 'dummy *do*' ("Do you like whiskey?"), and use continuous –ing verbs much less; conversely, Hindi uses them where English would not ("we are not wanting to see this movie"). German capitalizes much more, and favors longer sentences and paragraphs. The English ambiguity in how negative questions are answered:

> He is never on time, is he?
> No.

can be frustrating to speakers of other languages where one would logically agree with the statement by saying "yes"—that's true, he is never on time.

Much of my discussion for a while will be drawn from my experience teaching Koreans. I've previously mentioned Richard Nisbett's *The Geography of Thought*, which asserts that western thought focuses more on analysis, and eastern culture emphasizes context. This is equally so with languages. English is very careful to separate and categorize things using articles or prepositions to make these distinctions. Korean and many northeast Asian languages pay more attention to levels of respect and relationship distinctions, reflecting its concern with harmony and balance. This isn't a value judgment, but a difference which must be considered when writing.

For example, specifying who is doing an action is so natural to English speakers that we assume every language does so. In English this is usually done by pronouns or by word order ("the dog bit the man"). In Latin or other languages, endings or internal word changes tell us the relationship: in "canis hominem mordet," -*is* and -*em* tell us who bites who, and these words can be rearranged for different emphases. Korean does have such markers, such as 남자가 사과를 먹어요, boy-subject apple-object eat, but these endings are usually omitted where it's obvious. I have heard Korean conversations where once the subject or person is mutually clear, there are no further pronouns. Such languages are called high-context languages, whereas English is low-context, continually requiring details to convey meaning.

The result is that statements which seem obvious to Koreans confuse English speakers. If you've been talking about food and say "I'm hungry," to a Korean "stomach-empty" (배고파요) makes perfect sense. If you're going to the beach, one can say "beach-go" (바닷가 가요). To a Korean, an English speaker who doesn't understand these things could seem foolish or perverse—of course *I'm* hungry; I can't feel your stomach. Just as an English speaker is puzzled as to why one must use the correct ending or word for "woman speaking to wife of younger brother-in-law"—as my wife would use fluently without thinking about it—many Koreans find our mania for pronouns frivolous. But because they are expected from habit, English speakers are lost without what seem like superfluous referents.

Hence a common error pattern I see in Korean or northeast Asian writers of English is missing words. When I mark papers by such students, most of the corrections tend to be insertions of words necessary for the statement to make sense, and less crossing-out of wrong words. I may read sections of text and realize that I don't know what the subject is, or I become confused when the relationship between two subjects is unclear. This is also a reason why automated translation between these languages has in the past been very bad, as early AI can't subjectively pick up the context of the discussion in order to render English pronouns or referents.

For students writing from any first language, even when pronouns are marked, referents that may be clear to the writer may not be to the reader.

Gertrude Stein told Alice that she was informed about her mother's illness. **x**

Is the 'she' Gertrude or Alice, and whose mother? This is an artificial sentence for illustration, but I do see confusing or missing referents even in high-level papers by native speakers.

14.3 Articles A & The

'The' is both the statistically most frequent word in English, and perhaps the hardest one to master for learners of the language. In other languages which some form of 'the,' they may be used differently, as with Spanish. The Arabic definite article *al* gives us *algebra, alcohol, alchemy,* and *alcove*, reflecting the Arabic influence on science in the west (logically, "the the cohol" shouldn't make sense). Many languages have no articles, such as Latin, Russian, Chinese, Japanese, and Tagalog (used in the Philippines). Old English itself didn't have articles, only evolving them around

1100 from its demonstratives. The Romance languages did the same, evolving *el, il, la,* and *les* from Late Latin *illa* and *ille* (that).

Using indefinite 'a' and definite 'the' in English is probably the severest grammatical difficulty that my Korean students have in writing or speaking English, because their language has no equivalent. Korean has demonstratives *this* and *that*—proximal this bus (이 버스) and distal that bus (저 버스), and a sort of medial *this-there* (그) that is somewhat like 'the,' in being used for something already mentioned. But Korean needs no actual articles, and I have the feeling that its speakers the English "the" is like learning an alien language and having to continually grammatically indicate whether the speaker has blue or purple antennae. Why is this so important?

'A' is a Counting Word; 'The' is a Visual Word

One strategy to make articles more understandable is to learn their origins. *A* comes from Old English *an*, usually meaning 'one,' cognate to German 'ein.' We can logically think of 'a' as a counting word, so that *a* pencil means one pencil out of a possible group of pencils. 'The' comes from 'that.' Old English had several words for "that," including *se, seo,* and *pæt* (that). Sometime around 1100 *þe* (the) began to be used as a substitute for these words, eventually becoming modern '*the*,' while '*this*' and '*that*' continued on separately.

Essentially, 'the' is a visual word to point with to indicate something that the other person can 'see.' *A* bus is any one bus—but *the* bus which I am pointing to is unique, and I am differentiating it. The problem arises when we use 'the' for abstractions and things we can't see. We still use 'the' because they are distinct entities which can be mentally "seen." Often English has this pattern: "I went to a restaurant and it was very crowded." Think of this as a sequence: *A* restaurant causes an example restaurant to appear in your head, and then 'the' refers to that one mental restaurant presently in your mind.

So we have two conditions for needing 'the': the referent is unique, and is recognized by both you and the audience as so.

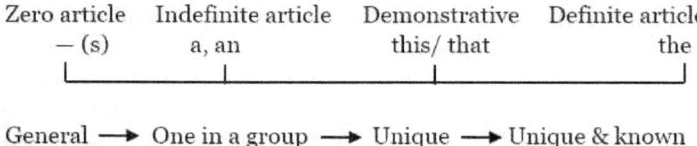

Another practice is to ask yourself when writing any noun: to which category does this noun belong along this continuum from generality to extreme specificity?

Printers are very useful.
I need to find a printer.
The printer on my desk is heavy.

In the last example, both the speaker and hearer mean one mutually-known printer. Similarly, in:

The electric car has changed the world.

The single and known 'idea' of the electric car, and not any unspecific group of electric cars is meant.
  Admittedly, real life is messier than these concepts can explain. There are innumerable exceptions that seem to defy logic—The Mississippi River, The Pacific Ocean, Lake Superior, The Philippines, Indonesia, Mount Everest, The Everglades. Articles are again one of the hardest facets of English to develop an intuition for, just as my German friends have an uncanny logic to know whether unfamiliar objects are male or female. My only advice is that if stuck, you Google these phrases and see whether they are commonly written with or without *a/the*.

14.4 Numbers, Prepositions, and Passives

Korean is again less fussy about plurality: two bottles is "two bottle" (두병, 병두개), and "there are some cats" could probably be handled by "cat-is" (고양이 있어요), unless the number of cats is for some reason significant. Many L1 speakers of various languages have trouble with English plural markers, and occasionally native speakers do also. Number agreement can get tricky in a sentence like "there is a box of oranges on the table." We say 'is' because the subject is the box and not oranges. Yet sometimes writers bend this rule to say "there is a box of oranges and they're on the table," with 'they're' referring to 'the oranges' and not the single box. It can be difficult to know how much flexibility is acceptable.

Another difficulty for new speakers is number agreement regarding uncountable and countable nouns.

> I do a lot of stuffs on the weekend. **x**
> I drink some coffees. **x**
> This is a nonsense. **x**

All of these nouns are uncountable and take no plurals. Unfortunately, there seems to be no logical reason why some nouns are countable and others not. As a rule, uncountable nouns tend to describe things which are difficult or impossible to divide. There are three common categories: liquids (*tea, rain, snow, beer*), abstractions (*love, war, peace*), and mass nouns which describe classes of objects (*furniture, cutlery, stuff*). Of course, English again has exceptions—we can speak of "the beers of Belgium," counting varieties of these liquids as a group. There are also situations where number agreement is flexible:

My favorite activity is going to cafes, drinking coffee, and meeting people.

My favorite activities are going to cafes, drinking coffee, and meeting people.

Which is correct—*is* or *are*? The answer is both, because the speaker might consider these three actions as connected and simultaneous, or they may be three separate activities.

Prepositions

Prepositions are also important in English because they indicate the relationships between parts of the sentence: I am going *to* school. The mail is *on* the table. She did it *by* working hard. They drove *through* the tunnel. As a last Korean example, the language indicates this function with particle endings: I am going home is "home-to go" (집에 가요). But Korean again might omit the preposition if the context is clear, or the pronunciation is awkward.

English does not permit omission of prepositions except for a few fixed expressions. "I am going home" is an idiom that is almost unique in the language, and plausibly has survived fossilized from Old English *Ic ga ham,* when the language used fewer prepositions. But "I am going shopping center" doesn't make sense.

Which preposition is used seems particularly arbitrary in English, and often reflects etymology or changes in technology. We ride *on* a bus but *in* a car because of historical reasons related to how these vehicles were made. The most inconsistent prepositional conventions may be those of time: "I will meet you *at* 2:00 *on* Tuesday *in* June *in* 2011." Similarly, usually *see* is used for movies and plays but *watch* is used for television programs.

Active and Passive

A related problem with prepositions is confusion of active and passive voice. An L1 speaker may contextually see that "I changed the oil in my car" means "I had the oil changed in my car," and that you are not the mechanic. But in writing it may be necessary to much more careful in stating who did an action. Additionally, for either logical or historical reasons some English verbs are rarely or never used in passive.

The problem might be occurred. **x**
He was disappeared. **x**

Neither makes sense in English, as things occur by their own force; no one can cause something to occur or disappear, except as a euphemism.

14.5 Word Class and Miscellaneous Errors

The last group of common problems is word class errors: the confusion of nouns, verbs, adjectives, adverbs and other categories. Sometimes I have students write that "I was very boring this weekend" **x** and it sounds unintentionally humorous. The writer meant "I was bored," a finished action (I had a feeling of boredom), but confused it with *bor–ing*, an action which affects others (I made other people feel bored). This error can easily happen because in English word types aren't well-indicated or uniformly differentiated by consistent endings. Adverbs usually have –ly endings, such as 'quickly,' but even there exceptions abound: "He will do it *soon*." As well, some non-adverbs end in –ly, such as 'costly.'

Similarly, many languages have a smaller number of modal auxiliaries than English does, and so students write "When the sun sets it should get dark." The sentence implies that the Earth has a choice and decides to get dark; in English there is a clearer distinction between modals of choice (should, ought to) and those of necessity (must, have to, will).

One way to combat language interference is to try to think directly in English rather than thinking out a sentence in your L1 language and then translating it. I won't pretend this is easy. But when students tell me they had a dream in English I know they're starting to do this.

14.6 Grammar and Native Speakers

Sometimes my native- or near-native English-speaking students do surprisingly poorly in my classes, for they are overconfident. A typical problem for such writers is that, having been steeped in popular culture in English, they confuse verbal and written modes. You can say things in spoken English that you seldom write, partly because usually others can see your expression and determine if you are serious, sarcastic, or playful. If you watch a foreign film and there are no subtitles, often you can follow much of the story by watching body language. These cues are absent in writing. A common problem I see on social media is people using sarcasm, and being misunderstood by others who didn't see they were joking. This is perhaps one reason why emoticons have become common.

Conversely, there are conventions used in writing but not in speech. Academic English often has a formality and sentence complexity that would sound stiff or artificial if spoken. You wouldn't normally say a sentence with multiple subordinate clauses, unless you are Jane Austen; spoken statements are shorter and linked with conjunctions and pauses. Compare the later books of the New Testament, which are mostly church letters, to the early books of the Old Testament. Even in translation, Paul's letters have a more complex syntax reflecting their epistolary nature, whereas the OT books have multiple paratactic clauses connected with "and then he…," mirroring their likely origins as oral narratives.

This also applies at the lower levels of spelling and grammar. Many native-English speakers write as they hear, so that they type "should of" **x** where "should have" is correct: "they should have been here." This is because "should have" often elides *'ave* into the preceding word, so that it sounds like /əv/, *of*. Similarly, 'than' and 'then' are confused: "Spain has a warmer climate then Iceland" **x**. A further depressingly growing error is using 'it's' rather than 'its': "I found the toothpaste but it's cap is gone." **x**

Grammatically, another key difference between spoken and written English is that the latter prefers more precision with verb tenses. In spoken discourse the context makes time relationships sufficiently clear, so that you might say, "I was wet because I didn't bring my umbrella." The hearer can predict the likely sequence, although whether it rained or you forgot your umbrella first wasn't stated. In written English, being more exact with verb tenses would make the order clearer: "I was wet because I hadn't brought my umbrella."

Similarly, "I was in the shower and the phone rang" is close enough in speech, but in writing the reader may be unclear about the sequence of events. A more exact statement would be "While I was showering, the telephone rang." This makes clear that an ongoing activity was interrupted by a momentary one. These are simple ideas; but where you are discussing complex ones, verb tense ambiguity may make everything worse. There is a joke that Latin is so complex, one wonders how the Romans learned it; but a street laborer probably didn't know every verb tense. Yet a Virgil or Cicero would certainly have known them, and a modern writer of scholarly English should also understand the fine points of usage that will add exactness to writing.

Slang and Obscenities

Somehow this comes up with native- or near-native English speakers, and seldom with learners. There are two broad types of students who use slang and vulgarities—those who do accidentally because, as mentioned, they have been brought up hearing it; the other type feels that coarse language is 'real' or 'honest,' and that I am being too old-fashioned—or that correct or formal usage is an elitist conspiracy to marginalize less-educated or foreign speakers. I won't get involved in such a debate here. But I will say that committees, editors, and employers may not be so open-minded when they make selection decisions.

It is true that some scholarly fields now have more tolerance for explicit language, whether merely as a naughty article subtitle, or in discussion. I suppose if one is writing a paper where the quoted source has curse words this can be done, and whereas my generation used asterisks (s**t) or dashes (f–k), many now don't. But I do warn that academics otherwise have a low tolerance for casual or unnecessary obscenities, and some more conservative disciplines might summarily reject papers with such vocabulary.

For those who don't want to use slang or clichés in writing and worry about doing so unintentionally, these are generally the worst offenders I see.

'A lot of x.' Instead: many, several, large numbers of, a considerable quantity of

'Let's face it/ make ends meet / put bread on the table.' These are stale clichés, and make the writer look amateurish.

'Literally.' The word means that it is not a metaphor. It is now misused as an intensifier: "It was literally a million degrees in there!" x It's unlikely that the room actually was 1,000,000 degrees Celsius inside.

Commas

An additional common problem that native speakers have is using commas as pauses, again mirroring speech patterns. Another is forgetting the final comma in lists, which is called the Oxford or serial comma.

After the rain, there were flooded basements, wrecked cars, and damaged roads.

Many journalists omit this final comma to save print space, but APA/MLA/Chicago all mandate it. But if you insist on omitting the last comma, at least check that the result isn't ambiguous: "There was a priest, and a soccer player, and a young girl eating a sandwich, and a moose." Without the last comma it sounds like the girl is eating the moose.

Contractions

In recent revisions of this book I am using contractions, in order to give the tone a more relaxed feel. I rarely do in my published scholarly work. This is perhaps a field-specific decision where you might follow the lead of others, but more often than not, 'don't' and 'isn't' and other forms should be spelled out. Curiously, I also had a reviewer comment that a paper manuscript had too many *italicized* words, and that this gave the text a too-conversational feel. I am trying to use fewer of them as well, as italicized words admittedly slow down reading speed.

FINAL COMMENTS

Afterword

I have at times spoken informally in this book, often using "I" references—but I can't discuss how to write scholarly text without sometimes stepping outside of doing exactly that. In this book I've discussed the planning, writing, and editing of academic research papers, moving from the basics to more abstract principles and complex projects, finishing with a detour into alternate genres and a brief grammar clinic. It is my hope that through these materials you have gained techniques for making your writing more efficient, lucid, interesting, and most important, more persuasive by cultivating trust in your reader. If so, you will be on your way to convincing him or her of your arguments and becoming a part of an academic discussion and community. Ideally I have also induced you to think about some of the concepts of the discipline of rhetoric and composition.

To return to some of the discussion beginning this book, academic argument writing involves some 'science' and some 'art.' By this I mean that there are aspects involving fairly arbitrary prescribed rules and conventions, or at least obeying the abilities, limitations, and proclivities of human cognition and emotions. To reiterate a final time, writing isn't a democratic pursuit; professors, disciplines, and style organizations set standards, and readers have choices. A paper which doesn't care if others understand it will likely get the readership it deserves. It is a good thing if writing is enjoyable; but fun is not itself the goal.

But writing also has, even if only to a limited extent in some applied or scientific fields, some latitude for personality and individual style. The paper's aim is to inform and optimally persuade the reader with precision and transparency. But you will have unique ways of conceptualizing or phrasing things, and or preferred euphemisms or allegories or comparisons. You will find certain sentence patterns or metaphors more natural than others; for example, you may gravitate towards adjectives of sight, or hearing, or touch, or smell, or taste. The argument looks fishy; it sounds fishy; it smells fishy; it tastes fishy. These differences are good things, and it would be a dull world if everyone wrote exactly as I do—or only computers wrote.

I am not sure academic writing is or should be 'fun,' but on a good day there is a sense of fulfilment or accomplishment in creating a text which adds to a community of readers, which is fixed and permanent, and which is yours, for the rest of your life or even beyond it. On a bad day, you will ask yourself, or others will ask you, why you are wasting your time on a tiny and apparently trivial corner of a subject. The reason you do so is that these subjects or problems are immensely complex and difficult, and when your tiny 'pixel' is added to those pixels made by other scholars and assembled, a beautiful 'photograph' of knowledge may result.

Works Cited

I won't cite my past students, as their sample segments are modified and anonymized, but I do again thank them collectively here. I also acknowledge the works listed below, which are either referenced in this book or are useful reading in the practice of academic writing or the discipline of composition studies.

Brown, Stephen. *Writing in the Margins*. Fountainhead Press, 2007.

Burke, Kenneth. *The Philosophy of Literary Form*. University of California Press, 1941.

Eckert, Kenneth. "Using Old English to Teach the Articles a and the in the Classroom: An Etymological and Visual Approach." *TESOL Review*, vol. 3, 2011, pp. 34-47. *ResearchGate*, https://www.researchgate.net/publication/266220286

Glasman-Deal, Hilary. *Science Research Writing: For Non-Native Speakers of English.* Imperial College Press, 2018.

Graff, Gerald, & Cathy Birkenstein. *They Say / I Say: The Moves that Matter in Academic Writing.* W. W. Norton & Company, 2014.

Hayot, Eric. *The Elements of Academic Style: Writing for the Humanities.* Columbia University Press, 2014.

Kaplan, Robert. "Cultural Thought Patterns in Intercultural Education." *Language Learning*, vol. 16, no. 1, 1966, pp. 1-20.

Marche, Stephen. "The College Essay Is Dead." *The Atlantic*, 16 Dec. 2022, www.theatlantic.com/technology/archive/2022/12/chatgpt-ai-writing-college-student-essays/672371.

Millward, C. M. *A Biography of the English Language.* Harcourt Brace Jovanovich, 1988.

Nisbett, Richard. *The Geography of Thought.* Free Press, 2003.

Roselle, Laura, and Sharon Spray. *Research and Writing in International Relations.* Routledge, 2011.

Strunk, William Jr., & White, E. B. *The Elements of Style.* Harcourt, 1920.

Swan, Michael, and Bernard Smith. *Learner English.* Cambridge University Press, 2001

FINAL COMMENTS

ABOUT THE AUTHOR

Ken Eckert is from Edmonton, Canada and lives in Korea. As an English professor most of his writing is academic, including articles on medieval romance, humor, Chaucer, and (post)modern literature, with a recently published book, *Middle English Romances in Translation* (Sidestone, 2015). He is an alumnus of Memorial University in Newfoundland and University of Nevada, Las Vegas, where he studied Chaucer. He has also published a humor novel, *Shorter of Breath* (2017), and *Learning to Crawl* (2020), both by the same press as this book.

www.ingramcontent.com/pod-product-compliance
Lightning Source LLC
Chambersburg PA
CBHW071259110426
42743CB00042B/1104